# THE GLOBAL TRADER

# WILEY TRADING

# THE GLOBAL TRADER

## Strategies for Profiting in Foreign Exchange, Futures, and Stocks

Barbara Rockefeller

John Wiley & Sons, Inc.

Published by John Wiley & Sons, Inc., New York.
Published simultaneously in Canada.

*Library of Congress Cataloging-in-Publication Data:*

Rockefeller, Barbara, 1946–
    The global trader : strategies for profiting in foreign exchange, futures, and stocks / by Barbara Rockefeller.
        p.   cm. — (Wiley trading)
    Includes index.
    ISBN 0-471-43585-6 (cloth : alk. paper)
    1. Investments, Foreign.   2. Financial futures.   3. Foreign exchange.
4. Portfolio management.   I. Title.   II. Series.
HG4538.R5767      2001
332.67—dc21
                                                                        2001045638

Printed in the United States of America.

10  9  8  7  6  5  4  3  2  1

To high school teachers, who said I could:
Gladys Buell, Evangeline Hogue,
Margaret Saunders, and Mary Jo Sargeant,
and to Desmond MacRae, who said I had to.

# Acknowledgments

A large number of people contributed to this book. Many are named in the text. Some who are not named but contributed much are:

Desmond MacRae, financial journalist, brilliant synthesizer of ideas, and supreme goad;

Ed Dobson, founder of Traders Press, who has gone to heroic lengths to republish trading books once out of print, and generous sharer of knowledge;

Angel Europa, hard-headed risk manager and research assistant extraordinaire;

Cedric Niguidula, a tech expert who can also speak a correct and useful English sentence;

Stephanie Haight-Kuntze, joke-lover and director of equity research at Bankgesellschaft Berlin;

Giles Kavanagh, from horsemouth.com, who *always* asks the extra question;

Vicki Schmelzer, financial journalist at MarketNews, who remembers with perfect clarity what the FX trading room at Citibank was like; and, not least,

Jim Sullivan, who knows a hawk from a handsaw (and runs the Fairfield County Technical Analysis Club).

B.R.

# Contents

## Contents

# THE GLOBAL TRADER

# Introduction

Trading and investing are not games, but you should think and act as though they are. You would not bet on a losing poker hand, and you should not bet on a losing investment position, either. Every time you put down money, it should be with an expectation of a gain. This is called "positive expectancy" and involves calculation of the probability of gain. It also involves calculation of the probability of loss. Every famous trader talks about loss. Some traders go so far as to say that when they sit down at their desk every morning, they say aloud: "how much will I lose today?" This is neither an unhealthy obsession nor a morbid emphasis on the dark side of life; it's a clear-eyed interest in the internal battle of the psyche when it stares failure in the face.

Positive expectancy is not just some vague idea that every trade will be a winning one; it should be a statement of a specific dollar number. Psychiatrist Ari Kiev finds that naming dollar targets improves results enormously. It is not true that results depend on "the market"—how trended it is, or how volatile. Results depend on the trader. A trained trader—or a natural-born trader—walks a tightrope spun out of self-confidence, and self-confidence is stronger than steel. Tightrope walking requires perfect focus and concentration; it is not a part-time hobby that leaves room for doing six other things at the same time. Self-confidence comes partly from doing the work that precedes the trade.

"Doing the work" of trading consists of finding the combination of analytical techniques for which you have an affinity.

1

These may be fundamental or technical, or rooted in sociohistorical insights—it doesn't matter. You cannot buy a winning technique in a book or a software program. Conditions will always be slightly different for you, and your implementation will always be slightly different from the next person's—because of you. No system is entirely rule based; some personal judgment is always needed. You will not be able to trade a system that embodies a holding period time frame or a win-loss ratio that you find unsympathetic. Discovering a trading methodology that is suited to your character and personality is a voyage of self-discovery.

The biggest obstacle to becoming a successful trader is your attitude toward losses. The value-investing school that is dominant in the United States today holds that losses don't count if you really have bought a value stock. "It will come back" is utter nonsense. You cannot know with certainty that you have a value stock, and there is no game in which losses do not count. Trading and investing are not games, and the theory of gambling and statistical logic is not arguable. The biggest con game in the world is the assertion, by stock brokers and mutual fund peddlers, that holding stocks for the long run will result in compound annual returns of 12 to 16 percent, as history has shown. There is no rate of return inherent in U.S. stocks—or in any other investment, except bonds.

Nobody knows where and when we started to accept a phony semantic distinction between "investing" and "trading." Old-time Wall Street legends like Bernard Baruch and Gerald Loeb would be appalled. *They viewed buy-and-hold as the real gamble.* You make actual money only when you sell. Moreover, you take no risk when you are out of the market. To say that you are investing your savings in the stock market and, at the same time, to say that trading in and out of the stock market would be too risky, is to accept an illogical proposition. This was blindingly obvious to commentators as early as 1870, when a large number of books about Wall Street started to appear. Many have been republished by the Fraser Publishing Company of Vermont, by Ed Dobson at Traders Press, and, in the 1990s, by big publishing houses such as McGraw-Hill and John Wiley & Sons. These wonderful books have titles like *The Theory of Stock Speculation* (1900), *Studies in Tape Reading* (1910), *Studies in Stock Speculation* (1924), and *The Art of Speculation* (1930). If you see these books at a garage sale, don't hesitate. They contain exactly the same advice and perspective as any trading book today, without the pious and false distinction between "investment" and "speculation." Trading stocks and commodities has inherent risks, and you might as well face them head-on, acknowledge that all market trading is speculation, and learn as many of the tricks of the trade as you possibly can.

Pointing this out is probably like preaching to the choir. After all, you are holding a book with the word "trader" in the title. But, like most people who have been brainwashed by the prevalent equity culture today, you are probably quite tentative and not fully committed to the idea that you will lose money on over half of your trades and it is the minority of trades that will make your stake grow—or it will be the one based on a lightning flash of insight, on which you bet big.

As Alexander Fleming found when he accidentally discovered penicillin, our brains achieve synthesis of a new idea after long, grinding analysis. You may have to trade for many years before you spot a trading opportunity so big that it is worthy of a big bet. Meanwhile, the best approach to trading profits is to make consistent small bets where the odds are in your favor but no single trade can be a catastrophe that knocks you out of the game. In this book, trading opportunities are named "inefficiencies." This is what professional traders are looking for, although they may not use that word. An inefficiency is any misperception by market participants of the true value of a security. It is the basis of Graham and Dodd's advice to buy stocks when they are temporarily at 60 to 70 percent of book value, and it is the basis of technical analysis trading, whereby you take a position when the price is temporarily off the trend. Academics mistakenly believe that markets are always efficient. They are not. They are inefficient more often than they are efficient. *Efficiency is a process, not a state.* This is why Value Line, which identifies undervalued situations and statistically projects the correction to true valuation, has been so successful for over 50 years.

We chose global markets because they are less efficient than equity markets in the United States. Let's face it, the U.S. stock market is thoroughly picked over and analyzed to death. In Europe and Japan—let alone emerging markets—the securities industry is less than 20 percent the size of the U.S. establishment, and that includes the number and quality of securities analysts. The citizens of foreign countries are not as involved in stock markets, either. Participation by individual Europeans is less than 20 percent (compared to 50 to 60 percent in the United States); and in Japan, participation is less than 10 percent. On the other hand, individuals in those countries are far more savvy about the foreign exchange market than Americans are, and foreign-currency-denominated accounts in both places are common. They are rare in the United States.

Americans are overinvested in the U.S. stock market. To diversify into foreign stocks is not necessarily the best answer, or the only answer. The stock markets in major countries are highly correlated with the U.S. market, or with one sector of the U.S. market. The Morgan Stanley Capital International index for Europe, Asia, and the Far East (EAFE), for example, was 50 percent correlated with the S&P 500 for the 30 years leading up to 1995, but 74 percent correlated with it in the five years from 1995 to 2000. The Taiwan Taipei index and the Korean KOSPI are highly correlated with the Philadelphia Stock Exchange Semiconductor Index (SOX). Other examples of correlation abound, but you won't find them neatly listed in a book or a financial periodical.

The diversification analysis performed by brokerage houses and Web-based services use long-dated correlations that are increasingly out of date, and many other untenable assumptions, such as the expected rate of return, also based on long-dated past returns. The result is that you have no idea what risk you are really taking. Portfolio theory is elegant, and impossible to refute. It's also impossible to implement without making a lot of assumptions and guesses. To diversify correctly, you would need to look at markets and securities as disconnected as possible from the S&P 500, the Dow, and Nasdaq, and evaluate their correlation—or the absence of correlation—on a one-by-one basis. Nobody is offering a "beta" today for each security in the world vis-à-vis the S&P 500, but this is not as hard as it sounds, especially since, as a trader (rather than an investor), you are no longer considering your holding period to be "forever." You can easily construct a correlation study in Excel or Lotus.

You can stay in stock markets, if you prefer, but you would be bypassing one of the great diversification opportunities of all time—the futures market. Leaders of the equity culture work very hard to keep you from noticing the futures market. They constantly issue warnings that the futures market is ultra-risky and nearly everybody who ventures there loses his shirt. But many securities in the futures market are *less* volatile than equities. What makes futures markets riskier is the use of leverage, or borrowed money. Most people cannot grasp the essence of leverage and do not apply sensible rules of trading, so horror stories abound. There is a vast difference in the mind-set of equity market participants and futures markets participants—and their brokers, analysts, software programs, and press. "Business" periodicals such as *Forbes, Business Week,* and *Barron's* focus exclusively on equities; when they write about futures trading, they are disapproving. This is partly because they view technical analysis, universally used in futures trading, as some kind of unproven voodoo that will inevitably lead the reader to ruin. And yet, unless you are going to "buy value stocks and hold forever," at least some rudimentary technical analysis is essential for trading success.

You will have to overcome the prejudice against futures trading that is widespread in the United States today. Futures trading is in fact a good place to practice trading any global security, whether it is a Chinese stock, German bond futures, or deep-discount Argentine sovereign debt. Futures trading forces you to consider the probable win-loss ratio *very* carefully, and that is the key to all trading success. The advanced academic work that is being done today on risk—measuring it, managing it, and systematically exploiting it—is being done in the futures markets. Technical analysis and its cousin, money management, are integral parts of futures trading precisely because they are the tools that help you calculate the probability of winning and the probability of losing. Technical analysis proponents sometimes claim too much for it; they say that it is like having inside information on what's going to happen next. You don't need to go that far to take advantage of a useful tool.

Don't think that you can bypass technical analysis and risk management if you chose to bypass futures trading. You still need an estimate of the probability of winning in any trade and an exit strategy when prices move against you. You probably do not speak and read Chinese, Hebrew, or Turkish—and you wouldn't necessarily be any the wiser about specific securities and markets if you did. Technical analysis is the one tool that transcends language. Fortunately, this means it also transcends BS and is thus very liberating.

Technical analysis cannot, however, predict a price shock. A price shock arises from a surprise event that was not on anyone's radar screen, except the few who are carefully imaginative. A price shock develops from a series of events and culminates in one big event, whereupon, with perfect hindsight, everyone recognizes what has been going on all along. This is why we *read*. We are seeking information to build two insights: first, what securities price development exaggerates true conditions, either overvaluation or undervaluation. Once we find an obvious case of mispricing, we can imagine that some shock or event must come along to reverse the perception. The best story to illustrate this process is Jim Melcher's realization that, after the Russian sovereign default in September 1998, at one point the entire Russian stock market was worth less than half the value of Yahoo! He bought near the bottom and booked a 160 percent gain in only a few months. No newspaper reporter had observed that the Russian market was so undervalued. If one had, he would have become a trader instead of a newspaper reporter. But news reports are the raw material for creating insights and, make no mistake, a creative process is involved. Much pompous bumf is written about the creative process, but let's just say that it is not entirely rational and logical.

The second insight we seek by reading is to guess what will influence institutional investors, who, collectively, are the real driving force in every market. Chat-room visitors mistakenly believe that what influences them is also what influences institutions. They err in falling in love with their stocks, forgetting that a stock is not the company. Institutional investors are far more hardheaded but are, at the same time, just as susceptible to herd instinct as anyone else. The phrase "herd instinct" is a semantically insulting way to describe group behavior. But professional institutional investors are required, by their own rules and their contract with their clients, to meet or beat benchmarks, which, by definition, are the grand sum of group behavior. An entirely contrarian institution may hit an occasional home run but is generally doomed to remain small. Individuals buy into professional management precisely because they want to meet or beat benchmarks. On the whole, professional managers fail to do even that, which raises the question again: what do we really seek when we trade securities markets? Is the goal to prevent the loss of capital (defensive) or to make money (active)? Anyone who made a first investment in the U.S. stock market in March 2000 failed to prevent the loss of capital one year later if he had bought into a standard index-tracking mutual fund. In what way is this defensive and protective of "savings"? What risk aversion means to the individual is very different from what risk aversion means to the institution. Risk aversion to the institution means avoiding anything that jeopardizes the ongoing existence of the institution. It does not mean maximizing *your* cash. Having said all that, we still need to be able to predict what institutions will do in the face of price shocks and watershed Events. There is no point in analyzing a situation correctly if the crowd does not also come to the same realization.

Economist John Moffatt, at Analytic Systems in New Hampshire, says that the price of stocks is determined by three factors: (1) 50 percent, market influences; (2) 25 percent, the macroeconomic background, and (3) only 25 percent, the fundamentals of the company itself. This suggests that picking a rising-star company in a falling market is likely not to yield the gains you might expect, especially if the company's home-country economy is in a slump. Further, you may want to keep the bulk of your investments in the United States, if only to avoid foreign exchange risk. The top-down approach would be: first seek a rising market, then make sure the economy is rising, then seek specific securities. Meanwhile, keep an eye on any situations that are bottoming or are oversold, because we can guess that the next wave of market sentiment will likely be upward—possibly, to an excessive degree. Many if not most of these situations will be high risk in the conventional way of looking at things. Country or sovereign risk may be high. Disclosure and transparency may be awful. Liquidity may be low and price volatility high. The currency may be a problem, including

convertibility (back into U.S. dollars). Nevertheless, these situations are where the high-probability gains are to be found.

The world is a big place, and trading is a zero-sum game—your
gain is someone else's loss. You need a well-stocked toolkit to
venture outside of a "strategy" of merely buying U.S. mutual
funds. Don't be a cheapskate. Get the tools you need. Nicholas
Darvas describes how he made $2 million from remote places in
the world with no tools except stale copies of *The Wall Street
Journal*, a hotel telex machine, and his theory of how prices move
(Nicholas Darvas, *How I Made $2,000,000 in the Stock Market*,
Lyle Stuart, 1971). You could do it, too. But the world is faster-
moving than in Darvas's day (the 1950s), and the tools are cheap.
If you are starting literally from scratch, you will need to get sub-
scriptions to the major world newspapers and business periodicals, a data service, several newsletters, and a technical analysis
software package, not to mention a PC to run the software and access the Internet. You will also need 10 to 20 books. The total
cost of all this is $2,500 to $5,000, depending on how fancy a PC
you get. Ongoing subscription and data costs will be about $100
to $300/month, or $1,200 to $3,600 per year. This may seem like
a big investment, but consider what you pay in fees to a mutual
fund—1 to 4 percent—and the return you expect to get on the out-
lay by doing the work yourself. You should be able to recapture
the capital investment in the first month or two, and you should
target your return to do precisely that (following Kiev's advice).

Almost every writer on trading has at least one valuable point
to make that you can use in your own trading. You can buy books
and file magazine articles for the rest of your life. At some point,
you have to choose which market, which specific security, and
which specific technique you will use. The secret of trading, which
a lot of people do not want to admit, is that everything works.
Cycle theories, with or without astrological overtones, work. Pattern recognition, once you train youself to see patterns (whether of
the head-and-shoulders variety, or Japanese candlesticks), works.
Statistical techniques, whether you use channels or arithmetic for-
mulations such as moving averages and momentum, work. Neural
networks, which find organization within apparent chaos, work.
Today, we have computers and software to help implement all
these techniques, and the techniques work.

No technique works all the time, and no technique works on every security, so you have to find what works on your security or pick a technique and find what securities it works on. In the end, the only really difficult question you have to address is the time frame of your trading. If you can see big-picture trends and therefore choose a long time frame, there is a set of long-term indicators that will work on your securities. Be aware that long-term trading, in which you hold a position for months and even years, is where big one-time gains are to be made—but also where big one-time losses may occur, too.

If you pick a shorter time frame—for example, today's popular "swing trading" of three, five, and eight days or weeks—you will use a different set of techniques and a different mind-set. You will need to be more opportunistic—that is, less emotionally committed to the trade—because, at this level, the market is throwing off a lot of "noise" (random moves). You therefore have to have a personality that is more accepting of high risk and of frequent losses.

Most individuals think that they need: first, a trading system; next, a money management system, and last, a way to train themselves to operate the trading and money management system with discipline and focus. This sequence is backward. The first thing you need to do is: take an inventory of yourself and find out what securities are suited to you. If you do not have the patience and the time to follow economic and market conditions in China, you have no business trading China Telecom, even if you are a world-class expert on the telecom industry. If you *have* the time and energy to follow conditions in China, it doesn't matter what trading system you adopt to trade China Telecom. Any number of equally valid trading systems will work just fine to give you buy/sell signals. Then, of course, you need to follow the signals scrupulously. Buying is easy, selling is hard. But as the great traders of history point out, you make money only when you sell.

It's important to acknowledge that the rules of the game are not what the brokerage and mutual fund industry would have you believe. A key theme of this book is that trading isn't what you think it is. Active trading is factually and logically far more defensible than index-tracking. Index benchmarks are meaningless because they are rigged to include the best and the brightest in a continual process of discarding losers. A company is not its stock, anyway. Once you realize that the "value" touchstones peddled by the securities industry are dross, you might as well go global, where the opportunities are. Because it is very difficult to determine intrinsic value in foreign securities and to become fully familiar with market conditions in foreign countries, you are liberated to trade foreign securities (or derivatives) on the price action of the securities themselves. It is a deductive and rational process fully divorced from false-belief systems.

This is a harsh message. If you want to be a global trader, you have to devote a great deal of time and energy to the effort. You have to hold two ideas in your mind simultaneously: (1) the big-picture opportunity, and (2) the price vagaries of your specific securities. If, for example, the Chinese stock market is the place to be and you have selected a Chinese telecom stock, but suddenly the entire telecom sector worldwide starts tanking, including your stock, you need an exit rule that will keep your head clear. Then you need to apply the rule and actually exit, even though you have persuaded yourself that the "story" is a good one and "it will come back." Things change. It may not come back, even if it "should." In the meanwhile, some other security is worthy of your attention, and if you can't find such an opportunity right away, there is only one place for your cash—short-term U.S. Government paper. This is why global professionals rank markets according to attractiveness, and retreat to the zero-risk security when none of them measures up to the sure return on cash. Notice that the fall-back position is not a U.S. securities-based mutual fund.

Above all, you have to be realistic about the gains that can be made in your chosen securities, and the losses that will inevitably accompany them. It is usually unrealistic to expect a security that has already risen 150 percent to rise another 150 percent. It is also unrealistic to expect to recover losses at a pace of 100 percent, which is what is needed if you lose 50 percent of your stake—unless you are specializing in a security that routinely and predictably changes by 100 percent and you are sure that you are on the right side of it. Target each gain—and each loss, too. That's what professionals do that makes them different from the average trader.

A global trader is different from an average trader because he sees a bigger universe of opportunities—one that includes foreign bonds, emerging markets, futures, and all manner of newly developed instruments and securities. A global trader targets the one with the highest positive expectancy—and nails it down by not holding it too long and always entering a stop-loss. If the highest positive expectancy is in U.S. equities, so be it—but we should not automatically assume that U.S. equities are the "safe way to save." If you want to protect savings, buy bonds. If you want to trade, start looking for positive expectancies.

# Chapter 1

# TRADING VERSUS INVESTING

*A mind stretched to a new idea never goes back to its original dimension.*

Oliver Wendell Holmes

"Global trader"—a glamorous and sophisticated-sounding title. What exactly does it mean? If you buy the stock of a multinational company that operates worldwide, like Coca-Cola, aren't you already a "global" trader? And what's the difference between a "trader" and an "investor"?

Let's start with "global." It's true that U.S. multinationals like Coca-Cola, IBM, and General Electric all derive a high proportion of total sales revenue from foreign countries. Warren Buffett has been quoted as saying that he gets all the international diversification he needs from owning U.S. multinational companies. This is not, strictly speaking, true diversification. For one thing, U.S. multinational stocks do not trade very differently from their purely domestic counterparts. Aside from an occasional divergence due to special circumstances, multinational stocks are highly correlated with the S&P 500.

Multinational companies also vary widely in their management of currency exposure, the chief cause of earnings effects arising from international operations. Some hedge all currency exposure; some hedge none. During the second half of 2000 and first half of 2001, the stocks of many multinationals fell on earnings warnings from companies that had failed to hedge their

13

exposure to the falling euro. In dollar terms, sales and profits both fell solely from the currency effect. Stock analysts almost always ignore the currency hedging policies, practices, and outcomes of U.S. multinationals until there is an emergency like this. It's possible that they may not understand currency effects, but it's also true that companies disclose very little about it. They are able to be tightlipped because U.S. accounting rules allow them to keep foreign exchange hedges off the balance sheet. (They may appear in a footnote, but only when the effect is "material.") It's not going too far to say that you are taking an extra and unknowable risk in holding a U.S. multinational corporation's stock.

Another way to look at "global" is to confine the term to non-U.S. companies. United States investors are comfortable with familiar-seeming but nonetheless foreign companies such as Sony (Japan), Nestlé (Switzerland), or Glaxo SmithKline (United Kingdom). They have major operations in the United States and their stocks trade on a U.S. exchange. Sometimes they are listed directly, but usually they are listed on the American Stock Exchange in the form of American Depositary Receipts (ADRs). It's easy to forget that these global companies are really foreign, that their stock price is most influenced by events in their home country's stock markets, and that although you pay and receive dollars when trading them, their underlying stock is priced in the home-country currency. The case of Nokia and the Helsinki Exchange is notable. The telecom industry and the euro both slumped at the same time. American investors got hit with a double whammy, and so did anyone who bought a Finnish stock directly in Helsinki, since Nokia dragged the whole index down.

A subset of foreign stocks is the small but growing class of hybrids, from the point of view of nationality. Daimler-Chrysler springs to mind, but before that merger we had Anglo-Dutch companies like Royal Dutch Shell and Anglo-French Airbus Industrie, as well as Anglo-Australian Rio Tinto. Cross-border mergers are becoming ever more common. In addition to the inevitable effect on earnings of the choice of "home" currency, hybrids pose some serious management and corporate-culture problems that professional securities analysts—let alone inspired amateurs—have a hard time wrestling with.

"Global" can also refer to the time frame of trading—meaning, essentially, 24 hours a day. This is a bit of an exaggeration so far. The only securities that can really be traded 24 hours a day are spot currencies and currency, bond, and stock index futures. But don't stick your head in the sand. The 24-hour trading of individual stocks, and of individual stock futures, will happen in our lifetime—perhaps as soon as five years from now. You may say to yourself that you don't want to be a slave to the quote screen, like spot currency traders who have to know, at 2:00 A.M., where their yen is. Markets that are open 24 hours are an inconvenience to those who prefer an orderly life and a full night's sleep. Even if you choose not to accommodate your schedule to the world's time zones, the very existence of price moves 24 hours a day will force upon you the need to sharpen your trading skills. Some very unpleasant surprises can occur overnight. Like all problems, however, 24-hour trading also offers opportunities, such as arbitrage between time zones—the strategy behind the Rothschild fortune in the nineteenth century—and intermarket analysis. (If the Nasdaq declines during U.S. hours, the Nikkei 225 index also declines, eight times out of ten, during Tokyo hours.) Many of these opportunities can be exploited without losing a minute of sleep.

## Organizing Principles

To take advantage of the emerging global market, you need well-thought-out organizing principles and trading rules. You want trading rules so well established that they become almost mechanical; otherwise, you can become so overwhelmed by information overload that you can't make any decision at all.

Books and magazine articles abound in trading rules promulgated by famous investors and traders. They all sound sensible until you realize that many of them are mutually exclusive. Don't throw up your hands in despair. There is a way to separate rules into two camps by what can be named the "holding period philosophy." Once you know the preferred holding period of the guru, you can deduce the chain of logic that leads to the rule. Some aphorisms are appropriate to "investing" (a long holding period) and some are appropriate to "trading" (an indefinite holding period). We think of "investing" as a process of identifying a temporarily mispriced stock that has intrinsic value, and holding it for such a long time that the market has a chance to come to its senses and price it higher. A value stock will fall less when the market falls because it is acknowledged as having high intrinsic value. It is "safe." "Trading," on the other hand, is perceived as more dangerous. Traders may place their money on securities without intrinsic value solely because they are rising, and they may risk losses because the prices of such securities are more volatile. Traders compound the risk of dealing in volatile securities by using leverage. Trading is a stressful occupation that is akin to gambling. Investing is a form of saving, and saving is a virtuous act.

This conventional differentiation is mistaken on many counts. The laws of probability and statistical logic apply to any venture in which money is staked on an unknown outcome, whether we name it "investing" or "trading." When we talk about trading, we use the semantically loaded language of gambling because the history of the study of probability and the most easily understood statistical models are exemplified by gambling cases. To illustrate a trading situation by using the language of gambling doesn't make trading itself "gambling." In fact, good traders place a portion of capital only on situations where the outcome is expected to be positive and the win-loss ratio has been estimated. Most "investors" place capital in situations where the outcome is not calculated statistically but is instead flavored with the nonspecific but equally loaded word "value." They bet without having a win-loss ratio in mind. Wise observers of this odd phenomenon, like Bernard Baruch and Gerald Loeb, marvel that it is the average investor who is, in fact, gambling.

## You Will Take Losses

It is often said that the "first rule of investing" is to preserve capital. You can't play if you have lost all your chips. Therefore, the central issue is what attitude you should take toward losses. Everybody takes losses at one time or another. Losses are inevitable. How should you think about them? There are two competing philosophies and they have associated rules about stock market losses. The value-investing school of thought shrugs off losses as a temporary inconvenience. If you have selected the right value stocks in the first place, losses should be only tempo-rary. The other school of thought, which might be termed the pragmatic school, holds that controlling losses is the key to suc-cess. You can preserve capital only if you limit losses to predeter-mined levels and let the winners run. The goal of trading and investing is to make money—a positive statement, rather than the more negative orientation of "preserve capital."

Both can't be right. It is essential that you decide which phi-losophy you will adopt. You can't pick a rule or two from one school of thought if your overall orientation lies with the other school. A great deal of confusion arises from not being able to dif-ferentiate between some apt-sounding rule that actually carries a lot of baggage with it in the form of a chain of assumptions.

## What's Wrong with Value Investing?

1. Markets are not efficient.
2. Value investing ignores risk management.
3. Analysts don't know how to do it, so how can you?
4. Companies are not stocks.
5. You invest to live, you don't live to invest. Value investing ig-nores personal risk management.

Value investing has, as its premise, that changes in the environ-ment—specifically, market sentiment (whether bullish or bear-ish)—are always temporary. This is true. There is no such thing as equilibrium in stock prices. The process of "price discovery"—the continuous action of supply and demand—is never at rest. Some-times prices are "too high"—given the P/E ratio or some other benchmark—and sometimes prices are "too low." The key to value investing is to acquire value stocks when they are temporar-ily "on sale," presuming that you can identify them in the first place. This is a function of financial ratio analysis and some other factors, such as the supremacy of a brand. Ideally, the true value of a stock is independent of what is going on in the market at large. If a stock should be valued at $25 and it is currently priced at $15, it is a bargain, and you should not care whether the S&P 500 is up or down at the time. Eventually, the price will be $25—but you will continue to hold it on the assumption that it will lead the market when the market is up (and lag price declines when the market is down). Because the stock market has a long-term upward bias, historically, buy-and-hold is the correct approach if what you have is a true value stock.

There are any number of problems of fact and logic in the value investing approach. The first is that it assumes the market is efficient—that all relevant new information is known by everyone, and prices adjust immediately to the new information. You cannot predict new information and therefore you cannot predict what the price adjustment will be. You can't "beat the market" by anticipating big moves. Because the market is so big and has so many participants with different interests, you can't influence or control prices, either. You are, by definition, a passive observer of the scene.

## 1. Buy-and-Hold Is Bunk

"Buy and hold" gets its legitimacy from the *efficient markets hypothesis.* This was most popularly voiced by Burton Malkiel in *A Random Walk Down Wall Street* (W.W. Norton & Company, 1973). The theory holds that all the information that contributes to a security's price is known by everyone, and new information is known immediately and universally. The incorporation of fresh news into the price is efficient. Any inefficiency will be instantly arbitraged away. Only new information that was not foreseen can move the price. Just as unpredictable news is the only thing that can change a price, we cannot predict which way the price will change—up or down, or by what amount. Random news causes random price moves. The new random price move is unconnected to past price moves. Therefore, you can't predict stock prices and, observing that, over the long run, equities are a superior investment to bonds and other instruments, you might as well simply buy and hold as a practical matter. Market-timing cannot, logically, work.

You are probably getting weary of seeing the efficient market hypothesis mentioned in every book on trading and investing. Talk of efficient markets is tiresome because the mathematical logic and statistical proofs offered by academics (and there are endless legions of them) are unassailable by the average investor. By the time you finish following the chain of reasoning, you are convinced that putting your money in an index fund is the only sensible and defensible course of action. Any other course of action is speculative, or at least embodies a risk that you can't effectively pin down. In short, academics and fund managers control the terms of the debate, and they structure it in such a way that it cannot be refuted. The efficient market hypothesis is now the "base case," and any other observation about the market is automatically relegated to the status of "minor side effect" or even "curiosity." Those who embrace the efficient market hypothesis have taken upon themselves the mantle of intellectual and moral superiority, and that can be very intimidating, especially when they have so much of what is obviously correct on their side.

The random walk argument seems beguiling, but it fails to address the observation that securities prices do move in trends, and some market-timers are systematically successful over long periods of time. *Any* random news may have a random effect, but not *all* random news has a random effect. The market does have a memory. We all know of cases where a stock that has been on a rising trend fails to fall on a bad earnings announcement, and rises instead in a "relief rally" after the bad news is out of the way. This may be irrational but it is not random. The response of securities prices to bits and pieces of news is not chaotic; it follows a pattern. If you can detect the main outlines of the pattern, you can outperform the benchmark indices.

Nonrandomness is also why we have 11,000 mutual funds in a universe of 7,500 stocks. In the "weak form" of the efficient market hypothesis, small companies, companies in certain sectors, and other groupings may have an advantage that will cause them to deliver higher earnings and higher stock prices. Concentration in these groupings may deliver higher returns than the benchmark. At the least, mutual funds seek to reduce the risk of the major indices or subindices without sacrificing the average return. But it would be a rare fund manager who would flatly say that the efficient market hypothesis is poppycock; instead, it is practically a religion. Hedge fund managers and managers of other "alternative investments" say that the efficient market hypothesis may be correct, but the majority draw the wrong conclusion from it. Instead of seeking temporary undervaluation of high-quality securities, hedge fund and alternative investment managers seek inefficiencies of *all* stripes, whether in momentary market perception of a specific stock or the largest mispricing in a very large universe of mispricings.

The line of argument supporting the principle of diversification is thornier, but equally tinged with religious fervor. The formal statement was made by William Sharpe in *Portfolio Theory and Capital Markets* (McGraw-Hill, 1970), and Sharpe won a Nobel prize in Economic Sciences. This followed work by Harry Markowitz in 1953—so the investment world has had nearly 50 years to enshrine the concept and the rules that arise from it. The problem is that all models make simplifying assumptions that do not reflect real-world conditions, and portfolio theory is no exception. No one will argue with the idea—let alone the mathematics—that "Diversification reduces risk." But the theory requires, among other unrealistic requirements, that the correlation between two securities does not change over the period under study—and we know that the world's stock markets are increasingly influencing one another. To buy the Nikkei 225 as a diversification play from the Nasdaq, for example, is a fool's errand because they are highly correlated. To use the past 5 or 10 years' average returns in a market as the forecast for the upcoming 5 or 10 years lacks credibility, too, because economies and companies are dynamic, not static—they *change.* In *CNBC 24/7, Trading Around the Clock, Around the World* (John Wiley & Sons, 2000), we cite a study by an economist at the Boston Federal Reserve, showing that you cannot force a global portfolio optimization to include an Asian (ex-Japan) fund, due to negative returns in 1998 and 1999 arising from the Asia crisis (www.bos.frb.org/economic/neer/htm). The only way to include Asian stocks would be to discard the historical 10-year return and make a forecast of the upcoming 10-year return. Even the most seasoned professional would blanch at having to make such a forecast. It's an insoluble problem: to predict the future, you must use the past, but the past is unreliable.

A smart diversification rule is not to accept old data as perfectly reflective of the future. Before embarking on a search for the country or region that offers the most opportunity, consider that recent research indicates that the best diversification comes not in the form of spreading money around in different countries, but rather in different industries. An International Monetary Fund (IMF) report (www.imf.org/external/pubs/ft/wp/2000/wp00216.pdf) shows that, over the past several years, industry-specific factors better explain global stock market returns than country-specific factors. This may partly be due to the higher weight of high-tech in many markets, such as Taiwan. Because over half of Taiwan's market cap is tech-related and those stocks rise and fall with the Nasdaq 100, you don't get diversification when you buy Taiwan stocks—even those that are not tech-related—because of the overall effect of "the market" on all stocks when high-tech founders. Logically, you want to find foreign small-cap stocks that are not influenced by global industry effects.

Another problem involves the calculation of indices themselves, and indices are universally employed to conduct diversification exercises. A corollary to "A company is not its stock" is the observation that an equity index is not its stocks, either. The continuous process of reconstituting indices to reflect the biggest names in a market or sector (or the "most representative" names, according to the index-compiler's judgment) results in what is called a success or survivorship bias. This is why the Russell 2000, for example, moves in odd spurts—its most successful companies grow out of it and graduate to the Nasdaq! Dimson, March, and Staunton, in *The Millennium Book, A Century of Investment Returns* (ABN AMRO-London Business School, 2000), recalculate U.K. stock returns to remove hindsight in share and sector selection and other factors, including researcher laziness (using data that is easy to get). They laboriously hand-collected data from the *Financial Times*, starting in 1899. The outcome is a new ABN AMRO/LBS equity index for the United Kingdom that "sets the record straight"—and the true performance is about half the figure generally accepted as the historic record. Applying the principle to other markets, they find that, on average, national stock market returns are exaggerated by 2.2 percent. There is wide variability, though: U.S. returns are overstated by only 0.8 percent, but the overstatement is 5.3 percent in France and 4.3 percent in Germany.

This is a bitter pill to anyone who paid $400 or more to a broker to concoct a personal optimum global portfolio. Over the past few years, brokerages and other vendors have offered optimum portfolio construction as a fee-based service to the public, and already the less-than-sterling results are attracting scathing criticism in the financial press. Again, the central issue is that adherents have taken the intellectual and moral high ground—and there is no competing theory. There are only two ways to deal with the shortcomings of portfolio theory: (1) roll up your shirtsleeves and work around the issues—which is little more than guessing in most cases—or (2) ignore them.

To ignore portfolio theory is to subject yourself to the charge that you are a financial ignoramus, adrift in a sea of unknown risks without an understanding of each specific risk you are taking or of the combined risk of every item you own. You have a "collection" of securities rather than a "portfolio." And yet, people were putting together portfolios before portfolio theory came along, and the principle that diversification reduces risk is hardly a novel and revolutionary idea. We like to joke that common sense is not common (i.e., not widespread), but in practice, only people who do no homework at all would assemble a collection of concentrated risks if they were actually seeking a diversified-risk portfolio.

Besides, what is so wrong about concentration rather than diversification? Gerald Loeb says, in the introduction to *The Battle for Investment Survival* (Simon & Schuster, 1935), "Diversification is a necessity for the beginner. On the other hand, the really great fortunes were made by concentration." It goes without saying that if you are going to put all your eggs in one basket, as Loeb also phrased it, they must be good eggs in the first place and you have to watch the basket very carefully.

Of course value matters. Nobody in his right mind would seek to place his hard-earned money in second-rate securities with a high probability of falling in price. Many gurus are available today to offer advice on the extent of value in individual U.S. stocks. The Web site www.validea.com will even use the techniques of some of the top gurus to score stocks of your choice. At www.stockcharts .com and other technical analysis Web sites, you can find specific recommendations with full explanations. But neither "value" investing nor pure technical analysis alone provides the one thing you need to know about a security: is it mispriced? What specific inefficiency or set of inefficiencies is at work? How much is it mispriced, and why? If you buy it, what can go wrong? If you short-sell it, what can go wrong? In short, what is the probable risk/reward ratio over a specific time frame? To determine the numbers, such as a $5 probable upside gain versus a possible worst-case $1 downside loss, you need to combine big-picture economics and market intuition, fundamental analysis, industry knowledge, and at least some idea of immediate support and resistance. The less you know or are sure you know, the shorter should be your trading horizon.

If you cannot synthesize all these factors and come up with winning trades in real time, then you should place your funds in bonds, where the rate of return is known.

### Selecting Good Eggs

We can believe that the market tends toward efficiency (i.e., it prices stocks correctly when fresh information is released), but is not always efficient. Efficiency is a process, not a permanent condition. Financial markets theorists confuse a flow with a state, like the comparison of a cash flow report to a balance sheet, which is a fixed snapshot of assets and liabilities that changes five seconds after it is completed. There are times when the market does not have information. The information may exist, but it isn't widely known. A second case occurs when the market has the information but is interpreting it incorrectly. (Information is not knowledge, and knowledge is not wisdom.) Both of these situations are so common that we may say efficiency is often the exception rather than the rule. In other words, the market is pricing the security efficiently on the basis of what it knows or thinks it knows, but in reality, an inefficiency exists in the form of not-known information or improperly processed information. Inefficiency is a catch-all term; it encompasses a cornucopia of information that is not known to all or is at least not interpreted the same way by all.

In the first instance, where the information does exist but the market doesn't know it yet, some insiders may know it (and some outsiders may guess it). Inside information is the very essence of an inefficiency. When the market gets to know the new information, it may be efficient in pricing the stock higher (or lower, as the case may be). Meanwhile, as long as the information is not known, the insider can exploit the inefficiency. The best way to select a stock that is sure to rise is to have inside information about an invention or patent, FDA approval, a merger or acquisition, or another major discovery. Actual trading on inside information is illegal in the United States, as various people have discovered to their rue (including printers of documents, and secretaries and their brothers-in-law). The illegality of insider trading means that assiduous study of insider transactions doesn't necessarily tip you to real inside information, although some claim it can come in handy, if only as an overall barometer of management confidence. Of course, it can also mean nothing at all.

The next-best way to pick a surefire stock is to get in on initial public offerings. In recent years, some 90 percent of IPOs have resulted in immediate gains (within the first three months). The problem here is that everyone knows this statistic, and there tends to be a shortage of IPO shares available to the general public. Those who are included in an initial allocation are big customers of the underwriter, or those able to return the favor. IPOs are an instance of inefficiency, too, not because of unknown news, but because of the supply constraint. As we noted in *CNBC 24/7, Trading Around the Clock, Around the World,* foreign companies that may have traded for years on their home exchanges often behave like IPOs when they are listed for the first time as ADRs. Supply constraints are typically less onerous then.

Inside information and IPOs are two examples of situations where almost no judgment is required to pick a high-probability trade. *Everything else takes work.* It seems ridiculous to mention it, but many people seem to feel that it doesn't take any special skills to pick winning trades. If you wanted to become an engineer, a gardener, or a cook, you would go to school, read books, and practice, practice, practice—but, for some reason, people feel they should be able to make investing and trading decisions with no preparation at all. In the real world, though, there are two essential paths down which you must go in order to succeed in investing and trading.

On the first path, you train yourself to identify the inefficiencies that offer profit opportunity. Warren Buffett, for example, has said that if electric utilities become deregulated, it's a business in which he would like to invest. This is a meaningful statement.

Buffett has identified an inefficiency (regulation) that inhibits electric utility companies from maximizing their performance. But he thinks it's a good business (and Mr. Buffett's judgment on company valuation is always worth consideration).

The second path is a form of self-discipline. It's conceivable that you could be given 10 insider tips and 10 first-round IPO allocations and still lose your entire capital stake if you failed to apportion correctly among the choices or if you failed to sell at the right time. Each trade has its own risk-reward characteristics that are roughly knowable in advance. You should apportion a higher percentage of total capital to the trade that has the higher win-loss probability ratio—but most people do not. If you are playing a game of chance in which the probability of winning is 3 to 1, you should put a higher proportion of total capital on each round of play than if the probability of winning is 1.5 to 1. If you have just had a big gain and your total capital is now doubled, you should continue to invest the same fraction of total capital in each probability category.

What is not so obvious is that when you have just had a big loss, you need to reduce proportionately the amount invested in each round of play. Instead, many people fall prey to the gambler's fallacy; after a series of losing trades, they increase the amount of capital on the next trade, on the assumption that "it's time" for a winning trade. This is simply nonsense. The market does not owe you a winning trade after a series of losing trades. In fact, the odds on a particular transaction have not changed at all or may have fallen, if it's the same security and if it is on a newly emerged falling trend. Moreover, a series of losing trades can easily happen even in a situation where the probability of winning remains at 3 to 1. The only way to stay in the game (preserve capital) is to trade a fixed fraction of total capital—and to trade only when the expected return is positive in the first place. It's always possible that your estimation of 3 to 1 is wrong, and a series of losing trades is the market's way of alerting you to that unhappy fact.

This raises another key issue of trading discipline. After you have discovered the market inefficiency that is your own special insight, you have to believe in it. True faith in your judgment can only come from having done exhaustive analysis, including an honest listing of all the things that can go wrong and a reasonable estimation of the gain/loss probability. If you don't truly believe in your idea and in your ability to create a realistic estimation of the win-loss probability, you will exit at the wrong time.

Buy-and-hold is bunk because of these two points: (1) you are supposed to buy value stocks when they are temporarily cheap *but (2) you are not supposed to sell them when they are temporarily overvalued.* This runs directly contrary to the most basic rule of trading, investing, or playing a game: risk a portion of your capital stake only if you have an expectation of a positive return. When a stock becomes overvalued, it no longer has a positive expectancy. You wouldn't buy it today on its present valuation, whether you are using its P/E or any other criterion. If you wouldn't buy it, why should you hold it? Some other security is undervalued. It makes more sense to sell the overvalued security and buy the undervalued one, doesn't it? This is, in fact, the formula that John Templeton used in developing his first successful mutual fund.

## 2. Value Investing Ignores Risk Management

The value-investing school of thought starts with a holding period of your entire lifetime. Warren Buffett says, "My favorite time frame for holding a stock is forever." Once you have found a stock that meets the value criteria, it can fall from $50 to $10 but you will continue to hold it, unworried. It will come back. True value stocks always come back. In fact, true value stocks weather bear markets better than glamour stocks. Because it is a value stock, you don't need to follow the stock or the news about the company very closely. Philip Carret, the founder of one of the first mutual funds (in 1928), said you should evaluate your stocks only every six months. If you do it more often, you are likely to sell too soon. It can take years for the stock market to appreciate your value choice, and after all, even the bluest of blue-chip companies has to issue negative news once in a while. As John Bogle, founder of the Vanguard Funds, puts it, "Think long term. Don't let transitory changes in stock prices alter your investment program. Stocks may remain overvalued, or undervalued, for years. Patience and consistency are valuable assets for the intelligent investor. The best rule is to stay the course." In other words, don't let a loss get under your skin. Be loyal to your stock picks. Bull markets follow bear markets and even the most beaten-down sector comes back eventually [*The Little Book of Business Wisdom, Rules for Success from More than 50 Business Legends* (John Wiley & Sons, 2001)].

Being able to hold a stock forever and to view losses as temporary requires that you really have identified a true value stock (i.e., it is not a buggy-whip stock in the age of the automobile). The first value investing rule is: "investigate before you invest." Warren Buffett's main source of information is the annual reports of the prospect companies and their competitors. Legendary investor Bernard Baruch said of the two principal mistakes made by nearly all amateurs, "The first is to have an inexact knowledge of the securities . . . to know too little about a company's management, its earnings and prospects for future growth." As a practical matter, most people do not have the time or the analytical skills to identify value situations. Thus, a huge industry of securities analysts, advisors, touts, and chat-room posters has sprung up.

To select a value stock on its internal criteria is to ignore its riskiness vis-à-vis the rest of the market (beta), and to ignore the riskiness of the market itself. When the luminaries of the stock brokerage industry appear on TV ads, they tell you that stocks are the only place to be, with a nod once in a while to bonds. But stocks are not the only class of securities available today to the average investor, nor the least risky. Stocks are far riskier than many other classes of securities, which is precisely why the average return on stocks is so high. You've heard of the one-for-one trade-off between risk and return. It is, roughly, true. In every other class of securities, especially futures, we hear that harsh risk-management discipline is needed to be a successful investor. But somehow, in "value investing," we need no risk management at all because "value stocks will come back." This is nonsense on the face of it. Companies change over time and can lose their intrinsic value through bad management, competition, failing to keep up with technological change, lost liability lawsuits, fraud, federal antitrust breakups, and for many other reasons.

## 3. Professional Analysts Can't Do It

Professional securities analysts who work for brokerage houses are trained in financial statement analysis, the heart of the investment decision. Criteria for selecting value stocks were laid down in 1932 by Benjamin Graham and David Dodd in *Security Analysis* (McGraw-Hill, 1997), and have been modified, refined, and added to ever since.

On the simplest level, we know what makes a winning stock. We get the highest rate of return over a long period of time when we buy stocks with the lowest price-book ratio, lowest price-cash flow ratio, and lowest price to sales. James O'Shaughnessy gave us Table 1.1 in *What Works on Wall Street* (McGraw-Hill, 1997).

We all have available today the ability to scan the universe of stocks for companies that meet these criteria. At www.multex.com and many other Web sites, you can quickly and easily screen all the stocks to find those that have the best ratios. You don't even have to do the work yourself; www.worldlyinvestor.com has already done it in its "Value Stock Screen." This uses a large-cap bias to embrace companies with a low price-to-book ratio, recent market performance that is below average, and good earnings prospects.

Notice that the price-earnings (P/E) ratio is not on the O'Shaughnessy list in Table 1.1. It is on the list of a sophisticated analytical approach taken by Yale University Professor of Finance Zhiwu Chen, whose www.valuengine.com offers modeling based on three factors: (1) trailing 12-month earnings per share (EPS), (2) the analyst consensus estimate of the company's future 12-month EPS, and (3) the 30-year Treasury yield to derive a company's "fair value." It also uses some important

**Table 1.1.**   The Best Ratios

|  | Annual Return, 1952–1994 |
| --- | --- |
| All Stocks | 14.6% |
| 50 Stocks with lowest price/book ratio | 17.5 |
| 50 Stocks with highest price/book ratio | **11.9** |
| 50 Stocks with lowest price/cash flow ratio | 17.1 |
| 50 Stocks with highest price/cash flow ratio | **10.8** |
| 50 Stocks with lowest price/sales ratio | 18.9 |
| 50 Stocks with highest price/sales ratio | **8.2** |

*Source:* Reproduced from Timothy P. Vick, *Wall Street on Sale* (New York: McGraw-Hill, 1999), p. 29.

technical indicators for short, medium, and long-term reversals. ValueEngine puts it all together to calculate the probability of a doubled stock price as well as the probability of meeting and exceeding any given investment target by a stock or a portfolio of stocks. You can also create portfolios that are aggressive or conservative. ValueEngine's track record is impressive, but notice that, again, we stuck with dependence on the consensus of analysts as to future earnings per share, which is a two-pronged forecast—not only earnings in absolute dollar terms (knowable, within a range), but earnings per share, with the price set by the market (not knowable).

Earnings per share is an awful statistic that gets just about everyone in trouble, whether they use it to make dire or rosy predictions. The P/E ratio is a snare and a delusion. A study cited in *The Economist* magazine (April 7, 2001, p. 84) states that the average profit forecast for stocks tracked by I/B/E/S (www.ibes.com) was 19.8 percent as of March 2001—but only 10 percent of firms *ever* had profit growth of 18 percent or more over any 10-year period during 1951 to 1997. Further, the median forecast growth rate for any three-year period was 14.5 percent over 1982 to 1998, when the actual number was 9 percent. In other words, analysts are consistently overoptimistic—and yet we accuse them of lowballing the numbers so that their stocks will rise when the company beats the consensus (Louis Chan, Jason Karceski, and Josef Lakonishok, "The Level and Persistence of Growth Rates," University of Illinois Working Paper, March 2001).

Securities analysts can't just name the stocks that meet the O'Shaughnessy criteria because new companies sometimes burn up the quote screen. Especially in the high-tech mania 1990s, analysts didn't have performance for five years, or even three years, as a basis on which to calculate the standard ratios, but the new companies were outperforming everything in sight. In many cases, analysts failed to separate out the "objective" value of the stock from their opinion on where the market would take the stock. It's not clear that this is a failure that can be avoided. During the early stages of the telecom and dot-com frenzies, just about any company associated with the Internet saw big stock gains. Individual stocks are heavily influenced by "the market," if only because index funds have to buy the market as new money comes in (or sell it as money goes out), so it's not entirely appropriate to divorce particular stocks from the overall market trend. The environment has an important effect on individual stocks. It is the context. How does one discriminate among them? Analysis can't take place in a vacuum, and valuing a stock like its peers in the same industry or sector is not *per se* a bad process, but it certainly can result in big mistakes.

Some professional securities analysts deserve the opprobrium and scorn heaped on their heads. In 1999, one analyst "valued" Qualcomm at $1,000 per share, which, multiplied by the number of shares outstanding, would have made the company's market capitalization $300 billion at a time when its sales were $4 billion. Common sense—let alone established value-investing concepts—makes a mockery of such a forecast. Analysts who issued exaggerated forecasts for dot-com stocks (such as amazon.com) got their comeuppance in the dot-com crash of 2000. Many publications, especially *Barron's*, publish barbed pieces that discuss the real numbers and how some analysts are missing the juicy revelations to be found by a thorough grinding of the facts—including accounting gimmicks and loopholes, such as merger and acquisition accounting and cash-flow timing, that pull the wool over the eyes of unwary analysts.

Of particular concern is a trend by companies to modify the meaning of "earnings" to exclude unfavorable items. According to generally accepted accounting principles, or GAAP, earnings are sales minus the cost of goods sold, depreciation, and operating expenses, including interest and taxes. "Earnings" is another word for "net income," or used to be. Now companies use new categories (not recognized by GAAP) like "operating earnings," "pro forma earnings," and "economic," "core," or "ongoing" earnings. By these definitions, earnings are anything the company wants them to be. JDS Uniphase, for example, reported "pro forma" earnings for the fiscal year ended June 30, 2001, of $67.4 million. According to *The Wall Street Journal*, it arrived at that number by excluding 98 percent of the $52 billion in operating expenses. Under GAAP, the company actually had a $50.6 billion full-year net loss (August 21, 2001). It goes without saying that professional securities analysts are hard to trust when they swallow whoppers like this.

The public has other reasons to distrust professional securities analysts, too. The most obvious is the hint of big-institution market manipulation arising from analysts' manipulation of certain numbers, especially earnings. When a company's earnings exceed the earnings estimates of the pros, the stock rises. Analysts may have an inherent conflict of interest that gives them an incentive to lowball earnings estimates, thus ensuring a stock rise when the actual earnings number is announced. They are accused of serving two masters: the companies that spoon-feed them the information on which earnings estimates are based, and their employers, which may, in other divisions, have business with the very same companies.

Companies are forbidden to announce earnings estimates (and stock-price targets) under Securities and Exchange Commission (SEC) regulations aimed at preventing companies from manipulating their own stocks. They do, however, make public other information (such as contracted future sales) that allows someone else to make earnings estimates. Until the SEC put an end to it with Regulation FD (for "Fair Disclosure") in late 2000, companies gave preferred treatment to securities analysts, disseminating more information and earlier information to them than to the public. The new regulation is intended to level the playing field for professionals and amateurs alike, although some professionals are squawking that corporate fear of running afoul of Reg FD has turned the spigot of company information and insight to a trickle insufficient to the job. Critics respond that now, perhaps, the analysts will have to look at actual numbers rather than junketing off to hear public relations hype.

A different charge is that analysts may actually own shares in the companies on which they are reporting. According to an article in *Institutional Investor* magazine (April 2001, pp. 60 ff.), one analyst owned 100,000 shares, worth about $10 million, in an IPO managed by his firm. His report on the company was glowing. Securities firms may state, in the fine print of an offering memorandum or elsewhere, that "the company and/or its employees may have an interest in the securities described," but the general disclaimer does not help you figure out whether the analyst of any particular report has a conflict of interest. You may think that it's just dandy if an analyst does have a position because it means he believes in his work—but what about when he starts feeling that the stock has reached a peak and he would like to sell it—but cannot because of his company's internal rule on his minimum holding period? If he says the stock is topping, he is working against his own self-interest.

Mistakes and incompetence are one thing, but venality is another. The uproar over whether the integrity of analysts is compromised has already resulted in formulation of a code of ethics by the Association for Investment Management and Research (www.aimr.com). The U.S. Congress held hearings on conflict of interest in June 2001. The Securities Industry Association (www.sia.com) is concerned, not only for the sake of its image but also because investor lawsuits—charging that analysts issued misleading "guidance" on some stocks, and underestimated risks—are starting to pile up. The U.S. Attorney General for New York has opened a case file on specific conflicts of interest.

It can be difficult to know whether professional securities analysts are competent to identify true value stocks that will always come back, and independent enough to be motivated to have that as their only goal. These analysts are trained in financial analysis. How can you hope to duplicate or surpass their skills, let alone find the time to exercise them? The answer is: you can't, and it's not clear that you should try. Possible solutions include buying newsletters of independent analysts with good track records. (The *Hulbert Digest,* which evaluates advisors on a risk-adjusted basis over long periods of time, is indispensable.)

At the least, learn the true meaning of financial terms. Books abound. A good one is John A. Tracy, *How to Read a Financial Report* (John Wiley & Sons, 1999).

## 4. A Company Is Not Its Stock

Of the 500 companies selected for the Standard & Poor's 500 index in 1957, only 74 were still on the list in 1998 and only 12 outperformed the index over those 41 years. According to *Creative Destruction* by business consultants Richard Foster and Sarah Kaplan (Doubleday, 2001), two-thirds of those on the S&P 500 list will be acquired or will die over the next 25 years due to their inability to keep pace with technological and other changes. This is because companies that are "built to last," like IBM, can become hopelessly rigid in their thinking. In fact, this already happened to IBM, which built the first personal computer and then failed (at least initially) to capitalize on it. IBM's stock lost half its value between 1990 and the end of 1993.

Arie de Geus, in *The Living Company* (Harvard Business School Press, 2000), agrees that the life span of a typical Fortune 500 company is not much longer than the average executive's career. Using a biological metaphor, strategic planner de Geus says that companies that survive longer than average are like living entities that perpetuate themselves as ongoing communities rather than "economic companies," which are in business solely to produce wealth for a small inner group. Living companies manage for survival; economic companies manage for profit. Like living creatures, living companies are sensitive to their environment (they learn and adapt), they have a strong sense of identity, they are tolerant of unconventional thinking and experimentation, and they conserve (financial) resources for a rainy day, gaining flexibility.

What this means is that stock picking on the basis of financial ratios—price/earnings, price/book, and so on—may have worked in the past, as amply demonstrated in many books and papers, but in an environment of unbelievably rapid technological and social change, the only thing that counts is management. That's why top executives like Jack Welch, CEO of General Electric (and before him, Lee Iacocca of Chrysler) are the subjects of endless interviews. But what about the other 499 companies in the S&P 500? How can the average investor learn whether senior management has the right stuff to push its company along the evolutionary path?

The determining role of top management is increasingly coming under the microscope. *Forbes* magazine (www.forbes.com /valueceos) has dedicated a portion of its Web site to a new CEO yardstick of its own devising. In its "First Annual CEO Value Survey," it looked at 278 CEOs who have been in place for at least five years at companies that did not post a loss in that time. The average annual pay of this group is a stunning $7.64 million. The *Forbes* formula divides each CEO's five-year pay package by something called a "total growth rate"—the average of sales, net income, and share-price growth, including dividends reinvested.

This results in what 1 percent of growth cost each company. Warren Buffett, for example, earned $500,000, and Berkshire Hath-
away had a five-year total growth rate of 26 percent. That means
he delivered one percentage point of growth for $19,000, which
makes Buffett the top value among CEOs. Citigroup's Sanford
Weill, in contrast, has compensation of $785 million for 33 per-
cent growth, or a $23.8 million cost of 1 percent of growth. To the
officers and staff at Citigroup, this must be hard to swallow. It's
not clear that Weill's overcompensation affects the stock price,
though.

*Forbes'* financial ratio is not the only way to measure management. We may also cite imagination, inventiveness, employee
stock plan generosity, and a hundred other hard-to-quantify factors. Is it a joyful place to work, or is it like Dilbert's job?

Looking at companies that deliberately seek to regenerate
themselves, Sony stands out, although it, too, is subject to some
of the same constraints as other large companies—mostly imagination versus bureaucracy. It was the first Japanese company to
list its ADR in the United States (1961). It invented or popular-
ized the transistor (1957), Trinitron TV tube (1968), Walkman
(1979), digital CDs (1982), and PlayStation game consoles (1990s
to today). It made a mistake with Betamax (1980) but recovered to
focus on content (Columbia Pictures). Sony stumbled in late 2000
and early 2001 by not producing enough game consoles, and now
faces heightened competition from others, including Microsoft.
Still, as of 2000, Sony was the most esteemed brand name in the
United States, according to a Harris poll. And its stock? From
February 29, 2000, to February 28, 2001, it fell from $156.80 to
$74.86, losing more than 50 percent of its value.

In contrast, we read that the same management at Motorola
that caused Iridium to fall from the sky, literally, is still in place.
Motorola stock made a new all-time high in March 2000, after this
awful fact was known. Xerox, one of the Nifty Fifty in the 1970s,
and inventor of the graphical user interface, ethernet communica-
tions, and digital printing, famously "fumbled the future" in the
early 1980s. Twenty years later, it is still under harsh criticism for
financial irregularities and almost unbelievable management mistakes. The stock hit a low of $3.75 in December 2000—but had
more than doubled less than six months later.

The business consultants and strategic planners propose convincing models of what makes a great company that will survive—but so what? It doesn't mean that the stock will do well, or that bad company stocks will do poorly. John Maynard Keynes said it best, in 1936: "the market is like a beauty contest. You shouldn't bet on the girl you think is the prettiest, but rather on the girl the other judges will think is the prettiest."

The market is usually willing to be influenced by hype and spin. We have all seen the range of responses to a bad earnings "outlook" by a CEO. If he comes to stage center with a gloomy air, semantically negative words, and discouraged body language, the stock falls. If he bounces around the stage and uses upbeat language, the stock rises. Similarly, the investing crowd is willing to overlook earnings downgrades from professional analysts based on a diminished earnings outlook if the company can create favorable sentiment. Maybe the stock "should" fall on the basis of objective ratio analysis, but what "should" happen to a stock is not necessarily what we get. In fact, it's seldom what we get. Nobody can untangle actual company and industry news (like awful earnings) from crowd psychology. This is the central failure of fundamental analysis. If economist John Moffatt is right, only about 25 percent of a stock's price has to do with its fundamentals, anyway. Another 25 percent is due to the macroeconomic environment, and a full 50 percent to market conditions. We might do better to find a stock with a beta of one (perfect correlation with the S&P 500, Dow, or Nasdaq) and simply buy and sell when the market is up or down by $x$ percent, known as a filter rule. It would certainly save a lot of time and grief.

## 5. You Don't Live to Invest

Another reason "value investing" doesn't work for most people is that you don't live to invest, you invest to live. In other words, you want to spend the money at some point. At the very least, you want to give to your heirs more money than you started out with. As long as you imagine that your holding period is indefinitely long, it's comforting to think that the compound interest function is in your favor. But to apply the compound interest function retroactively to historical returns and then to turn around and apply it to the future is bad logic. Technically, the only time you actually earn compound interest is in a security with a stated interest rate, such as a savings account, CD, T-bill, or bond. Those instruments carry a rate of interest and you can compound the interest going forward in time at various rates as interest rates change. Stocks do not carry an inherent rate of interest. You are not lending money to the company. You become an owner when you buy stock in a company. You are owed no rate of interest at all. You might be owed a dividend, but any company can terminate its dividend payout at any time. While it may be true that over $x$ number of years, you are likely to earn a rate of return in stocks that is similar to the return over the past $x$ number of years, you cannot and should not count on it. *To repeat: stocks do not have an inherent rate of return.*

Finally, we circle around to personal risk management. In value investing, you don't need risk management because value stocks "always come back." Let's say you buy a stock and it immediately falls by 50 percent. You now need to make 100 percent on that stock in order to get back to your starting point. If you are counting on the usual 15 percent per annum long-term "normal average return" in stocks, this is going to take you several years— 4.8 years, in fact (using the Rule of 72s). *A bad first period can never be made up except by expecting a higher return than the market can be expected to deliver.* The hold-forever value investing philosophy has an internal inconsistency: it's okay for a value stock to fall 50 percent, because it will "come back." But if you hold the stock for a long period of time, it will come back to the long-term average rate of return of the total market or a bit more—from a permanently reduced level. Logically, if you are the poor soul who has a bad first period, the correct response is to dump the so-called value stock that just gave you a 50 percent loss, buy a so-called speculative stock that is already rising, and hope for a 100 percent return to get back to your starting point. Such an action, of course, invalidates the principle of the entire value-investing process. Remember, it took 25 years for the Dow to recover the prices that were at the peak in 1929.

# Inescapable Conclusions and a New Definition

The five objections to buy-and-hold are a justification of active trading. This is the inescapable conclusion. It's the same conclusion arrived at by the great traders and investors of the past, who used the negatively charged word "speculation" without apology. As each of them noted, of the many investors who try, few excel at speculation. It takes a combination of skill, talent, and imagination. As Philip Carret wrote, in *The Art of Speculation* (*Barron's*, 1930):

> Speculation is no simple business. The amateur cannot take a few thousand dollars' capital, fifteen minutes a day of time, treat it as a side-line and be any more successful than he would be in any other business. Indeed, speculation requires broader knowledge, closer attention, sounder judgment than the average business. Prices on the New York Stock Exchange are affected by French politics, German banking conditions, wars and rumors of war in the Near East, the Chinese money market, the condition of the wheat crop in the Argentine, the temper of the Mexican Congress as well as by a host of domestic influences. The successful speculator must carefully weigh the effect of all these influences, set down the pros and cons and arrive at a sound conclusion as to the side on which the balance lies. When he has done all this, he has only made a beginning. If he concludes that the balance favors an upward movement, he must still decide which stocks he is to buy for maximum profit.

Seventy years after Carret wrote this, we find mention in the *Financial Times* of every single one of the factors he named. Carret was referring to domestic stocks under these influences; today, the individual can buy and sell securities directly affected by those influences instead of domestic securities more remotely affected.

In practice, trading foreign securities is still quite difficult. You can easily trade foreign stocks listed on a U.S. exchange as ADRs, but they are subject to almost the same level of scrutiny as other U.S. stocks, meaning opportunities have already been seized *under normal conditions.* You would want to trade an ADR only when conditions are not normal. To buy and sell foreign stocks as they trade on their home-country exchanges is just as difficult today as it was 12 and 18 months ago, when we first started to hear about it. Every broker and data vendor promising foreign stocks by 2000 or 2001 has so far failed to deliver. Foreign stocks are still the exclusive property of the professionals. This is not really surprising; U.S. regulatory authorities believe that foreign stocks are not adequately regulated in their home countries as to disclosure, insider trading, and so on. The brokerage industry (quite rightly) fears liability in offering such securities to an aggressively litigious public. Unless you are a high-net-worth individual with a big account at one of the major brokerages, you will find it difficult or impossible to trade (say) a Greek stock on the Athens exchange. This is a one-sided situation. Many U.S. stocks trade on exchanges overseas. Microsoft, for example, is listed in Argentina, Hong Kong, London, and probably, by the time you read this, the new Nasdaq Europe.

Similarly, you can buy and sell foreign bonds, but the brokerage industry doesn't make it easy for you to do small lots, and you may feel that the exchange rate, over which you have no control, is rigged against you. It would be far easier to trade developed-country bonds in the futures market, and emerging-market bonds off the established exchanges altogether in the newly developing market for "emerging market" securities. Once you start looking at foreign or global securities, meaning those that can be traded around the clock and around the world, foreign exchange as an asset class has to come to your attention, and so we spend rather a lot of time on it in this book. It is not as mysterious and difficult as it may seem on the surface.

Our new definition of the global trader is one who is not afraid of the word "speculation," who appreciates that it's hard work and not a hobby, and who is aware that, in this area, more persons fail than succeed. The global trader never goes into a position expecting to hold it forever—in fact, he has an exit strategy. The global trader may never venture outside U.S. stocks, but by understanding as many of the outside influences named by Carret as possible, he is a better big-picture investor all the same. The quintessential global trader is George Soros. What exactly did he do that people are still talking about 10 years later? The answer may surprise you.

## The Ultimate Inefficiency— What Soros Really Did

Ten years ago, George Soros reasoned that the British pound would fall dramatically against the German Deutschemark (DM) and U.S. dollar, and he invested $10 billion in his reasoning. He was correct, and the market rewarded him with a $1 billion gain during the course of only a few weeks. Many people today misrepresent not only what happened, but what it means to the investing world. A CNBC anchorwoman, for example, said in April 2001 that the Soros "gamble" had "bankrupted" the Bank of England.

This statement is a complete misrepresentation of the situation and a misunderstanding of what global trading is all about. It was not a gamble. It was an investment decision as carefully and thoroughly researched as any stock purchase for a portfolio by an experienced investment professional. The counterparties who bought British pounds from Soros may or may not have taken a loss on their purchases—depending on whether they sold the pounds right away or waited until later, when they were worth a lot less— but the counterparties did not include the Bank of England, at least initially. The Bank of England is the central bank of the United Kingdom. It did not go bankrupt and is in operation today.

The Bank of England was not a direct counterparty to Soros's transactions, and it is inaccurate to set the scene as though Soros were sitting across a table from the Bank of England and playing a single hand of poker in the Wild West. Soros's counterparties were banks acting on their own account or for the accounts of their customers. The Bank of England comes into the story only because the U.K. government had signed a treaty with other European countries to defend the price of the U.K. pound at a particular level. The Bank was the instrument to implement a government policy. It was not entering into a transaction with Soros or anyone else, in which the terms of the transaction were negotiable (as in the case of the auction of government bonds, for example). It was, however, in the background as a potential counterparty to the banks with which it had a relationship, in the event that the pound rose or fell too far from the level mandated in the treaty. In the end, it became an actual counterparty, just like any other commercial or speculative buyer and seller of pounds.

Why is the event so widely misunderstood? Possibly because it makes a better story to display the lone cowboy who brings down the self-important and wrong-headed forces of authority. Possibly also because going short is still viewed as wildly risky, whereas to couch the transaction as buying the Deutschemark or U.S. dollar would not be seen as risky—even though in the foreign exchange market, if you are buying one thing, you must be selling another. To go short a currency is no riskier than buying or selling any security using the same level of leverage. And that's the third part of the glamour—leverage in the foreign exchange market can be, literally, infinite when trades are conducted with no money on deposit with the counterparty.

Unfortunately, glamorizing the story has resulted in just about everybody missing the point. This must be a terrible disappointment to Mr. Soros, who in fact won a billion-dollar vindication of his theory of how markets work, only to see a different theory win the mind of the majority. The winning theory (the efficient market hypothesis) ended up costing the market $3.6 billion when Long-Term Capital Management collapsed in 1998, only six years later.

George Soros was a successful equity-market investor long before he earned the $1 billion. Most accounts would say he "won" the money, but this was not a game and was not viewed as a game by any the participants, least of all Mr. Soros. Once you understand Soros's way of looking at how the world works, you see that there was nothing of a gamble about it. In gambling, the outcome of each toss of the coin is independent of the one that came before (and the one that will come after). The player cannot control or even influence the outcome. According to Soros, however, in markets as in life, price outcomes are deeply influenced by what comes before. In fact, price events develop in a predictable way if you can only discern the bias inherent in market participants.

In classical philosophy, Plato questioned whether objective reality exists, and if it does, whether anyone can perceive it. Soros believes no one can see the world objectively, and thus everyone operates with a perceptual bias. A prime influence on markets is the players' own imperfect understanding of what is going on. Market participants are not capable of being solely rational; their beliefs influence their thinking. Perceptions flawed by beliefs in turn influence market prices when participants act on them. Market participants do influence the outcome of price behavior, unlike the coin toss. The price behavior (the fact) is again interpreted in the light of beliefs, which cause the next price, and so on. Soros named this feedback loop "reflexivity" and reasoned that, in a long chain of belief-influenced price outcomes, prices could journey very far from where they should be on the basis of a bias-free analysis.

Reflexivity is akin to the Heisenberg uncertainty principle, which states that you cannot accurately measure subatomic particle movements because the act of measuring alters the movement. (This is why Soros named his fund the Quantum Fund, referring to quantum physics.) Reflexivity never caught on as a commonly used concept in the market. Some thought it was too obvious a phenomenon to deserve a name. Some claimed they couldn't understand it, although *The Alchemy of Finance* (John Wiley & Sons, 1994) is no more unreadable than many other books. Soros's explanation of what caused the stock market crash in 1987 is still the clearest and most plausible of all the scenarios proposed over the years.

At the time *The Alchemy of Finance* was published, the market was increasingly embracing a contradictory idea: the investor is rational and solely rational. Moreover, all investors are rational all the time, and they discount expected future events according to a numerically accurate and appropriate table of net present values. Thus, market prices are always "right." This is not possible in Soros's eyes because the chain of causation is not fact to fact, but fact to perception to fact. Prices are not a passive reflection of value; they are an active ingredient in forming the perception of value. Thus are born booms and busts; both are functions of a self-reinforcing process of misconceptions and mistaken perceptions. Markets are capable of becoming unstable and chaotic when the chain of mistaken perceptions leads prices to extremes. Then you get a one-way market, known as severe disequilibrium.

The phrasing may be in the form of economic theory, but the idea is to identify *crowd behavior.*

This is precisely what Soros did in shorting the U.K. pound in September 1992. He saw a chain of mistakes being made by the U.K. government in the management of monetary and fiscal policy, and foresaw a scenario in which eventually the market would wake up and say, "The emperor has no clothes." By perceiving how the government was deluding itself and carrying the market along in the same cloud of mistaken thinking, Soros predicted a crash. The delusion was in the form of an unworkable institutional arrangement whereby Britain had agreed, in the Maastricht Treaty, to maintain the exchange rate of the pound within a narrow band against the Deutschemark (with a central parity of DM 2.95 for each pound). But Germany had just reunified West with East, which was an expensive undertaking that pushed up inflation. The Bundesbank, the inflation-obsessed German central bank, accordingly kept interest rates high. High rates were not appropriate for the British economy, though; by the summer of 1992, it was falling into stagnation, if not recession. The government, which at the time controlled the Bank of England, was not willing to lower interest rates and thus potentially weaken the pound to the point where its value in Deutschemark terms would have to be defended—according to the exchange rate treaty just signed in February—in the form of the Bank of England's buying pounds from all comers. The alternative would have been to raise interest rates, exactly the opposite of what a central bank should do in the face of an economic downturn.

Soros's great achievement was to listen and to hear what the head of the Bundesbank was saying—it would not cut rates against its own self-interest in order to help out Britain. If Britain had to spend billions to defend the agreed-upon rate, well, tough, that's what the treaty called for. Soros also perceived that the British government was not facing unpleasant realities. It hoped, perhaps through respect for its sovereign authority, to achieve two mutually exclusive goals: (1) membership in the European Rate Mechanism established by the treaty and the associated uneconomic pound/Deutschemark rate and (2) the freedom to manage interest rates for the best interests of the British economy. Alternatively, the British government could have goosed economic activity by increasing government spending or reducing taxes, but these fiscal options were not seen as politically acceptable by the Conservative government.

Economists and traders were saying the same thing as Soros at the time. Whenever a government interferes with the free-market setting of prices, distortions appear in the allocation of resources. This is why California has had an energy crisis in 2001. It is a well-known fact of economic life that capital, the resource in question in this context, will flow to the highest expected real rate of return. If the nominal rate of return is perceived to be eroding through inflation or devaluation, capital will flee elsewhere. The price of capital happened to be denominated in pounds in this instance. All Soros did was apply this simple rule of market economics, which in itself is no great feat. And he was certainly not alone; his special triumph and his act of courage was that he invested such a large sum in the expected outcome. (Later, he was to say that the crisis occurred earlier than he had expected, or he would have done more.)

The exact chain of events that led to the U.K.'s abrogating its treaty responsibilities started when many foreign exchange trading houses—commercial and investment banks, as well as hedge funds like Soros's—sold pounds both spot and forward (i.e., for later delivery). The bandwagon very quickly gained momentum as market participants observed that bids to buy pounds were falling drastically, minute by minute. Exactly the same thing happens when bad news or an unfavorable rumor about a stock starts spreading through the equity market. Everyone wants to sell, no one wants to buy. Just as the designated specialist serves as the ultimate market maker on a stock exchange, a nation's central bank serves as the ultimate market maker in foreign exchange. The Bank of England became the only party willing to buy pounds; it paid for them out of its foreign currency reserves of dollars, Deutschemarks, and other currencies. The Bank of England bought £24 billion over the course of two days (September 15 and 16, 1992), and raised interest rates twice in a single day (from 10 percent to 15 percent), before formally announcing that it was withdrawing from the European Rate Mechanism. Robert Slater, in *Soros—The Life, The Times & Trading Secrets of the World's Greatest Investor* (Irwin, 1996), reports that the United

Kingdom had £44 billion in reserves to start with, so the intervention wasted more than half of the country's savings.

Slater notes that Soros was not alone in shorting the pound, and names other hedge funds that made hundreds of millions, including Paul Tudor Jones, not to mention Citicorp, J.P. Morgan, and Chemical Bank, which together made $800 million more, in that quarter, than the normal amount. A glance at Figure 1.1 shows that this was a runaway train that anyone could jump on, especially if he was using two moving-average-crossover technical analyses (as shown). But it was Soros who got the spotlight. In fact, he made about $2 billion, or double the amount usually mentioned, on other related transactions at the same time, mostly by buying British equities that would rise once the pound fell. As Soros himself said, the principles behind his analysis of the situation were no different from any other analysis of

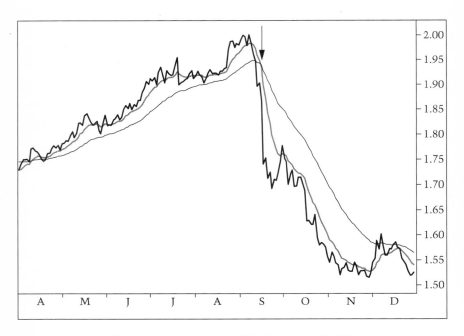

**Figure 1.1**   Devaluation of the British pound, 1992.

whether a security is undervalued or overvalued, the central purpose of all securities analysis.

When observers say that "Soros broke the Bank of England," what they are really saying is that lots of people, personified by Soros, correctly detected that a security was artificially overvalued and therefore vulnerable to a price decline. A trading decision is not a moral judgment or a political statement—it is a price estimate. The British government broke itself by having made a political decision (the treaty) that had unintended consequences. Its intentions may have been honorable, but its economic analysis was wrong. The same thing happens every day to die-hard holders of mispriced securities. In this instance, the holder of the security happened to be a government. The market does not care. Short-selling in equities is considerably harder to achieve, but companies that write to shareholders asking that they forbid their custodians to lend shares for shorting are acting in the same spirit as the Bank of England. Actually, the Bank of England did have another arrow in its quiver that it did not use this time, although it was known to have used it in the 1967 devaluation: calling up the banks where ultimately all foreign exchange transactions reside, and urging the banks not to take such big positions. Governments theoretically control bank licensing, so there is an implicit threat in such "moral suasion." It is increasingly harder, however, for governments that wholeheartedly embrace raw capitalism in public to revert to such authoritarian measures behind the scenes, especially since the chief outcome would be for banks and brokers merely to relocate outside the sovereign boundaries of the annoying sovereign.

## A Change in Perspective

This most successful speculation of all time seems to stand in blinding contrast to the Buffett mode of investing—buy undervalued but top-flight securities and hold them forever. Buffett says you should buy securities and not object if the stock market were to close for five years. Soros, of course, was following every tiny movement of the pound moment by moment, looking for the optimum exit point. To hear Buffett, there is never an exit point, although he may be exaggerating this issue—Buffett does sell stocks (such as Disney). What is central, though, is that, in both cases, the investment decision is made on the basis of deep and thorough research. The purpose of the research is to identify a market inefficiency, whether it is information not yet known or information not correctly perceived by the rest of the market.

Three other issues obscure the centrality of the inefficiency thesis. First, Soros was not involved in the equity market, but rather the currency market in this instance. Aside from their purchasing power, currencies do not have intrinsic value. Companies do. Currencies do not manufacture products, deliver dividends, or have any of the ownership characteristics of an equity. Well, so what? *The nature of the security is secondary to the act of identifying a tradable inefficiency.* Soros had been an equity analyst—and a highly successful one—for many years. To choose a currency trade was only to recognize that the profit potential in that case was far higher than in any of the other equity, bond, or commodity trades available at the time. In terms of inefficiencies, the Maastricht Treaty had created a whopper. In terms of probabilities, the short sterling trade was a million-to-one gain/loss ratio, while everything else on offer had a lower gain/loss ratio. To invest in a fall in the pound was an act of supreme rationality.

The essence of successful trading or investing is to take a position in an inefficiency, with a high expectation of gain and a high gain-loss ratio. To recognize this can be tremendously liberating. It frees you from semantic servitude to the common usage of the word "saving." If you invest in a stock as an act of saving, and it falls 50 percent, you have lost 50 percent of your savings. To say "It will come back" because it is a value stock is to delude yourself that because you named it "savings," it has some kind of permanent value. In practice, only cash or near-cash should be considered savings, and even then it is at risk of diminution from inflation. About the stock that has fallen 50 percent, you can legitimately say "It will come back" only if you have a specific reason for believing such a thing. If you do, then the gain-loss ratio must be even better today than it was when you initially bought it—and you should buy some more. This is called "averaging down," a practice frowned on by everyone because a big price decline prompts a reevaluation of the security by the market at large. To use a stale evaluation in the face of new information is to be irrational and nonadaptive.

The second issue is Soros's use of leverage. To many, this is what made him a speculator rather than an investor. Leverage, however, is not necessarily an essential part of the trade. The U.K. pound futures contract was worth $125,550 at the beginning of the move (September 8, 1992) and $62,499 at the end of the move (February 12, 1993). An individual could have sold the contract at the beginning and bought it back at the end for a gain of $63,051, or 50.22 percent, with no leverage at all.

The third issue is that Soros was shorting the security. We think of "investing" as always buying something of intrinsic value in the expectation of a rise in that intrinsic value through the work and value-added of land, labor, and capital. But this is a limited and limiting point of view. If the purpose of investing is to make money, it makes no difference whether we make it when the security is rising or when the security is falling. The prejudice against shorting is a moral judgment, not a business judgment. It arises (in large part) from stock exchange rules that were implemented to prevent competitors from driving one another out of business, or to prevent a selling panic from getting out of hand. The minute we understand that to hold forever is against our best interests, and that to hold only securities with a high win-loss expectancy is the superior approach, we are liberated from the "intrinsic value" fiction. Instead of owning a shareholding, which makes us a part owner of a business, we hold a *position in a security*. It doesn't matter whether the position is long or short, as long as we have a positive expectation of gain.

## Summary

To "invest" is to buy an equity with an indefinite holding period and to ignore risk management—specifically, the rule that says you should hold a security only if you have a positive expectation of a gain. Traditional "value investing" does not acknowledge any inefficiency except the one that temporarily put your stock on sale and provided the buying opportunity. You are supposed to

**Table 1.2.**   Trading versus Investing

|  | Investing | Trading |
|---|---|---|
| Goal | Preserve capital | Make money |
| Holding period | Indefinite | Not determined in advance |
| Fundamental research | Intensive | Maybe |
| Technical analysis | No | Maybe |
| Orientation | Intrinsic value—long only | Price trend—long and short |
| Worldly outlook | No | Yes |
| Risk management | None | Dominant |
| Leverage | None | Maybe |

ignore an inefficiency that makes the same stock temporarily overvalued.

To "trade" is to seek any inefficiency in the market pricing of any security (not just equities), regardless of intrinsic value, with the goal of exploiting the price disparity over some time frame not determined in advance, and with a positive expectancy of a gain.

To "speculate" is to take an unusual risk with the expectation of an unusual gain; to trade with leverage is to speculate, since leverage constitutes an usually high risk of loss. Good speculators work extra-hard at identifying the unusual risks that may deliver the unusually high return. Bad speculators are buyers of lottery tickets, where the positive expectancy is infinitesimal (see Table 1.2).

# Chapter 2

# INEFFICIENCIES GALORE

*There is a tide in the affairs of men, which,*
*taken at the flood, leads on to fortune . . .*
William Shakespeare, *Julius Caesar*

As the Soros story illustrates, a trading opportunity opens up whenever we can identify a market inefficiency that has resulted in an extreme mispricing. Warren Buffett complains that it's hard to find bargains, but he is constraining himself to domestic U.S. companies rather than the entire universe of countries and instruments. He is also looking for stocks alone, and he selects those he can hold for a long time. Buffett seeks ownership in companies. The trader seeks winning positions. The minute you widen the investment horizon and shorten the holding period, you can find inefficiencies galore. Try it. Read the *Financial Times* and *The Wall Street Journal* for one week, with an eye out for inefficiencies. They may not be tradable in an obvious way—or you may not wish to learn the ins and outs of trading a security associated with a particular inefficiency—but they abound.

## Classifying Inefficiencies

One way to organize inefficiencies is by class of risk. We tend to think only of price risk, but risks come in all stripes, from sovereign risk (the risk of default by a government) to the risk of fraud. A U.S. investor in U.S. securities can safely forget about U.S. sovereign risk, except to the extent that we might consider a change in taxation of capital gains as arising from "the sovereign." In the United States, while we have plenty of fraudulent schemes perpetrated by the immoral upon the unwary, we have in place, in securities markets, a regulatory structure that goes out of its way to protect the individual. Even so, other regulatory issues may provide investment opportunities because any government meddling with free market pricing always creates inefficiencies. A reduction in regulation therefore provides a profit opportunity.

Another form of fraud risk is that a company does not properly disclose its financial condition, despite regulations requiring outside audits. In any case, some risk is inherent in existing accounting standards that allow basically dishonest practices to masquerade as "according to generally accepted accounting principles." Sometimes the perpetrators of accounting fraud are unmasked only long after the fact, as in the case of "Chainsaw" Al Dunlap, CEO of now-defunct Sunbeam, whose auditors were able to call phony profits of $8 million "not material." Finally, legal risk is generally seen as stemming from product liability—think of Firestone—but also can arise from disputes over intellectual property (copyrights and patents).

Above all other risks is market risk, the subject of this chapter. We don't ordinarily think of market risk as embodying an inefficiency, and yet the extremes of market sentiment are just that—misperception of true conditions. When markets rally to extremely high levels, we say that greed is supreme and market participants are neglecting to heed historical price-earnings ratios (P/Es), money supply, or some other factor that realistically should make them feel fearful. When markets are crashing, we say that market participants are overly fearful and are neglecting to heed historical verities like P/Es, money supply, or some other factor that realistically should encourage them to buy. In short, the ebb and flow of market sentiment is itself the primary risk in trading and investing, with a weight double the weight of the fundamentals of a particular company.

## Market Risk

In all markets, we have something called "systemic risk" or "market risk," referring to the phenomenon of how a move in the overall market affects individual securities within the market ("a rising tide lifts all boats"). This is a risk that cannot be diversified away, except by adding securities from another market altogether; it applies to all securities within the same universe. The degree of correlation of individual stocks to the market is beta, and no stock has a beta of zero. Market risk arises from a number of sources, chiefly psychological phenomena like manias and panics (and their lesser cousins, greed and fear), but also from mundane causes like tax payment and tax refund periods, month-end and quarter-end window dressing by mutual funds and others, and so on.

Manias and panics have been at the forefront in the press since the dot-com and high-tech crash in March 2000. Charles Mackay's *Extraordinary Popular Delusions and the Madness of Crowds* (Harmony Books, 1980), originally published in 1841, has been quoted just about everywhere, and it is indeed a delightful book. Academic economists are so annoyed by the irrationality of manias and panics in a world where investment decisions are supposed to be rational (and markets, efficient) that we even have a book debunking asset inflation in historical bubbles and claiming they were not extreme (Peter Garber, *Famous First Bubbles: The Fundamentals of Early Manias*, MIT Press, 2000). The author argues that the price put on tulips by Mackay—long after the event—was wrong. The price of a tulip was far less than the price of a house in Amsterdam, as Mackay said. Moreover, tulipmania and the South Sea bubble did not cause or even immediately precede economic recessions in their day. These started long afterward. Garber's effort is worth mentioning to show the grip of the rational decision-efficient market theory on academia (which includes business schools) and the press. The ideas are all-pervasive, and you have to be careful to detect the bias when you read and even more so when you subscribe to advice.

The rational decision-efficient markets majority believe that the only reason prices could become inflated is "the greater fool theory," that is, people buy an obviously overvalued asset because they believe some other fool will take it off their hands. The next buyer thinks the same thing. So each is rational and the market is pricing the asset efficiently in the sense that demand for the asset still exists. Of course, the last guy left holding the asset is truly the greater fool. If we have a hard time evaluating when a security is undervalued, is it easier to spot when it is overvalued?

Yes. As noted in Chapter 6, in 1995 the press delighted in reporting that the land under the Imperial Palace in Tokyo was worth all the real estate in California at the then-current rate of exchange (about ¥80 to the dollar). How can you hear a statement like that and not immediately run out and sell the yen? The answer, of course, is that other equally ridiculous comparisons were being made at ¥100 and ¥90. Who is to say where a mania will end?

In the U.S. stock market, John Templeton was one. According to a story in *Forbes* magazine (May 28, 2001, p. 54), Templeton shorted 84 high-tech stocks in January 2000, ahead of the Nasdaq crash in March. He said, "This is the only time in my 88 years when I saw technology stocks go to 100 times earnings, or when there were no earnings, 20 times sales. It was insane, and I took advantage of the temporary insanity." In some cases, he used a double-pronged strategy—not just identifying general overvaluation, but also timing short sales to take effect 11 days before the lockup expirations on the specific stocks, meaning just before company insiders were allowed to sell. In half of his sales, he bought back the stocks to cover his short sale when prices reached 5 percent of his sale price. In other cases, he closed when the price fell below 30 times trailing earnings. In the lockup expiration cases, he got out right after the expiration. *Forbes* reports that his gain so far is $86 million.

As we note over and over again throughout this book, the bias against short-selling among the general stock-buying public is a psychological drawback in the trading landscape today. Rules against short-selling of stocks were put in place to protect companies from unscrupulous competitors and malicious enemies, as well to make it more difficult for a panic to develop. Nobody would argue that we still do not need the constraints today. The issue is not regulatory obstacles, but the psychological environment that has developed, under the unceasing encouragement of brokers and mutual fund sellers. To buy and therefore to participate in capitalism at its highest pinnacle, the stock market, is morally and ethically correct; to sell short is morally reprehensible and against the public welfare. This point of view serves only to foster irrational behavior, such as plans that automatically invest a portion of the monthly paycheck in stocks, reinvest stock dividends, and so on, no matter where stock prices are at the time.

Pretend that you receive a piece of inside information from an employee that his company is not manufacturing the product it claims to make, falsifying sales and earnings reports, and in fact getting money only from the sale of stock. The company has wonderful public relations and has been accepted in the securities analysis and brokerage industry as an up-and-coming "growth stock." Nobody has actually verified that the sole source of revenue is the sale of shares (in complicated deal structures executed by dishonest brokers), but by dogged persistence in reading the company's financial statements (and perhaps a visit to the factory floor), you are able to verify the employee's charge of fraud. What can you do? What should you do? Aside from the public-welfare issue of reporting the situation to the SEC and other regulators, you should sell the stock short. It is, literally, worthless. You have discovered an inefficiency of extreme value; you know something the rest of the market does not. When the rest of the market wakes up to the true situation, they will dump the stock, and you will be ready to buy it from them at far lower prices than the price at which you sold short, for a tidy profit. This is what professional short-seller Manuel Asensio does for a living. In *Sold Short: Uncovering Deception in Markets* (John Wiley & Sons, 2001), Asensio describes that short-selling of fraudulent company shares performs a public service and can also be highly profitable. So why does *Forbes* magazine write laudatory pieces about Templeton shorting overpriced tech stocks and fail to celebrate Asensio's unmasking of astounding gall by crooks? It's a mystery having something to do with not wanting to believe that "the establishment" makes such mistakes as to be gulled by con artists. Templeton, by 2001, was long part of "the establishment" and so he is deemed clever. Asensio, as an upstart newcomer who seeks the opposite of "value," is ignored or vilified in the financial press. Nowhere than in consideration of short-sellers is the essential irrationality of the market more visible.

## The Cause of Manias and Panics

Economist Charles Kindleberger makes fun of the rigid efficient market theorists who can't see irrationality and inefficiency when they are standing in front of them. The historical record is clear; economists have long known that the anatomy of a typical crisis is everywhere the same. Manias start with "displacement"—some shock to the economic system. It can be a war or the end of a war. It is often a new technological invention that changes everything, like the automobile, the railroad, or the personal computer and the Internet. Kindleberger wrote *Manias, Panics, and Crashes, A History of Financial Crises* (John Wiley & Sons, Third Edition, 1996) in 1978, but he probably wouldn't object to adding "the Internet" to the list of displacements. Then the availability of money and credit permits the mania to develop. Next there appear swindlers who prey on the greedy in a greedy atmosphere. People "overtrade," although we don't have a clear definition of what that is. Finally, some Event happens to wake everyone up, and prices crash. If you are going to read one book on this topic, Kindleberger's is the one to get.

The point to take away from the historical perspective is that the underlying cause of manias is the availability of money and credit. Virtually every top macroeconomic analyst and advisor today starts his review of a market with this one factor. One of the top advisors in the United States is Ned Davis Research, which sells its reports only to institutions (for $15,000 per year) but is often quoted in the press. In *Being Right or Making Money* (Ned Davis Research, Revised Edition 2000), the analysis of the bubble of 2000 starts with charts of personal savings and household debt, total credit market debt, nonfinancial corporate debt, money supply, foreign ownership of U.S. debt instruments, and so on. Similarly, the Amernick Letter (available on request via e-mail from amernick@home.com) starts its analysis of global markets with liquidity and interest rates, especially relative bond yields. Worldwide, cash flows into the region with the highest real risk-adjusted rate of return. After that, we have to consider special situations. For example, the U.S. Bank Index (BKX) often reflects changes in the Argentine stock market—and the yield spread of Argentine sovereign debt over U.S. Treasuries—because

American banks have large exposures in Argentina. The main stock index in Hong Kong, the Hang Seng, is highly correlated to the S&P 500—partly because the Hong Kong dollar is pegged to the U.S. dollar, and a rate change in the United States is almost always followed by the same change in Hong Kong. When the Fed is liquefying the United States with rate cuts, making the cost of borrowing cheaper, the Hong Kong Monetary Authority does the same thing and both markets rise.

To track changes in domestic market liquidity and in relative international capital flows is a big task. The major banks, broker-ages, and fund managers all conduct this kind of research, which is seldom made available to the public but can sometimes be found at various Web sites, including www.multex.com. The Conference Board (www.globalindicators.org) offers in-depth information on a limited list of countries, but at a hefty annual charge ($500 per country per year). At www.economagic.com and at www.globalfindata.com, you can find just about every economic and financial time series ever collected, for less expensive annual fees, depending on what you download—but you have to do the thinking yourself. The same thing is true of the data available at www.imf.org, where trained economists go. Data, essays, and current analysis are also to be found at www.yardeni.com. If that kind of modeling appeals to you, you need *The Research-Driven Investor, How to Use Information, Data, and Analysis for Investment Success,* by Timothy Hayes (a Ned Davis research associate, by the way; McGraw-Hill, 2001). One of the best resources, monthly reports on 117 countries from the Economist Intelligence Unit (EIU) (www.eiu.com), is priced for institutions: $435 per country per year, or $195 for a single report. The EIU says 95 percent of their customers are transnational institutions. Well, no wonder. *The Economist* magazine itself, however, issues special country reports a few times a year, and a subscription is cost-effective (about $100/year).

Unless you have an affinity for global macroeconomics and an appetite for managing a large amount of data, you might be better off starting to learn about foreign markets by looking at their internal dynamics. This means studying the indices themselves for clues to market risk—an empirical approach rather than a macroeconomic approach.

# The Amazing Calendar Effect

A lot is known about market risk in the United States. Calendar effects are probably the best known market risks—but seemingly, they are not as respected as they should be. Yale Hirsch, publisher of the *Stock Trader's Almanac* starting in 1967, performs exhaustive analyses of historical stock market behavior and cycles in differing political and economic environments, using data going back, in some cases, over 80 years. He discovered the "January Effect," which states that as January goes, so goes the rest of the year. This indicator has an impressive record of accuracy: correct in 45 of the 50 years since 1950 (and no errors in odd years when new Congresses convened). He also discovered the "Santa Claus Rally" and the "Best Six Months of the Year," also known as "Sell in May and go away." Hirsch discovered the Presidential cycle, as well as the amusing fact that, since 1901, $10,000 has grown to $270,930 under Democratic administrations but to only $94,675 under the Republicans. Hirsch is the author of *Don't Sell Stocks on Monday*, now out of print (the *Stock Trader's Almanac* updates the information). From 1952 to 1989, Monday was the worst trading day of the week; the S&P 500 rose only 44.5 percent of the time. In 1990, Monday became the best trading day of the week, rising 57.5 percent of the time (up to December 1999). The *Almanac* is packed with facts like this. The Hirsch Organization also publishes three newsletters. (Visit Hirsch at www.stocktradersalmanac.com and www.hirschorganization.com.)

Does the study of statistics pay off? You bet. In his October 1974 newsletter, "Smart Money," Hirsch wrote "Buy!" on the exact bottom day of the market. In December 1974, with the Dow just below 600, he predicted "Dow 800 By April." This 33 percent gain in four months was reached as Hirsch had forecast. Many other successes like this have come about from empirical study of how the market behaves (as opposed to the more common normative approach of describing how it "should" behave).

The six-month cycle is perhaps the most impressive. In 1986, Hirsch discovered that practically all the gains to be had in the S&P 500 are made between November 1 and April 30, and, even with some alterations caused by the 1990s' bull run, this has been true for 50 years. If you invested in stocks on November 1 and sold them on April 30 in favor of bonds for the rest of the year, and did that every year since 1950, on a $10,000 initial investment you would have made $363,353 over the 50 years, compared to being invested in stocks in the May 1 to October 31 period, where you would have made a paltry $11,574.

Sy Harding, author of *Riding the Bear: How to Prosper in the Coming Bear Market* (Adams Media Company, 1999), uses the six-month cycle together with another observation: the market tends to rise from the last trading day of a month to the fourth trading day of the next month. Combining the two patterns, you would want to buy on the day before the last trading day of October and sell everything on the fourth trading day of May. Following this rule, from 1964 to 1999, you would have nearly doubled the return of the Dow. Since you would have been out of the market half the time, you also would have had half the risk. Further, by using a single technical indicator, moving average convergence-divergence (MACD), you could have tripled the return on the Dow by moving up or postponing the stipulated entry and exit dates. Notice that with only two trades per year, the seasonal trading system is thrifty. In Table 2.1, the seasonal timing system is investing in index funds.

Chuck Hughes is another market guru who makes a study of seasonality in the stock market (www.chuckhughes.com). He offers home study courses and software, as well as online advisories, focusing on option strategies in a Guaranteed Real Income Program (GRIP) that relies on seasonality. Hughes also finds that

**Table 2.1.** Seasonal Timing System

| Year | Dow Jones Industrial Average | Seasonal Timing System—Dow | S&P 500 | Seasonal Timing System—S&P 500 |
|---|---|---|---|---|
| 1998 | 18.0% | 33.2% | 28.7% | 41.8% |
| 1999 | 27.2 | 34.5 | 21 | 26.5 |
| 2000 | −4.7 | −2.6 | −8.9 | −7.3 |
| 3-year compounded | 43.1 | 74.5 | 41.9 | 66.3 |

*Note:* Includes dividends in index funds and interest earned when out of the market in Seasonal Timing System.

*Source:* www.syharding.com.

**Table 2.2.**   Probability of Seasonality

| Benchmark | Years Tested | Number of Winning Years | Number of Losing Years | Profitability |
|---|---|---|---|---|
| Dow Jones Industrial Index | 50 | 40 | 10 | 80% |
| S&P 500 Index | 50 | 39 | 11 | 78 |
| Nasdaq Composite | 30 | 24 | 6 | 80 |

*Source:* Chuck Hughes, "Seasonal Tendencies in Stocks," Chapter 2, *Guaranteed Real Income Program Home Study Course,* p. 23.

moving money into the S&P 500 (on the next-to-last trading day in October) and out again (on the second trading day in May) would have returned $1,663,178.75 over the 50 years that ended in September 2000, with the money invested in T-bills when out of the market. In contrast, staying invested in the S&P the entire time would have returned only $607,853.76. Employing seasonality as a strategy is about 2.5 times better than buy-and-hold—and it can be improved by moving out of the S&P when the 100-day moving average is breached during the period between February and May, where, historically, anomalies in the October to May seasonal pattern have been seen. (See Table 2.2.) Finally, the technique is refined further to adjust the entry date to October 28. With these refinements, the gain on the S&P is raised to $2,273,967.80, or 3.74 times buy-and-hold.

## Seasonality in Foreign Markets

Statistical analysis of foreign markets is essential. Unless you read German, Japanese, Spanish, and a host of other languages, you will have a hard time reading online newspapers and other content from foreign countries. Business and market coverage of foreign markets is skimpy or nonexistent in most U.S. newspapers, the exception being the *Financial Times,* now widely available in the United States and online (www.ft.com). *Barron's* and *The Wall Street Journal* offer limited coverage of foreign stocks and foreign markets. At the beginning of 2001, *The New York Times* initiated coverage of foreign markets in its own section.

Foreign markets display the same kind of calendar effects discovered by Hirsch. In Figure 2.1, we can see a double peak in the
Deutsche Borse DAX index, for example, first in mid-July and
again at the end of December.

The technique for constructing a chart like this is simple. We
first determine the price range of each year, the lowest low sub-
tracted from the highest high. Each day's close is expressed as a
percentage of the range. Then all the percentage values for a single
date are averaged over 10, 15, or 20 years, depending on how much
data we have. (The more data, the better.) The charts shown here
were prepared for this book by Duane Davis, president of Financial
Software Systems (www.seasonalprojections.com), the firm that
provides much of the seasonality research to the industry today.

Note the difference between the German DAX and the French
CAC indices in Figures 2.1 and 2.2. They both bottom in mid- to
late January each year, but, in France, the CAC rises much faster

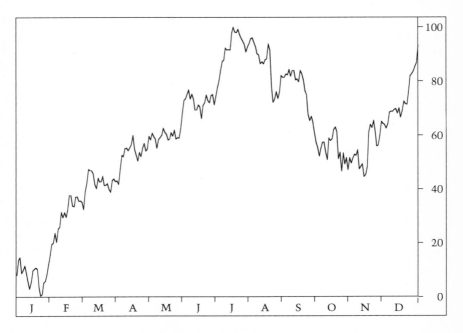

**Figure 2.1**    German Borse DAX Seasonality, 1987–2000.

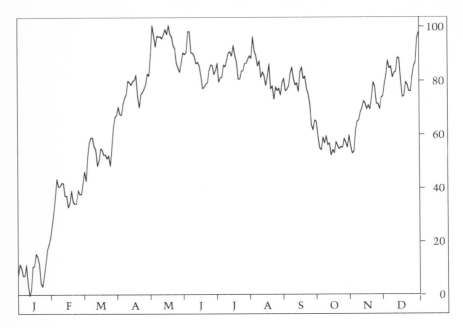

**Figure 2.2**    French CAC Index Seasonality, 1988–2000.

and peaks in May (instead of mid-July, as in Germany). They both tail off into October before rising again into the year-end.

Now look at the Madrid index in Figure 2.3. It peaks in May and June, like the CAC, but has a much more distinct correction around the end of April, before resuming the uptrend. It also corrects far more steeply than the DAX or CAC going into the end of October.

The United Kingdom's Financial Times Stock Exchange Index (FTSE) 100, on the other hand, looks nothing like the Continental bourse indices. (See Figure 2.4.) It starts January low, goes lower, and peaks at the end of December. Notice that we have a little more data for the FTSE.

Japan's Nikkei 225 index has been the subject of much discussion since it crashed starting in 1990, the biggest and longest-lasting major stock decline in the world since World War II. From a peak of ¥38,951 on January 4, 1990, it fell to its lowest low, ¥11,434, on March 15, 2001. (See Figure 2.5.)

You wouldn't know from looking at a regular time-series chart of the Nikkei that it conceals an important seasonal pattern. In

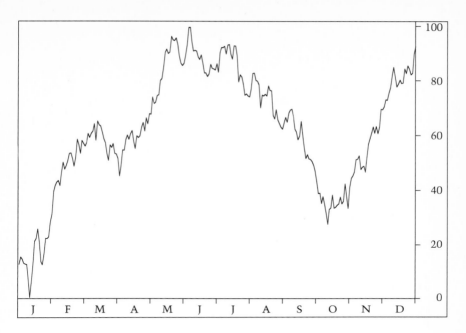

**Figure 2.3**   Madrid Index Seasonality, 1990–2000.

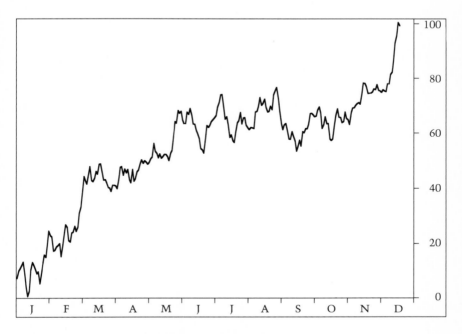

**Figure 2.4**   FTSE Seasonality, 1985–2000.

**61**

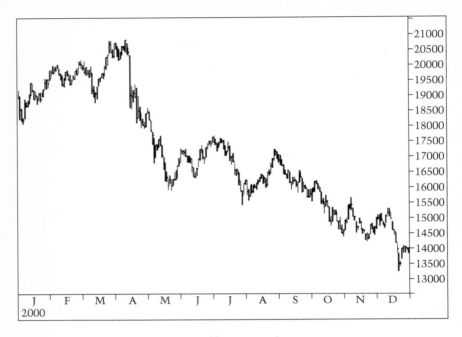

**Figure 2.5**   Nikkei 225 actual prices, 2000.

Figure 2.6, the Nikkei tends to rise from January to the end of June, sags a bit, peaks again in early July, and then collapses into the first week of November, with a small rally into December.

Remember, the left-hand axis is the average percentage change of each year's *range,* not the percentage gain or loss in dollar (or euro or yen) terms. One conclusion to be drawn from the distinctive seasonality patterns of each national stock market is that omnibus indices and securities including stocks from each of them, such as the S&P Europe 350 (which covers 70 percent of the market capitalization of 15 pan-European markets), are subject to push-me/pull-you influences. The FTSE Eurotop 100 and FTSE Eurotop 300 are two others in which national seasonalities would presumably conflict.

Sources of information on seasonality include www .thomsonFN.com, which offers a seasonality "tracker" for individual stocks and the market at large, and www.trade-futures .com, where you can review Jake Bernstein's many publications

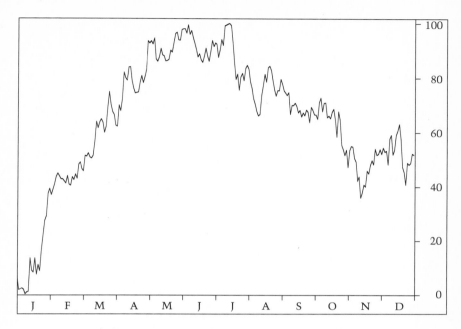

**Figure 2.6**    Nikkei Index Seasonality, 1985–2000.

and books, including *Seasonality: Systems, Strategies, and Signals* (John Wiley & Sons, 1998).

## Event Trading

Within the seasonality phenomenon is another class of trading decisions that specifically targets the efficient market effect. It is a third approach to markets—different from fundamental analysis and from technical analysis. Just as "earnings surprises" can generate exceptional returns when the actual release differs substantially from expectations, so, too, economic data can surprise and offer profit opportunities. The question is whether one can create a consistently profitable system substituting economic data for corporate earnings, on a risk-adjusted basis and with gains larger than transaction costs. In *Event Trading—Profiting from Economic Reports and Short-Term Market Inefficiencies* (Irwin Professional

Publishing, 1996), Ben Warwick tests the idea and finds that, on the whole, it works. Warwick is testing futures contracts, but the principle is what counts. He offers four case studies (the S&P Index, the T-bond, Eurodollars, and the Dollar Index) and tests whether each of nine indicators moves these markets to such an extent as to create a profitable trading environment. The nine indicators are: (1) Producer Price Index (PPI), (2) Consumer Price Index (CPI), (3) gross domestic product (GDP), (4) Industrial Production Index (IPI), (5) durables, (6) retail sales, (7) trade balance, (8) National Association of Personal Management (NAPM) index, and (9) employment. All are monthly and all except the NAPM index are released by government agencies on a scheduled basis. Warwick constructs a hypothetical trading model that buys or sells the futures contract if its price "breaks out" to the upper or lower 20 percent of its average true range after the release, and maintains the change for a "holding period" of same-day to five days.

Warwick analyzes upside and downside breakouts separately, and finds that durables move the U.S. bond in the first two days (including the release day) with a confidence level of 97 percent. The same indicator moves the S&P in the first four days with a confidence level over 99 percent. Retail sales are good for generating a breakout in bonds and the S&P, but GDP and employment are low confidence indicators. The work covers the 1989 to 1994 period, and it goes without saying that indicators wax and wane in ability to move markets over time. In this period, trade was never a good indicator; it was correlated with the Japanese yen, but failed to generate breakout trades in the Dollar Index. After developing event trading rules, Warwick applied them to real-world situations and got better than 50 percent winning trades and high win-loss ratios with a low risk ranking. The S&P turned out to be the most susceptible to the event trading approach.

Event trading is now an established technique. Sandi Lynne (www.wallstreetinadvance.com) is the provider of the calendar of events in the *Stock Trader's Almanac*. She provides analysis at her site of events likely to affect the U.S. and foreign stock markets. At www.wallstreetinadvance.com, you will find, for example, international conferences in Europe and Asia as well as the United States, pertaining to biomedical research, information technology, electric automobiles, and so on. Important announcements, constituting "events," are often made at these conferences. Event-driven trading seeks to identify a near-term catalyst for the market. Traders buy on the first dip a few days before the event, then sell into the enthusiasm created by the "news" (or the other way around, as the case may be). As noted by Warwick, we have about 10 potentially market-moving events at any one time (on a shifting slate). In foreign markets, often there is only one or two economic releases that has such a big effect that it becomes tradable from the United States.

In Germany, for example, the attention getter is the release of the "business conditions" index by a research institute named Institut fuer Wirtschaftforschung—Institute for Economic Research (IFO)—more precisely, it is the extent of divergence between the expected IFO index number and the actual number. (See Figure 2.7.) A component of the business *conditions* index is another index of "business *expectations.*" This index can become quite confusing. If business expectations had been abnormally high (because of the advent of the euro or some other factor) and then fell after that event came and went, the entire "business conditions" index will fall, even though no other change in actual conditions has occurred. Therefore, the IFO index of business conditions is often interpreted as a confidence indicator. You would think that authentic confidence (meeting corporate earnings goals, for example) would cause higher expectations, but it doesn't always turn out that way when suddenly a new negative factor comes along. In other words, expectations are more volatile than conditions, but can give the appearance of volatility to a conditions index.

In Japan, the major event that shapes and conditions the Nikkei index is the quarterly "Tankan" report, a survey of business conditions that also includes an expectations component. (See Figure 2.8.) Because it is released on a quarterly basis, the Tankan is the subject of much discussion ahead of the event. Reuters and Bridge News both go so far as to conduct their own Tankan surveys of many of the same companies surveyed by the Bank of Japan in the official release, and they have a good track record of anticipating the changes.

In each country, you need to find the financial and economic news that has a consistent effect on the stock (and bond) markets. In many cases, it is a business sentiment indicator like the IFO

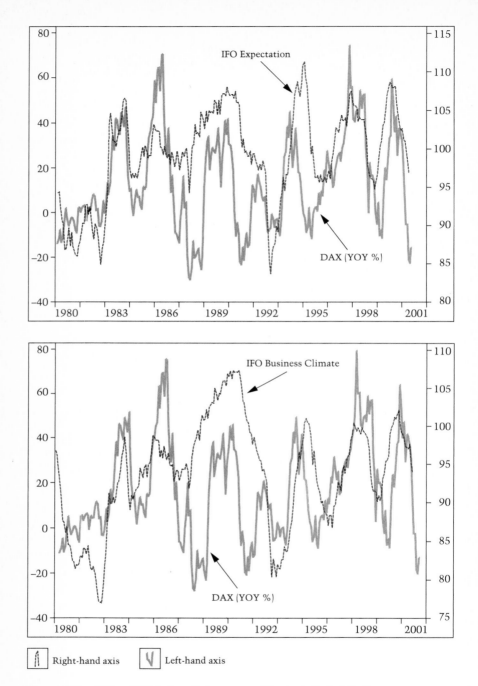

**Figure 2.7** DAX and IFO Indices. Data courtesy of Bankgelsellschaft Berlin Economics Department.

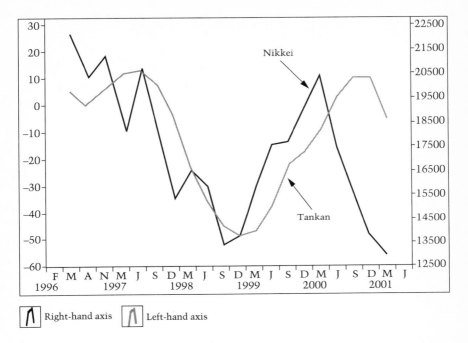

Nikkei

Tankan

 Right-hand axis   Left-hand axis

**Figure 2.8**  Tankan and the Nikkei 225.

and Tankan indices, or it may be GDP or one of the many money supply/inflation indicators. As a general rule, consumer sentiment and consumer-related indicators (such as household durable goods) are of less importance in foreign economies than in the United States.

## The Way the World Works

Worldwide, a very large amount of money is devoted to mimicking one index or another. No one knows how much money is devoted to tracking the S&P 500, the Nikkei, the FTSE 100, and the hundreds of other indices worldwide, because in addition to mutual fund and pension fund managers who set out to reproduce an index, we also have futures on indices, options on futures, exchange-traded funds, hedge funds, and individuals—all involved one way or another and all having an effect. Even some who claim not to weight their holdings according to an index are really "closet indexers." Thus, the estimate of 30 percent of U.S. funds invested directly in index-tracking vehicles—upward of $3 trillion—is probably low. Because the United States has the largest stock market, and equity market participation is broad and deep, estimates for other countries are lower. The estimate is thought to be around 10 percent in the United Kingdom, for example.

Index preparers such as Dow-Jones and Standard & Poor's revise their indices periodically to reflect structural changes in a market. Revisions are usually kept secret until the very last minute because demand for a new index member will automatically rise, and demand for a company being kicked out will automatically fall. When the Dow Jones Industrial Average was reconstituted in November 1999, each of the four new members rose, often on a gap up. The reweighting of indices reveals a major inefficiency in the way markets work, and offers opportunities of a structural nature as industries, sectors, companies, and countries are reevaluated.

Anyone who can anticipate how an index is going to be changed has an advantage. The composition of the S&P 500, for example, was changed an astonishing 286 times in the past 10 years. The S&P 500 makes up about 70 percent of the value of all U.S. stocks, so it pays to attend to these changes. In the year 2000, 18 new companies were added, and over half of them were technology companies. Because the market "permits" technology companies to have higher P/Es than nontech companies, to say that the new S&P 500 average P/E, at 24, is too high compared to the historical average of 15 is to compare apples and oranges. The S&P committee that judged these companies more "representational" than the ones kicked out of the index changed the rules of the P/E game—and P/E is reportedly not even one of the criteria used by the committee. Moreover, as of May 21, 2001, a mere 40 stocks made up half the value of the S&P 500 index, according to *Money* magazine (July 2001, p. 89). This means that investors in the stocks occupying the 498, 499, and 500 slots have a right to be nervous. All investors have a right to be annoyed that only a handful of stocks can bring the entire index down, and, as noted, 50 percent of the price of any particular stock is a function of "the market," and only 25 percent is due to its own merits.

With all their faults, indices allow us to keep track of "the market," especially over long periods of time. This poses problems of construction (dividends reinvested or not; arithmetic versus geometric means, and so on), and comparability, and distortions of all sorts creep into the indices. The most glaring problem is the use of market capitalization to construct an index. If you add up the market cap of the top 100 companies in a market and then allocate weightings to each individual stock according to its proportion of the total, you have a fair and reasonable process as long as anyone can buy and sell each of those shares. But, in many situations, not all the shares counted in the market cap are actually available to the market. Let's say the largest company in a market, measured by market capitalization, has 1 million shares outstanding—but 999,000 are owned by the founder of the company (which may be the government) and are not for sale. The "free float" of the company is actually only 1,000 shares. Because index trackers will definitely need to own that stock in order to mimic the index, they compete like mad to get the few shares that are available, and they artificially drive up the price. In the United States, insider ownership is the chief reason that market cap and free float diverge. In other countries, government ownership can be an influence, as can "cross shareholdings," whereby companies own shares in one another. Cross shareholdings are particularly large in Japan, France, and Germany.

Morgan Stanley Capital International (MSCI) is a company that devised benchmark indices for countries, country groupings (such as Asia ex-Japan, North America, and Europe ex-United Kingdom), geographic regions, and the world, on the basis of market capitalization (www.msci.com). Many fund managers are evaluated on whether they meet or beat the MSCI indices, and about $3.5 trillion worldwide is devoted to tracking the indices directly. As a practical matter, we care about the MSCI weightings because the MSCI index for each country is the basis of the country's iShares traded on the American Stock Exchange—at present, one of the best ways for an individual investor to participate in foreign markets.

In 2000, MSCI announced it would adopt the free-float methodology in place of the market-cap version, and would introduce the changes in a two-phase process so as to prevent market disorder.

The first stage will occur in November 2001, and the second stage, on May 31, 2002. In addition to the methodology change, MSCI will also deepen each index by including companies making up 85 percent of market cap rather than the 60 percent covered today.

The first announcements about the new weightings were made on May 19, 2001. So far, we know that the United States and the United Kingdom will gain the most as country weightings in the international indices. In the "All Country World Index," for example, the weight of the USA Index will rise to 55.3 percent, compared with 49.1 percent in the market-cap version. The weight of the United Kingdom Index will rise to 10.4 percent, compared with 9.3 percent. Japan's weight will be reduced by 1.3 percent (from 10.71 percent to 9.38 percent), France's by 1.2 percent, and Germany's by 1 percent. The immediate effect of the announcement when markets opened on May 21, 2001, was the U.K. pound's rising to a five-month high against the euro—but the Nikkei stock index rose 2.2 percent because the market had factored in an even worse reduction—to 9 percent—in Japan's weight. Therefore, 9.38 percent looks good.

The weight of developed markets in the new All Country World Index will be 96.9 percent (up from 95 percent), and emerging markets will comprise 3.1 percent (down from 5 percent). This is a more realistic assessment of higher-average free float, less restrictive foreign ownership limits, and greater availability of liquid securities in developed markets over emerging markets. On another front, industry groups are reweighted, too. Technology Hardware & Equipment is raised from 10 percent to 11.5 percent, and Telecommunication Services is reduced from 8.2 percent to 7.2 percent. To figure out what this means over the long run, we can imagine that a telecom company in an emerging market just lost a certain amount of demand for its stock solely from the double reweighting of the sector and the designation "emerging market." Meanwhile, Cisco, which is a technology hardware company in the United States, just got an automatic increase in demand for its stock, entirely independent of the business cycle and the company's fundamentals.

It may or may not be true that Cisco stock is now more attractive because of the double change in the MSCI index, just as it may or may not be true that interest in emerging markets will now be at a relatively lower level. How do we evaluate a high-tech stock in an emerging market like Taiwan or Korea? The indices in both those countries are highly correlated with the Philadelphia Semiconductor Index (SOX). In fact, about half the market capitalization of the Taipei index in Taiwan consists of semiconductor companies. So, as illustrated in Figure 2.9, we have a hodgepodge of factors: a cyclical downturn in the semiconductor sector; emerging market stocks of less interest to the big institutional investors who are so important to any index; political issues in Taiwan with China; and the overall outlook for U.S. and world growth or recession.

One of the odd outcomes of the MSCI reweighting was the exclusion of China Unicom from the MSCI China Free index on the

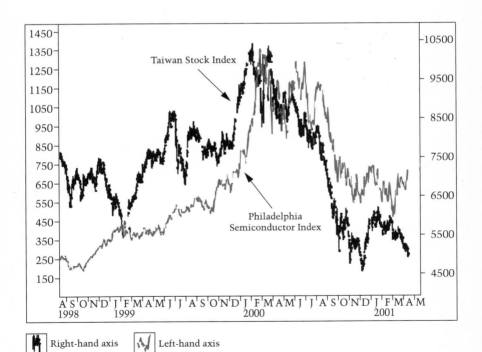

**Figure 2.9**   Taiwan Stock and Philadelphia Semiconductor Indices.

grounds that its competitor, China Mobile, represents about 85 percent of the mobile-phone industry. China Unicom became a constituent of the Hang Seng on June 1, 2000, however. Meanwhile, Hong Kong's weighting fell from 0.93 percent to 0.66 percent—actually, less than had been feared because many stocks are family-controlled and closely held. If you had been struggling to decide which stock to buy, China Unicom or China Mobile, MSCI may have made the decision for you. Even if you preferred China Unicom, you should heed Keynes's advice about picking the beauty-contest girl the other judges like, not the one you find the prettiest.

Like many research providers, Morgan Stanley Capital International serves only the institutional market. The average individual cannot get its correlation studies among sectors and countries, nor even the list of stocks in each index. You can get the company names, however, by asking for the annual report of MSCI index-tracking mutual funds (such as those at Fidelity, State Street, and elsewhere).

## Structural Inefficiencies

The reweighting of indices is conducted by the private agencies that invented them, and that makes indices a free-market phenomenon. Other structural aspects of market conduct involve governments and cultures. This includes everything from accounting standards (and how strictly they are applied) to stamp taxes on securities transactions, and customs and practices. Some structural issues properly belong in the category of sovereign risk (arising from government actions), and some belong in the more general category of country risk.

## Transparency

A critical component of country risk is transparency. When transactions are conducted behind closed doors, we suspect that a market is rigged in favor of insiders. At one end of the transparency scale is "crony capitalism," whereby the elite in a country tip each other off about significant transactions, mergers and acquisitions, and other inside information. At the far end of the transparency scale is outright corruption, whether by government or corporate officials. The lack of transparency is an inefficiency that works to the detriment of foreign investors. According to the Transparency International Web site (www.transparency.de),

> Corruption damages a country's development in several ways. It reduces growth, it scares away foreign investment and it channels investment and loan and aid funds into "white elephant" projects of little or no benefit to the people but which carry with them high returns to the corrupt decision-makers.
>
> According to research conducted by the World Bank, widespread corruption can cause the growth rate of a country to be 0.5 to 1.0 percentage points lower than that of a similar country with little corruption. Widespread corruption can also radically reduce inward investment. A study based on the TI Corruption Perceptions Index shows that a rise in corruption levels from that of Singapore (very low) to that of Mexico's (very high) is equivalent to raising the marginal tax rate by over twenty percent. As a single percentage point increase in the marginal tax rate is calculated as reducing inward foreign investment by about five percent, in the instance given corruption has cost the country and continues to cost the country virtually all of the foreign direct investment it might otherwise have expected to receive.

Since that piece was written, conditions have changed dramatically in Mexico with the election of a new president in the summer of 2000. Vicente Fox promised to end corruption, open up the economy to more foreign investment, reduce civil strife, and many other commitments. Fox was the first head of state met by the new U.S. president in January 2001. Even before he was elected, the peso reflected market approval of Fox. Although the Mexican peso fell ahead of the July 2, 2000, presidential election, as usual, it turned around and rose, starting three days before the election itself as Fox was shown by polls to be leading. Aside from some temporary weakness associated with financial problems in Brazil and Argentina that spilled over into perception of the Mexican peso, the peso has been on a strengthening trend for over six months (to end-May 2001). The case of the peso in Figure 2.10 demonstrates the valuable observation that development of confidence in changing conditions can often be seen in the exchange rate before it becomes obvious in economic statistics or even stock prices.

Then, in May 2001, Citigroup announced its acquisition of the largest independent bank in Mexico for $12.5 billion. Note that one of the top officials at Citigroup is Robert Rubin, who had been the U.S. Secretary of the Treasury during the Mexican government's debt crisis in 1995 and was the architect of a $40 billion bailout plan. This plan was erroneously seen by some as a handout; instead, it was carefully structured to be anything but, and all the debt was repaid in full, with interest, in very short order. Citigroup's acquisition was "widely hailed as the biggest vote of confidence by a U.S.

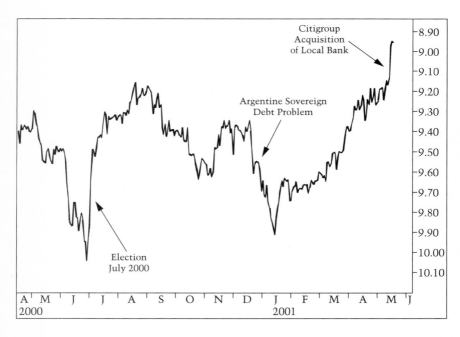

**Figure 2.10**    Mexican peso.

company in the Mexican financial system in 50 years" (*Los Angeles Times*). The peso rose 2.5 percent on the day of the announcement, and the stock index also jumped up dramatically—4.75 percent in a single day. (See Figure 2.11.)

Things change. These developments do not mean that the risk of investing in Mexican securities or the Mexican peso has now vanished. A society and an economy accustomed to a high level of nontransparency and corruption does not change overnight, but, at the same time, we need to be on the lookout for a change in this type of inefficiency. Compare the emerging situation in Mexico with the situation in Brazil. There, the country's president, Fernando Henrique Cardoso, found it necessary to deny a report that his government had covered up an insider trading scheme conducted by the *president* of the central bank, who allegedly sold advance information about the December 1999 devaluation of the currency to his cronies in return for $1.6 million in a secret offshore account in his name. The central bank has now

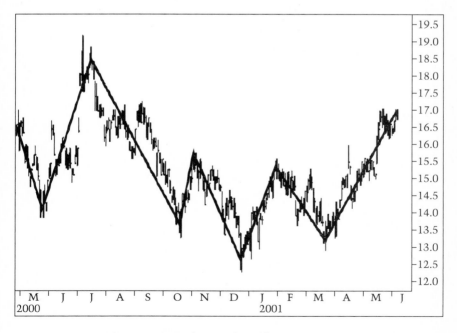

**Figure 2.11**   iShare Mexico and 10 percent ZigZag.

confirmed that it sold currency at off-market prices to the suspected insider institutions. The central bank president was dismissed two weeks after the incident, and is now accused in the press of having been blackmailed by the cronies into bailing them out of other difficulties.

You can get an idea of the drag of corruption on an economy and a market at the Internet Center for Corruption Research (www.gwdg.de/~uwvw/icr.htm), a joint venture between a European university and Transparency International, which publishes a "Bribe Payers Survey" as well as the "Corruption Perceptions Index" reproduced in Table 2.3.

**Table 2.3.**  The 2000 Corruption Perceptions Index

| Country Rank | Country | 2000 CPI Score | Surveys Used | Standard Deviation | High–Low Range |
|---|---|---|---|---|---|
| 1 | Finland | 10.0 | 8 | 0.6 | 9.0–10.4 |
| 2 | Denmark | 9.8 | 9 | 0.8 | 8.6–10.6 |
| 3 | New Zealand | 9.4 | 8 | 0.8 | 8.1–10.2 |
|  | Sweden | 9.4 | 9 | 0.7 | 8.1–9.9 |
| 5 | Canada | 9.2 | 9 | 0.7 | 8.1–9.9 |
| 6 | Iceland | 9.1 | 7 | 1.1 | 7.3–9.9 |
|  | Norway | 9.1 | 8 | 0.7 | 7.6–9.5 |
|  | Singapore | 9.1 | 11 | 1.0 | 6.2–9.7 |
| 9 | Netherlands | 8.9 | 9 | 0.6 | 8.1–9.9 |
| 10 | United Kingdom | 8.7 | 9 | 0.6 | 7.3–9.7 |
| 11 | Luxembourg | 8.6 | 7 | 0.7 | 7.4–9.3 |
|  | Switzerland | 8.6 | 8 | 0.3 | 8.1–9.1 |
| 13 | Australia | 8.3 | 10 | 1.0 | 6.7–9.3 |
| 14 | USA | 7.8 | 10 | 0.8 | 6.2–9.2 |
| 15 | Austria | 7.7 | 8 | 0.7 | 6.2–8.5 |
|  | Hong Kong | 7.7 | 11 | 1.2 | 4.3–8.6 |
| 17 | Germany | 7.6 | 8 | 0.8 | 6.2–8.4 |
| 18 | Chile | 7.4 | 8 | 0.9 | 5.7–8.4 |
| 19 | Ireland | 7.2 | 8 | 1.9 | 2.5–8.5 |
| 20 | Spain | 7.0 | 8 | 0.7 | 5.9–8.0 |
| 21 | France | 6.7 | 9 | 1.0 | 4.3–7.7 |
| 22 | Israel | 6.6 | 8 | 1.3 | 4.3–7.9 |
| 23 | Japan | 6.4 | 11 | 1.3 | 4.3–7.8 |
|  | Portugal | 6.4 | 9 | 0.9 | 5.3–8.1 |
| 25 | Belgium | 6.1 | 9 | 1.3 | 4.3–8.8 |
| 26 | Botswana | 6.0 | 4 | 1.6 | 4.3–8.2 |
| 27 | Estonia | 5.7 | 4 | 1.6 | 4.4–8.1 |

**Table 2.3.** *Continued*

| Country Rank | Country | 2000 CPI Score | Surveys Used | Standard Deviation | High–Low Range |
|---|---|---|---|---|---|
| 28 | Slovenia | 5.5 | 6 | 1.1 | 4.1–7.3 |
|  | Taiwan | 5.5 | 11 | 1.4 | 2.5–7.2 |
| 30 | Costa Rica | 5.4 | 4 | 1.9 | 3.8–8.1 |
|  | Namibia | 5.4 | 4 | 0.8 | 4.3–6.1 |
| 32 | Hungary | 5.2 | 10 | 1.2 | 3.9–8.1 |
|  | Tunisia | 5.2 | 4 | 1.5 | 3.8–7.1 |
| 34 | South Africa | 5.0 | 10 | 0.9 | 3.8–6.6 |
| 35 | Greece | 4.9 | 8 | 1.7 | 3.7–8.1 |
| 36 | Malaysia | 4.8 | 11 | 0.6 | 3.8–5.9 |
| 37 | Mauritius | 4.7 | 5 | 0.8 | 3.9–5.6 |
|  | Morocco | 4.7 | 4 | 0.7 | 4.2–5.6 |
| 39 | Italy | 4.6 | 8 | 0.6 | 4.0–5.6 |
|  | Jordan | 4.6 | 5 | 0.8 | 3.8–5.7 |
| 41 | Peru | 4.4 | 5 | 0.5 | 3.8–5.0 |
| 42 | Czech Republic | 4.3 | 10 | 0.9 | 3.3–6.2 |
| 43 | Belarus | 4.1 | 3 | 0.8 | 3.4–4.9 |
|  | El Salvador | 4.1 | 4 | 1.7 | 2.1–6.2 |
|  | Lithuania | 4.1 | 4 | 0.3 | 3.8–4.4 |
|  | Malawi | 4.1 | 4 | 0.4 | 3.8–4.8 |
|  | Poland | 4.1 | 11 | 0.8 | 2.8–5.6 |
| 48 | South Korea | 4.0 | 11 | 0.6 | 3.4–5.6 |
| 49 | Brazil | 3.9 | 8 | 0.3 | 3.6–4.5 |
| 50 | Turkey | 3.8 | 8 | 0.8 | 2.1–4.5 |
| 51 | Croatia | 3.7 | 4 | 0.4 | 3.4–4.3 |
| 52 | Argentina | 3.5 | 8 | 0.6 | 3.0–4.5 |
|  | Bulgaria | 3.5 | 6 | 0.4 | 3.3–4.3 |
|  | Ghana | 3.5 | 4 | 0.9 | 2.5–4.7 |
|  | Senegal | 3.5 | 3 | 0.8 | 2.8–4.3 |
|  | Slovak Republic | 3.5 | 7 | 1.2 | 2.2–6.2 |
| 57 | Latvia | 3.4 | 3 | 1.3 | 2.1–4.4 |
|  | Zambia | 3.4 | 4 | 1.4 | 2.1–5.1 |
| 59 | Mexico | 3.3 | 8 | 0.5 | 2.5–4.1 |
| 60 | Colombia | 3.2 | 8 | 0.8 | 2.5–4.5 |
|  | Ethiopia | 3.2 | 3 | 0.8 | 2.5–3.9 |
|  | Thailand | 3.2 | 11 | 0.6 | 2.4–4.0 |
| 63 | China | 3.1 | 11 | 1.0 | 0.6–4.3 |
|  | Egypt | 3.1 | 7 | 0.7 | 2.3–4.1 |
| 65 | Burkina Faso | 3.0 | 3 | 1.0 | 2.5–4.4 |
|  | Kazakhstan | 3.0 | 4 | 1.2 | 2.1–4.3 |
|  | Zimbabwe | 3.0 | 7 | 1.5 | 0.6–4.9 |

*(continued)*

**Table 2.3.**   *Continued*

| Country Rank | Country | 2000 CPI Score | Surveys Used | Standard Deviation | High–Low Range |
|---|---|---|---|---|---|
| 68 | Romania | 2.9 | 4 | 1.0 | 2.1–4.3 |
| 69 | India | 2.8 | 11 | 0.7 | 2.3–4.3 |
|  | Philippines | 2.8 | 11 | 1.0 | 1.7–4.7 |
| 71 | Bolivia | 2.7 | 4 | 1.3 | 1.7–4.3 |
|  | Côte-d'Ivoire | 2.7 | 4 | 0.8 | 2.1–3.6 |
|  | Venezuela | 2.7 | 8 | 0.7 | 2.1–4.3 |
| 74 | Ecuador | 2.6 | 4 | 1.0 | 2.1–4.3 |
|  | Moldova | 2.6 | 4 | 0.9 | 1.8–3.8 |
| 76 | Armenia | 2.5 | 3 | 0.6 | 2.4–3.5 |
|  | Tanzania | 2.5 | 4 | 0.6 | 2.1–3.5 |
|  | Vietnam | 2.5 | 8 | 0.6 | 2.1–3.8 |
| 79 | Uzbekistan | 2.4 | 3 | 0.9 | 2.1–3.7 |
| 80 | Uganda | 2.3 | 4 | 0.6 | 2.1–3.5 |
| 81 | Mozambique | 2.2 | 3 | 0.2 | 2.4–2.7 |
| 82 | Kenya | 2.1 | 4 | 0.3 | 2.1–2.7 |
|  | Russia | 2.1 | 10 | 1.1 | 0.6–4.1 |
| 84 | Cameroon | 2.0 | 4 | 0.6 | 1.6–3.0 |
| 85 | Angola | 1.7 | 3 | 0.4 | 1.6–2.5 |
|  | Indonesia | 1.7 | 11 | 0.8 | 0.5–3.2 |
| 87 | Azerbaijan | 1.5 | 4 | 0.9 | 0.6–2.5 |
|  | Ukraine | 1.5 | 7 | 0.7 | 0.5–2.5 |
| 89 | Yugoslavia | 1.3 | 3 | 0.9 | 0.6–2.4 |
| 90 | Nigeria | 1.2 | 4 | 0.6 | 0.6–2.1 |

*Source:* www.transparency.org. Reprinted with permission.

# Event Risk

You wouldn't want to buy a security issued in one of the countries near the bottom of the list—such as Colombia (60) or Russia (82)—if you expected to hold it for a long time. But if you were closely following the news in a particular country and noticed an excess of negative sentiment, you might continue to pay attention in the hope of picking up a security at a deep discount. This high-risk way of approaching global markets is not suited to everyone. In fact, experts in emerging markets (such as Mark Mobius, author of *Passport to Profits,* Warner Books, 1999) say you should be even more careful in selecting stocks in these countries and plan to hold them for at least five years, to give economic development a chance to work its magic on stock prices. Mobius has recently become a shareholder activist in emerging market stock markets, specifically targeting transparency and corruption.

As we know, however, market sentiment moves in big swings, and when we see negativity at an extreme, an opportunity may not be far behind. Turkey (50 on the Corruption Perceptions Index) recently went through a financial crisis that necessitated a bailout by the International Monetary Fund (IMF). (See Figure 2.12.) As is usually the case in emerging markets, Turkey had too many banks, the banks were noncompetitive, and bank failures started the chain effect of corporate failures, more bank failures, and so on. The economy had suffered the usual overexpansion of money and credit. Inflation was high and rising, which caused a certain amount of hot-money outflow to more stable currencies (and depleted government reserves of hard currencies). The Turkish lira needed to be propped up in the currency market by the central

**Figure 2.12**    Istanbul 100 Index.

bank, and eventually devalued. The effect on the Istanbul stock market was predictable: an accelerating decline as conditions worsened and investors withdrew. But after a restructuring plan was agreed on with the IMF, which then started to disburse funds, capital flowed back.

Over the past 20 years, Turkey has twice had the best-performing stock market in the world. Conventional risk-averse investment advisors would steer the average American investor away from Turkish securities. And yet, with good timing and a short holding period, the intrepid global trader could have made 56 percent in five weeks (March 30 to May 4, 2001). Actually, a U.S. investor would not have been able to trade the Istanbul 100 directly as a security; he would have had to find a specific stock instead. This is not easy. To find stocks by country, you can go to www.adr.com, the ADR Web site of J.P. Morgan, one of the major ADR sponsors; or to www.bankofny.com/adr, the site of Bank of New York; or even to the New York Stock Exchange (www.nyse.com). The Morgan site names many Turkish stocks traded outside Turkey, but only one seems to trade in the United States (Turkcell, a telephone company). Others, including banks, textiles, and energy companies, trade on various European exchanges. To get access to them, you need to have a full-service brokerage account at one of the big houses. Merrill Lynch says it is the largest broker of international stocks, and a broker there will send you company profiles, charts, and analysis reports. International ECNs are still in development (www.globeshares.com and www.intltrader.com) and the big brokerage houses are still promising access to foreign stocks "next year." As a practical matter, to get involved with international stocks, you need a full-service broker.

"Strategic investing" like this is a distinct alternative to stock picking among domestic U.S. companies. A well-known practitioner (to viewers of CNN) is Jim Melcher at Balestra Capital, Ltd. (www.balestracapital-ltd.com). His interest in Russian equities was aroused when he realized, in December 1998, that the entire Russian stock market was worth less than half of the dollar value of Yahoo! at the time. This was after the default, in August 1998, by the Russian government on its sovereign debt (a situation still not resolved in the spring of 2001). He committed funds to an open-ended fund specializing in the situation: the Third

Millennium Russia Fund, which bought ADRs such as Lukoil and
Gazprom. The gain within the first six months was over 160 percent. The gain in the RTS Interfax index was more—about 250
percent—but it contains small stocks with low liquidity that are
not really available to a foreign investor. From a low of $14.35 in
December 1998, the RTS Interfax Index has risen as high as
$52.24 (in August 2000) and is at $46.15 at the end of May 2001.
(See Figure 2.13.)

   If you go to the ADR Web sites today, you will not find Russian
stocks—even the famous ones like Lukoil and Gazprom. Your Merrill Lynch broker will give you the symbol, but you cannot get a
chart or a profile at Yahoo!Finance or other major U.S. Web sites.
You can't even get the historical price data from Reuters Online. In
some instances, you can get the information at www.bigcharts
.com, which is the charting service used by the *Financial Times,*
the best source of hard information on foreign stocks outside of
their own Web sites—if you can find the company names in the

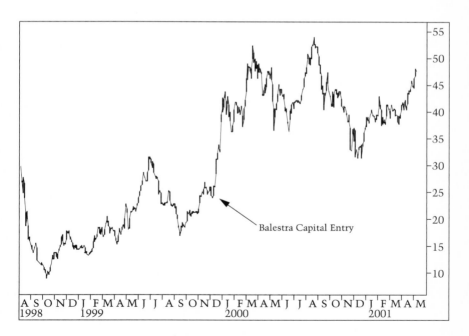

**Figure 2.13**   Russian RTS Index.

first place. This is frustrating; it serves to make the point that big-picture international-event trading is a very specialized field visited by few individuals. This is why Balestra's latest addition to its selection of services (managed accounts and two hedge funds) is multimanager allocation. Strategic investing requires specialists.

## Strategic Specialists

Each of the big management firms has a bevy of specialists hired to produce intelligence on sectors, countries, and regions, and, in some cases, classes of securities (such as emerging market bonds and foreign exchange). Many are independent boutiques staffed by only a few people. Some economics consulting firms will sell their reports only to institutions—chiefly because the "retail market" is too demanding of limited time. High-Frequency Economics, in Valhalla, New York, is a well-known and oft-quoted weekly service that forecasts the major world economies, stock markets, bonds, and currencies. The Amernick Letter, mentioned earlier, is one place to get broader coverage that includes emerging markets. Condor Advisers publishes a thoughtful monthly report on emerging markets, available by writing to jpg@condoradvisers. (None of these sources has a Web site.)

The best way to get started is to carefully read the mainstream press, such as *The Economist* magazine, the *Financial Times* newspaper, and some of the regional periodicals such as *The Far Eastern Economic Review.* If you happen to be in New York, the New York Institute of Finance offers a course named "Introducing the Global Financial Markets." It is cosponsored by the *Financial Times.* The course outline includes technical analysis, global bond strategies, and foreign exchange markets, as well as macroeconomics and derivatives.

You can also get information from the stock exchanges in each country, although the quality varies enormously and following links to "research" is often a time-consuming dead end. Many experts on foreign stocks, and especially emerging markets stocks, are to be found at brokerages in the countries themselves, or at the big global investment and commercial banks such as Goldman Sachs. Getting access to these experts is very difficult, but they can sometimes be found at www.multex.com, albeit usually for a hefty charge ($25 and up, per report). In many cases, only institutional clients may access the reports.

You can easily find information on developed countries in the mainstream press and in reports sent to clients by the major brokerage houses. The challenge is to find information and insight on emerging markets. The best entry into emerging markets from the point of view of availability of information is not stocks—although many are available as ADRs—but bonds, the subject of the next chapter.

## Putting It Together—A Practical Application

In the spring of 2001, you could read in the *South China Morning Post* (www.scmp.com) the news that China Unicom (CHU), the state-owned Chinese telephone monopoly and a stock traded as an ADR on the New York Stock Exchange, may be listed on the Shanghai exchange as a Class A stock, available only to Chinese citizens in local currency. It sometimes happens that a new listing of an existing stock on a different exchange acts like an IPO—it goes up. This is a correction of a supply inefficiency. A new listing with additional issuance will dilute the value of all the existing shares, but the net outcome is not necessarily a general price drop. In this case, Chinese citizens do not have access to the United States ADRs, so the market for the stock is effectively partitioned.

If the "art" of investing is the inspiration that the new listing could be an opportunity, the "craft" consists of finding out everything there is to know about the Chinese and Hong Kong markets in general, and the facts of the Chinese telephone companies specifically. Right away, we discover that all listed companies in China so far are state owned, and the state is a communist one. Domestically, Chinese stocks are traded on two exchanges—one for citizens and one for foreigners. Historically, communist governments have had an awful track record toward foreigners. They are prone to expropriation and other ploys that effectively deprive foreign asset owners of their property rights. The current Chinese government, however, has shown itself well aware of the benefits of foreign capital inflow, thereby reducing sovereign risk *at the moment.* Ford, for example, in April 2001, announced a joint venture to produce cars in China. We have to assume that Ford carefully evaluated the sovereign risk. Then we have the issue of evaluating the companies themselves. To be listed as an ADR, China Unicom (CHU) was required to state its financial condition according to U.S. accounting principles and rules, and therefore we can look at its financial condition. We may not believe every statistic we see, considering the source and its incentives to paint the lily, but the company is not completely unknown. We immediately find that China Unicom, the state monopoly in the People's Republic of China, has as its chief competitor a company named China Mobile (CHL), formerly China Telecom, a Hong Kong-based company that provides cellular services in Hong Kong and some mainland provinces. China Unicom also provides cellular and paging telephony as well as land lines. China Mobile, listed in Hong Kong but with most of its business in China, is a so-called red chip stock.

The holders of China Unicom include mutual funds with total dollar holdings (as reported by Yahoo!Finance at the end of April 2001) of $348.5 million worth of shares. They include two Janus funds (Pacific Growth and Global Technology), three Fidelity funds, and funds managed by other big names such as Vanguard/ Morgan. Mutual funds add and subtract shares mechanically, depending on fund additions and withdrawals, but, generally, the relative allocation to specific companies will remain in proportion to the whole. (See Figure 2.14.)

China Mobile also has ownership by U.S. mutual funds. In this case, one fund (Janus) owns $1.4 *billion* worth of shares, or a total of four times as much U.S. fund ownership by a single fund as all the U.S. mutual funds together have in China Unicom. In other words, some professionals at Janus like China Unicom, but some other professionals at Janus like China Mobile better, although you would have to do the arithmetic on each of the Janus funds to find out the relative proportion of China Unicom to the total funds, compared to the relative proportion of China Mobile to that one Janus fund. The dollar amount is not necessarily an accurate gauge. Assuming that you can't buy both stocks, how do you select a Chinese phone company for your portfolio? What you really need to know is which company is a better company—and

**Figure 2.14**   Telecom Index versus China Unicom.

whether the two stock prices reflect the difference between the
quality of the two companies. You can learn at Yahoo!Finance
that, up to 2000, China Mobile had revenue growth of 55.02 percent per annum, and China Unicom had revenue growth of 16.67
percent per annum. (See Figure 2.15.) For the year 2000, China
Unicom claimed a 285 percent jump in net profit to $390.2 mil-
lion, led by gains in the mobile-phone subscriber base. China Mobile, which actually has a bigger subscriber base on the mainland,
reported net profit up 276 percent to $2.2 billion.

　　Of course, you could consider that the sovereign risk of Hong
Kong is lower than the sovereign risk of China itself, although
that argument loses weight when you consider that, technically,
Hong Kong belongs to China despite having a different adminis-
tration (one of the great ambiguities of history). China could (un-
fairly) pass regulations or taxes that would favor its own company
over the Hong Kong-based company, thus throttling the latter's
growth in China. If such an event were to happen, how would the
management of China Mobile respond? We may assume that

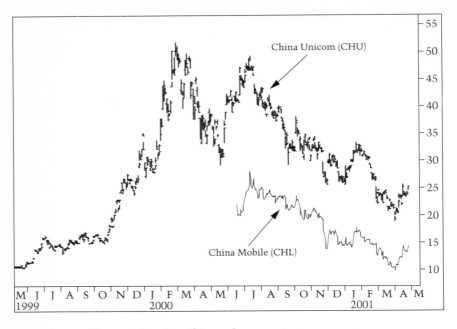

**Figure 2.15**　Two Chinese telecommunications companies.

China Mobile's management is less provincial and bureaucratic and more dynamic, and would simply turn to another market in Asia to expand—but does it have the capital to do so? Now we are back to craft, that is, analyzing the financial ratios and examining past management decisions such as strategic alliances with other companies, technology initiatives, and so on.

The point is that to evaluate this situation, you would have to become as expert as the mutual fund analysts to judge the market for telephone services in China, the likely government behaviors, the technology, the two company managements, the stock markets in China and the United States where the ADRs are traded, and the outlook for the telecommunications sector overall. How much of this work you are willing to do depends on your expected gain as a proportion of your total capital, and that, in turn, has a relationship with your expected holding period. At some point, Chinese citizens will have as much telephone service as they want or can afford, whereupon the growth of the sector there will slow down, as will the growth of earnings. Meanwhile, your investment could be trashed by a general exodus from Chinese stocks because of political events—escalating tension between the United States and China, Chinese troops invading Taiwan, or some other unforeseen event. Because you will be buying your shares as ADRs traded in the United States, you will have a time zone disadvantage—catastrophic news would probably be released during Chinese daylight hours—and that may pose a liquidity risk, or the risk that there are no buyers of your stock at any price.

The most important events will probably occur in China itself. China has two stock markets, in Shanghai and in Shenzhen, and each, in turn, has two classes of stock. Class A is available only to Chinese citizens for local currency, and Class B is available only to foreigners, for hard currencies. Shanghai's stocks are denominated in U.S. dollars; Shenzhen's are denominated in Hong Kong dollars. The Shanghai Exchange was reopened in 1990 (after 40 years of suspended stock trading) and Shanghai considers itself the financial capital of China, but Shenzhen is closer geographically to Hong Kong and is a rival for the title. Starting in the spring of 2000, there was talk of merging the two exchanges, or, in the spring of 2001, of putting the big companies in Shanghai and leaving IPOs and smaller companies in Shenzhen. The big event, though, was the government's allowing citizens to invest in Class B shares in both places in February 2001. Over $1 billion of new money flooded in during the first few weeks, accounting for the surge in prices. (See Figure 2.16.)

In fact, analysts suspect that the $10.4 billion increase in official government hard currency reserves (to $176 billion) was partly a function of Chinese citizens' repatriating foreign exchange specifically in order to invest in Class B shares. The market capitalization of the 114 listed B-share companies more than doubled—from about $7 billion at year end to more than $18 billion by April 1, 2001. Official local currency savings are estimated at about $80 billion, and, in the second quarter of 2001, citizens were allowed to set up new foreign currency accounts to use for buying B shares. This substantially reduces the sovereign risk of B shares. Any suggestion of "fleece-the-foreigner," as Mark Mobius calls it, would also hurt the interests of citizens.

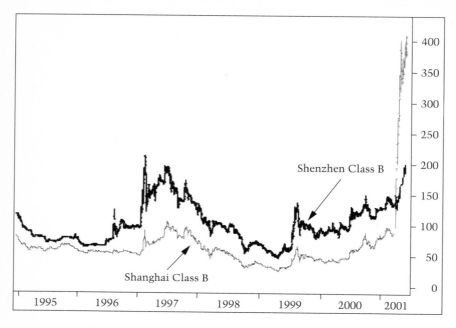

**Figure 2.16**    Shanglai and Shenzhen Class B stock indices.

Type in "Shanghai Stock Market" at www.business.com and you get zero Web sites named. On other searches, Microsoft MSN has 168,102 entries on "Chinese stock markets," but over half are in Chinese. The first 20 in English are dead ends. "Shenzhen-stockexchange.com" takes you to www .australian-stockmarket.com," evidently because it mentions a Shenzhen index, but the site is being rebuilt and that's all there is—a mention. www.virtualchina.org has a "Guide for Beginners" that leads directly to the U.S. Securities and Exchange Commission home page. It is very frustrating to research stock market conditions in China.

You can register (for a free subscription and newsletters) at the site of the *South China Morning Post* (www.scmp.com) and also at *Not the South China Post,* the site of a satirical newspaper that contains some very interesting insights on social and political matters (www.members.xoom.com). At www.english.peopledaily.com, you can get the official party line on businesses, and also "The Selected Works of Deng Xiaoping," if you are of a mind to read it.

**Figure 2.17** The Shenzhen Class B Index versus the Hang Seng—Cumulative percentage change.

You might think that because Shenzhen Class B shares are denominated in Hong Kong dollars, they might attract the most interest from Hong Kong, where the Hang Seng index is the main barometer of stock prices. (See Figure 2.17.) In practice, however, the Shenzhen Class B Index seems to have a life of its own, independent of the Hang Seng. The Hong Kong dollar is fixed to the U.S. dollar in a tiny trading range around 8.9, so there is no currency effect, either. Similarly, the Shanghai Class B Index, denominated in U.S. dollars, is independent of the S&P 500. (See Figure 2.18.)

China Mobile, traded on the Hong Kong market and in New York as an ADR, seems to have an independent life from both of those markets. (See Figure 2.19.)

We would need to learn a lot more about the behavior of Chinese stocks, but, on a superficial review, it would seem that a new listing for China Unicom—the removal of an inefficiency

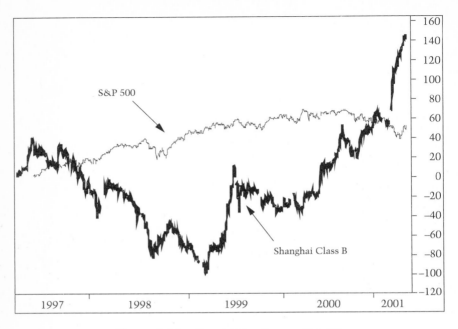

**Figure 2.18**　Shanglai Class B versus S&P 500.

that is our starting point—will not have a dilutive effect on China Unicom in New York, may not pull investors away from China Mobile, and, in fact, may result in a rise in *both* Chinese telecom companies as attention is drawn to telecom companies generally. Separately, Chinese stocks are rallying on their own and, at some point, can be expected to correct, or pull back, as some investors take profit. After a market top is reached and the index starts to slide, we need to reevaluate whether to continue to hold. Other inefficiencies, such as the shortage of U.S. dollars and Hong Kong dollars to would-be domestic stock buyers, may encourage holding through a correction. Any suggestion that China may devalue the renmimbi would also be a good reason to buy Chinese stocks, since we would expect the would-be domestic stock buyers to make a greater effort to get hard currencies and place them at work in stocks. Because of sovereign and country risk, though, we would not consider either stock as a buy-and-hold-forever item.

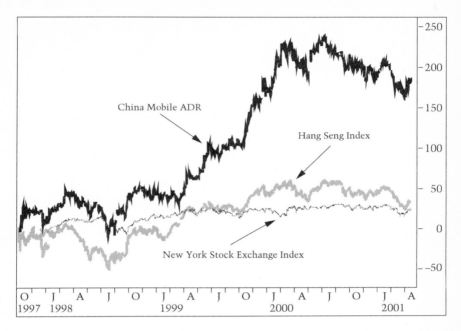

**Figure 2.19**   China Mobile versus Hang Seng and NYSE Indices—Cumulative percentage change.

Finally, we have to consider the driving force behind important market moves: the behavior of the big institutions. Worldwide, the performance of major fund managers is judged against the Morgan Stanley Capital International Index for the region, and we already know that, by June 2002, the MSCI index for China will include China Mobile and will not include China Unicom.

Before then, however, the FTSE International, a provider of in-dices like the FTSE 100 in London for U.K. shares, and China's Xin-hua news agency will have jointly launched an index of Chinese stocks in May 2001. It remains to be seen whether the index will compete, as intended, with the MSCI Index for China. The new FTSE/Xinhua China 25 Index seeks to better reflect the Chinese market for foreign investors because single-company weightings are capped at 10 percent, and this reflects free float better (as well as the holding restrictions within many funds). China Mobile, for

example, accounts for more than half of the MSCI China Free
index, but is 8.3 percent of the FTSE/Xinhua China 25. The
FTSE/Xinhua agency plans to reevaluate the holding with greater
frequency than MSCI, too, given the pace of change in China. If
the new index becomes popular, or when MSCI rejiggers its Free
China index to free float instead of market cap, shouldn't we expect China Mobile to fall as institutions reallocate? Yes. It will be
an Event. Since we have already figured it out, though, will it not
be fully discounted? Perhaps.

*Chapter 3*

# WHY NOT BONDS?

*To accept an orthodoxy is always to inherit unresolved contradictions.*

George Orwell

We take it as a matter of course that, over any length of time, stocks are the superior vehicle for total return. In *The Millennium Book, A Century of Investment Returns* (AMB AMRO/LBS, 2000), we see that equities consistently outperform bonds and "bills" (shorter-term government bills) in every major market.

Don't let the negative numbers in Table 3.1 confuse you. They are the result of calculating the real return, meaning the nominal or face return minus the rate of inflation.

Bonds are not as attractive as equities over the long haul, but they can be very interesting over shorter time periods. Even high-yielding bonds, rated junk or near-junk, can be less risky than stocks if you analyze the situation correctly. Once you have determined that your holding period is opportunistic rather than "forever," you are liberated to seek exceptional circumstances wherever they lie. So don't neglect bonds.

Among the mature economies with low sovereign risk, the opportunity lies in correctly forecasting whether interest rates will fall or rise. When they fall, the price of a bond rises in order to equalize the total nominal return of all the equivalent-tenor bonds in the same market. Price moves inversely to yield. Conversely, when a central bank detects impending inflation (or a currency crisis), it will raise interest rates, and even though this happens at the very short end of the yield curve (such as the Fed funds or

**Table 3.1.**  Annualized Real Return: 1900–2000

| Country | Equities | Bonds | Bills |
|---|---|---|---|
| Australia | 7.6 | 1.6 | 0.4 |
| Canada | 6.4 | 1.8 | 1.7 |
| Denmark (from 1915) | 5.4 | 2.7 | 2.8 |
| France | 4.0 | −1.0 | −3.4 |
| Germany (98 years ex-1922–23) | 4.4 | −2.3 | −0.6 |
| Italy | 2.7 | −2.3 | −4.1 |
| Japan (from 1914) | 4.2 | −1.5 | −2.1 |
| Netherlands | 6.0 | 1.1 | 0.7 |
| Sweden | 8.2 | 2.3 | 2.0 |
| Switzerland | 5.0 | 2.1 | 1.1 |
| USA | 6.9 | 1.5 | 1.1 |
| UK | 5.9 | 1.3 | 1.0 |

*Source:* Elroy Dimson, Paul Marsh, and Mike Staunton, *The Millennium Book, A Century of Investment Returns* (AMB AMRO/LBS, 2000), p. 19.

overnight rate), the action tends to shift the entire yield curve upward, including the bonds at the long end. A rise in yield causes the price to fall. The Web site www.smartmoney.com contains an animated yield curve that illustrates the effects of interest rate changes. It also describes tricks of the trade in "Ten Things Your Broker Won't Tell You About Bonds."

Bonds are generally offered on the basis of yield to maturity. Note that yields quoted in the financial pages of newspapers represent yields for only some of the available bonds, and those are rates that apply to institutional-size trades. Larger, more active issues tend to fluctuate less in value and are more liquid for redemptions. The U.S. bond market is the largest in the world, but opportunities exist in foreign bond markets as well. This is worth considering because studies have shown that, over the past 10 years, the U.S. bond market has ranked first in terms of performance in only one year. (See Table 3.2.) Total performance is the combined yield and price appreciation over one year.

## Tricks and Gimmicks

Aside from U.S. Government savings bonds or bond funds, most people have no familiarity with bonds. The first thing to recognize

**Table 3.2.** Bond Market Performance

| Year | Best Market | U.S. Rank Out of 10 Major Markets |
|------|-------------|-----------------------------------|
| 2000 | United States | 1 |
| 1999 | Japan | 3 |
| 1998 | France | 9 |
| 1997 | United Kingdom | 2 |
| 1996 | Australia | 6 |
| 1995 | Sweden | 7 |
| 1994 | Belgium | 9 |
| 1993 | Japan | 8 |
| 1992 | Japan | 4 |
| 1991 | Australia | 4 |
| 1990 | United Kingdom | 10 |
| 1989 | Canada | 2 |
| 1988 | Australia | 3 |
| 1987 | United Kingdom | 10 |
| 1986 | Belgium | 9 |

*Source:* www.troweprice.com.

about bonds is their promise of a rate of interest. As noted elsewhere, there is no rate of return inherent in stocks, although people talk about stocks as though there were. They are really referring to past average returns, and not something that is inherent in the instrument. When a bond is issued, you are promised a specific rate of return, and if you hold the bond to maturity, that is exactly what you will get—as long as the issuer does not default on the payment terms.

Our overriding goal is to buy something that is temporarily on sale because the majority of market participants don't yet see its true value, or to find something that is mispriced because of an inefficiency. The bond market offers many instances of mispricing, from the very small to the very large. A good example is convergence trades. One of the classic convergence trades in bonds arises because freshly issued bonds are deemed more desirable than already-issued ("on-the-run") bonds, which sell at a slight discount to the new ones. Over time, the new ones become old ones and their price converges to the yet-older on-the-run bonds. Most convergence trades work because some initial uncertainty over one of the bonds fades with the passing of time (and the payment of the coupon). The advantage of one over the other was not very serious to begin with, but in sufficient size (or with sufficient leverage), juicy low-risk gains are to be had. This was a central strategy of Long-Term Capital Management.

A much bigger convergence trade occurred when the original countries of the European Monetary Union (EMU) got closer to the launch date of the new single currency, the euro, which replaced the national currencies on January 1, 1999. Although there is no central political authority in the eurozone and each country is still an issuer in its own sovereign name, the European Central Bank replaced the national central banks as the interest-rate policy-setting body. The need for each country to manage its interest rate in the direction of the central rate occasioned convergence trades. The same thing happened when Greece joined in January 2001. The Greek central bank progressively lowered interest rates ahead of joining the EMU, to meet the level of the European Central Bank. As the EMU enlarges itself to include Poland, the Czech Republic, Hungary, the Baltic states, and so on, convergence trades will again come into play. Dates are not yet set, but these countries are expected to join during the period from 2003 to 2010. The present higher interest rates in those countries will most likely fall, to converge to the eurozone level, and prices will rise. Other effects have to be considered, though. The very fact of joining the EMU should reduce the sovereign risk premium (raising prices even more), although if the transition to the euro is not well managed (double accounting systems in place, and so on), the opposite could happen.

## Global Bills, Notes, and Bonds

For our purposes, we want to talk about situations where you can conduct global trading in the relative safety of the bond market. (Remember that inherent promised return.) Let's say you want to diversify your portfolio with 10 percent or 20 percent bonds, as most advisors recommend. *The bonds don't have to be U.S. governments.* We consider that the probability of default by the U.S. Government on its bonds is effectively zero. But we may also judge that the probability of default by (say) Great Britain is practically zero, too. So the first task is to seek a country that has yields higher than those in the United States, an effectively zero risk of default, and one other factor that makes the bonds a relative bargain. Atop the list of factors is the currency. Whenever you buy a foreign security, you are taking a foreign exchange risk. So what is the most undervalued currency and why do we expect it to rise, giving us a nice little extra gain on top of the bond yield?

## 1. Undervalued Currency

Let's say that you like the yield on Australian bonds: 7 percent versus 5.8 percent in the United States. The Australian Reserve Bank lowered interest rates over the course of late 2000 and the first half of 2001, so the total return on a portfolio of Australian bonds over the past year (to June 2001) is about 18 percent, including the price rise that accompanied the drop in interest rates. Meanwhile, the Australian dollar has been the most undervalued of the major world currencies for over three years, into the spring of 2001. A holder of an Australian-dollar-denominated asset like a bond (or an iShare) has a positive expectancy of a currency gain, on top of whatever gain he gets from the asset. So far, the A$ has not delivered on this promise, but the consensus of opinion remains that, over the long run, the A$ should rise. (See Figure 3.1.) From around 50 to 52 cents at the beginning of June 2001, the consensus forecast of foreign exchange analysts is 70 to 85 cents over the next two or three years.

Investors are able to buy Australian bonds today from many of the big brokers (such as Merrill Lynch), or by putting an order through the trading desk at an online broker. (Among the major online retail brokers, Charles Schwab, E*Trade, and CSFBDirect offer bond-trading capability at their Web sites, but bond quotes accessible online are restricted to U.S. issues only.) Keep in mind that, unlike stocks, availability and prices vary from dealer to dealer, depending on their inventory. You may not be entirely thrilled with the exchange rate at which your U.S. dollars are converted to Australian dollars, but you can buy a bond for as little as $5,000, and the broker will even mark it to market for you every day on the brokerage Web site.

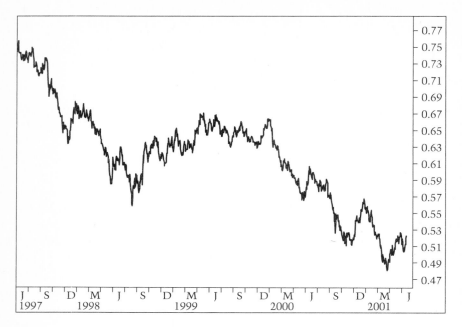

**Figure 3.1**   The Australian dollar.

On your own, tracking bond prices is not easy. Despite the ubiquity of the Internet, free information on bond prices, particularly foreign bonds, is inadequate. Whatever information is available is typically designed for professional traders rather than retail investors. The lack of transparency is due to the fact that bonds trade less frequently than stocks. Bonds typically are purchased for their income stream rather than for capital appreciation. True, trading is done by professionals who buy and sell bonds to profit from changes in interest rates and credit quality, but most bond investors buy and hold issues until they mature.

Indicative prices of the yields of foreign bonds can be obtained from certain Web sites, including those of the domestic exchanges. Unfortunately, in the United States as well as in other countries, bond prices are scarce compared to stock prices, and not all foreign sites have an English version. The sites listed in Table 3.3 have some information on foreign bonds (and all are in English).

Countries like Australia, Canada, and Great Britain are not hard for the average person to evaluate in terms of sovereign

**Table 3.3.** Global Bond Web Sites

| Name | Link | Comments |
|---|---|---|
| Financial Times | www.ft.com/cgi-bin /pft/bengov.pl/report | The Markets section lists yields and coupon rates of benchmark government bonds of the major OECD* countries, and Eurobonds. |
| Bloomberg | www.bloomberg.com | The Internet edition is nowhere near as comprehensive as a real Bloomberg box, but you can still access world news headlines and some market commentary, although these tend to be geared toward finance professionals. Benchmark prices are available on government bonds issued by Canada, France, Germany, Italy, Japan, and the United Kingdom. Currency rates are just a click away if you are thinking of investing globally. |
| BradyNet | www.bradynet.com | Only a few features of the site are free, but, for $99.95 a month (Basic Service), you can obtain historical data of up to six years' worth of prices and yields for benchmark Bradies and worldwide indices, and charts. There are chat rooms, analytic tools, links to market research and analyses produced by securities firms, and portfolio management tools. Real-time prices, yields, spreads, and intraday charts are available by upgrading to Premium Service for $199.95 a month. The site offers a 14-day trial period (credit card information required). Response time is acceptable, but we experienced some technical glitches when using the charting feature as well as the corporate research database. |

*(continued)*

**Table 3.3.** *Continued*

| Name | Link | Comments |
|---|---|---|
| BondAgent | www.bondagent.com | BondAgent is an online brokerage affiliated with Morton Clarke Fu & Metcalf, a Seattle-based broker-dealer. Registration is free and allows you to view bond prices. We were able to find "Yankee bonds" (foreign bonds issued in U.S. dollars). There is a bond search tool: type in the desired characteristics (type of issuer, minimum/maximum tenor, rating, coupon, price, yield) and the site will identify bonds that fit your specifications.<br><br>The dealer's markup is included in the price of the bonds, but the site's creator claims the markup rarely exceeds 0.6 percent of the par value of the bonds. (Large brokerage firms typically charge 3 percent or higher.) An initial investment of $10,000 is required to open an account and trade online. |
| Citytext | www.citytext.com | Provides high/low, closing price, and yield on gilts (U.K. Treasuries). |
| Sao Paulo Stock Exchange | www.bovespa.com.br | Provides closing reference prices on five domestic corporate bonds. |
| Hong Kong Stock Exchange | www.hkex.com.hk | Lists latest indicative prices (bid/ask, yield), coupon rates, maturity date, and next interest-payment date of Exchange Fund Notes (EFNs) issued by the Hong Kong Monetary Authority. |
| Swiss Exchange | www.swx.com | Provides closing price, high/low, and volume of bonds traded on the exchange. You can download 30 days' worth of daily closing prices into a spreadsheet. |
| Australia Stock Exchange | www.asx.com | Provides bid/ask, closing prices, coupon rate, and maturity date of domestic corporate bonds. Background information available on some listed companies. |
| Bond Exchange of South Africa | www.bondex.co.za | Lists all domestic bond issues available, but no prices. |

*OECD: Organization for Economic Cooperation and Development.

risk. They are highly unlikely to default. Even countries that have less than the highest ratings, such as Japan, can be deemed unlikely to default. Other countries (like Brazil) are harder to evaluate. Rating agencies are in the business of providing an independent and reliable assessment of the credit risk of issuers and/or specific issues, thus contributing to market efficiency. Quality ratings assist in the marketability of instruments, and since they have a direct influence on the interest rate required to attract investors, they can lower the borrower's cost of raising capital. Critics of the ratings agencies feel that they are a day late and a dollar short in downgrading sovereign ratings when it is sometimes perfectly obvious that a country is getting into trouble. This happened in the Asia crisis of 1997 to 1998, when the agencies were very slow to downgrade Thailand, Malaysia, Indonesia, Korea, and the Philippines. As is often the case, currency market specialists foresaw the crisis before the ratings agencies, because the currencies were under pressure.

Understandably, issuers are hesitant to publicize their ratings unless they are top-of-the-line. It is not difficult to get hold of the information, however. Investors can go directly to these rating agencies themselves:

- Standard and Poor's (S&P)
  www.standardandpoors.com
  Current ratings for specific issues or issuers can be obtained by downloading quarterly counterparty ratings guides available in Adobe Portable Document Format (PDF). Sovereign ratings are updated weekly, and each country's rating history since 1975 can be viewed.
- Moody's Investors Service
  www.moodys.com
  If you run an inquiry by typing in an issuer name, CUSIP, or ISIN (International Securities Identification Number), the site automatically takes you to a page that lists not just the Moody's rating but all prior rating action and, for searches by issuer name, all outstanding rated issues for that issuer.
- Fitch IBCA Duff & Phelps
  www.fitchibca.com

You can look up a rating by the issuer's name or by the security's CUSIP or ISIN. Historical ratings are not available from the Web site.

Table 3.4 illustrates the meanings of specific bond ratings. The rating systems of the three major services are similar in the way they label bond quality or issuer creditworthiness. Modifiers are used within each country to fine-tune the ranking. Moody's uses a numerical system (1 for higher end, 2 for midrange, 3 for lower end). Standard and Poor's (S&P) and Fitch use + or −.

If you are considering investing in bonds, don't disregard junk bonds right away. It is interesting to note that characteristically cautious U.S. pension funds have increasingly been investing in emerging-market (non-investment-grade) debt to diversify their

**Table 3.4.** What Bond Ratings Mean

| Moody's | S&P and Fitch | Definition | |
|---|---|---|---|
| Aaa | AAA | Highest quality. Issuers have exceptionally strong capacity for timely payment of financial commitments. | |
| Aa | AA | Very high quality, with slightly higher degree of risk over the long term. | **Investment Grade** |
| A | A | High-medium quality, with many strong attributes, but may be vulnerable to changing economic conditions. | |
| Baa | BBB | Good quality, currently satisfactory financial condition, but perhaps unreliable over the long term. | |
| Ba | BB | Speculative, possibility of credit problems in case of prolonged adverse economic conditions. | |
| B | B | Highly speculative, significant credit risk but with a limited margin of safety. | |
| Caa | CCC | Poor quality, default of some kind appears probable. Ability to meet financial commitments is dependent on favorable business, financial, and economic conditions. | **Junk or Non-Investment Grade** |
| Ca | CC | Highly speculative, highly vulnerable to nonpayment | |
| C | C | Poor prospects of repayment, though may still be paying (e.g., bankruptcy petition pending, but payments are being continued). | |
| | D | In default. | |

portfolios. According to Capital Access International, a research firm that specializes in tracking the fixed-income markets, 82 U.S. pension funds held emerging-market debt during 2000, up from 63 in 1999.

This trend does not necessarily violate regulations. ERISA (the Employee Retirement Income Security Act) requires only that fund managers apply the "prudent man rule." Instead of specifying grades, investment restrictions are defined in the fund's prospectus or in the fund manager's investment management contract. As you would expect, pension funds typically invest in very high quality securities to ensure preservation of capital. The 82 pension funds that do invest in emerging-market debt are the exception (there are about 600,000 pension funds in the United States) rather than the rule. In its simplest form, the prudent man rule restricts investments in a fiduciary account to transactions that a reasonably prudent person might conduct for his own account, taking into consideration a reasonable expectation of income as well as safety of capital. According to the International Financial Risk Institute, the origin of the term can be traced to 1830, when the Supreme Court of Massachusetts articulated, in the case of *Harvard College v. Amory*, that a trustee is required to conduct himself faithfully, exercise sound discretion, and observe how men of prudence, discretion, and intelligence manage their own affairs. A variation on the principle is the "prudent expert rule," which is based on the same tenets but differs in its implication that fiduciaries are subject to more than simple prudence. A person with fiduciary responsibility over other people's money has to hew to a higher standard. In the past, court decisions applied the prudent man rule to individual investments rather than to an entire portfolio. The message was: good portfolio performance does not excuse a single bad decision. More recently, other provisions of the law, and U.S. Department of Labor regulations, suggest that a portfolio approach may be applicable—that is, there may be some circumstances in which a position that is not prudent in isolation is acceptable in a portfolio context.

This legalistic approach to professional management is useful to individuals. First, it means that in the quest for yield, institutions are increasingly getting interested in bonds that, previously they dismissed as too risky. Over time, that will make the markets more liquid. More importantly, it confirms the view that one or two high-risk bond holdings do not constitute an unacceptable risk when a preponderance of less risky assets is in the same portfolio at the same time. For example, consider state-owned Petroleo Brasileiro, known as Petrobras, which issued a $450 million, seven-year bond in May 2001. The issuance amount was raised from $300 million due to demand. The bond is called a "eurobond," meaning it was issued simultaneously in several international financial centers, including London and New York. The 9.875 percent coupon represents a spread of 4.75 percent over the equivalent U.S. bond—and is less than the government of Brazil has to pay. This is because it received an investment-grade rating by Moody's Investors Service (Baa-1 local-currency issuer rating), a high level that was partly attributable to Petrobras's having obtained political risk insurance covering foreign exchange payments. This removes some of the sovereign risk associated with buying a bond of a state-owned company, not to mention that oil companies sell their product for U.S. dollars in the first place. Moreover, Petrobras plans to use the money to pay off more expensive bank debt, a virtuous use of funds.

## Drawbacks

Foreign bonds can have drawbacks. Currency fluctuations can cause the value of a bond to rise/fall in terms of U.S. dollars and directly affect overall return. Hedging currency risk is time consuming and doesn't automatically do the job. Political and economic instability in the underlying country could flare up unexpectedly, even if investors are tracking conditions in that country. On a more mundane level, outside of U.S. Treasuries, small lots of bonds (less than $10,000 worth) are expensive to buy and sell. Purchase costs can amount to about 1.5 percent to 2 percent of the bond's price. If you sell, you may incur a 2 percent to 3 percent commission because brokers usually don't have use for such small amounts. This is why brokers advise retail investors that they will be better off if they buy and hold bonds to maturity.

If you are making (say) a 30 percent return on a short-term position, however, you may feel less annoyed by a total 4 percent commission. Finally, as with foreign stocks, the tax considerations involved may reduce the return on your investment, complicate the paperwork, and increase your tax preparation costs.

None of these drawbacks was enough to stop the Mexican *cete* business, which was popular with investors not only along the southern border, but also in New York, Miami, and Los Angeles during the 1990s. A *cete* is a short-term (28-day or 91-day) Treasury bill issued by the Mexican Government. Going through both banks and brokers, individuals would buy *cetes* outright at an annualized yield of 25 to 35 percent, roll over the position every month, and exit as soon as the Mexican peso came under pressure. Some investors continued to hold. After all, if you have doubled or tripled your money in under a year, you are prepared to give back 20 percent of it in the form of a devalued currency. It was purely an arithmetically determined trade-off. The investor was taking the risk of default—which was not zero at the height of the Mexican crisis in 1995—and the risk of devaluation. Today, the situation has changed. Now the peso floats, and Mexico's finances have improved so that it doesn't need to offer 30 percent to get short-term funding. In fact, the Chicago Mercantile Exchange has a futures contract on both the 28-day and the 91-day Mexican Treasury bill, and you can't get a quote on the contract because there is no market for it today (i.e., no need for *cete* holders to hedge).

Investors who thought they were getting the same situation in the Russian crisis in 1998 were in for an unpleasant surprise. Then, too, Russian short-term paper for one and two weeks was yielding up to 50 percent per annum, and even higher on some days. Again, investors were taking both the risk of sovereign default and the risk of ruble devaluation. They got both. The default was a particularly unhappy outcome because the International Monetary Fund (IMF) and creditors were busily working to find new funds for Russia, and agreements—and some disbursements— had been made when Russia defaulted. Afterward, we found out that the fresh Western funds had flowed straight through the government into private hands in offshore banks—in a word, stolen. Investors knew Russia was corrupt, but were stunned at the extent of the robbery. Long-Term Capital Management (LTCM) lost billions of dollars betting that this would *not* happen, and had to be rescued by a capital infusion (demanded by the Fed from other market makers) to prevent a domino effect in the global capital market. LTCM failed to appreciate sufficiently that traders would not behave rationally in a panic situation, which is exactly what developed in September 1998. The story is told beautifully in Roger Lowenstein's *When Genius Failed, The Rise and Fall of Long-Term Capital Management* (Random House, 2000). You also learn quite a lot about bond markets and the mentality of traders in this book, and if you want to consider bonds, foreign or domestic, the book is a better investment than a textbook. Equally compelling, if a bit less colorful, is Nicholas Dunbar's *Inventing Money* (John Wiley & Sons, 2000), which is practically a primer—and a readable one—on swaps and other complex bond-based transactions. Both books also explore the downside of leverage in detail, which is a valuable lesson.

The Mexico and Russia stories are extreme cases. Most recently, we had a less extreme situation that offered a substantial profit opportunity—if you correctly interpreted the intent of the IMF and the World Bank to prevent another emerging markets crisis. This opportunity, in Argentina, came in the form of a political issue arising from a faltering economy and the inability of the government to devalue the currency and export its way out of recession. In 1991, the peso had been pegged one-to-one to the U.S. dollar and was backed by U.S. dollar reserves. The use of the "currency board method," as this pegging is named, was experimental. It is used by a few countries—notably Hong Kong—and although it has the virtue of preventing runaway inflation, since the government cannot print local currency and expand the economy without having the reserves, it also has the drawback of holding the currency-board country hostage to the monetary policy of another sovereign—in this case, the United States.

As Argentina's economic troubles grew (and were reflected in political events), the bond market swiftly began to doubt its ability to hang on to the currency board and thus to keep the peso pegged. A peso devaluation would put into doubt the ability to repay U.S. dollar-denominated government bonds. After all, Argentina has a long history of default. After February 2001, when the 10-year Argentine government bond was priced at 93.59 (yield of 6.41 percent), the price fell to a low of 75.31 (yield of 24.69 percent) on April 23, 2001. (See Figure 3.2.) Anyone reading the newspaper carefully, however, could have guessed that the major world leaders and the IMF would almost certainly come to Argentina's rescue. Its troubles were not the fault of bad policies, corruption, or other ignoble acts; besides, when one Latin American country fails, others historically have had a tendency to follow. By lending the country more money and allowing a restructuring of the debt profile (swapping fixed-rate debt for now-cheaper floating-rate debt, and swapping short-term debt for longer-term debt, for example), the probability of default would be lessened. Anyone perceiving this perspective could have made almost 20 cents on the dollar by buying Argentine bonds at the low point and selling them about one month later. Remember, these trades are opportunistic. Later in the summer of 2001, Argentine bonds fell again.

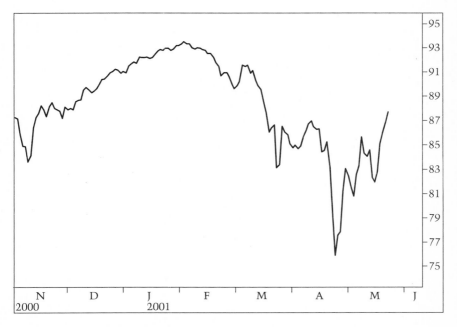

**Figure 3.2**    Argentina 10-year government bond price.

## 2. Underappreciated Country

We may say that Argentina was an underappreciated country, or that the price of its bonds was not commensurate with realistic expectations. We had the same situation in Turkey as of late spring 2001. The IMF came to the rescue, and the global emerging markets' fixed-income departments of major banks and brokers now recommend Turkish bonds. They also recommend Pakistani bonds, for the same reason, although it would be easy to argue that Turkey is a far better bet, given its proximity to Europe and its deep desire to join the European Monetary Union someday. Pakistan's economic and financial history is a saga of one disaster after another, unrelieved by the success stories that Turkey can boast.

How can you find these situations? One place to start is www.debttraders.com, where up-to-date prices and analytical reports are available on deep discount bonds issued by corporates as well as sovereigns and sovereign agencies. One recommendation, for example, is the bonds of the port authority of specific cities in the People's Republic of China. We know that China is very sensitive to its need for foreign capital for development purposes, and for perception, by foreigners, of its willingness and ability to pay. This may be worth researching. Table 3.5 illustrates the top gainers and losers among the bonds.

**Table 3.5.**   Deep Discount Emerging Market Bonds: Top Gainers and Losers, Seven Days to 05/31/01

|  | Price | Change | Percentage Change |
|---|---|---|---|
| **Top Gainers** | | | |
| Regal Cinema Inc. 9.500% 06/08 | 14.000 | 3.00 | 27.273% |
| Int'l Container Terminals 1.750% 03/04 | 123.250 | 21.50 | 21.130 |
| Tianjin International Trust 2.375% 12/01 | 62.500 | 10.50 | 20.192 |
| **Top Losers** | | | |
| ZhuHai Highway Co. 9.125% 07/06 | 27.500 | 27.00 | 49.541 |
| Teligent 11.5% 12/07 | 2.000 | 1.00 | 33.333 |
| Tiwi Kimia Int'l Finance 13.250% 08/01 | 17.000 | 4.00 | 19.048 |

*Source:* www.debttraders.com.

You can find a lot of free information on emerging markets in the *Financial Times* and *The Economist* special country reports. To stay up-to-date, you have to subscribe to newsletters by specialists who follow conditions daily and will usually see big changes in the works long before they get to the mainstream press. The place to start is www.bradynet.com, where you can read a great deal for free and get access, on a trial basis, to various newsletters and background research, including www.ideaglobal.com. At bradynet.com, you can chart issues with data updated daily, run an updated portfolio tracker, speak with other people in the industry, and find links to the majority of research and service providers in the industry. An excellent newsletter is *The Emerging Markets Monitor*, a weekly published by Business Monitor (www.emerging-markets-online.com and www.businessmonitor.com).

Worthwhile for tracking is a new exotic-markets index prepared by Wesbuin Capital in Old Town, Alexandria, Virginia. It tracks the prices of deep discount and distressed assets in each region and compiles a composite global emerging-markets index. You can get a free two-week trial at bradynet.com. Henry Avis-Vieira, president of Wesbruin Capital, believes that timing an emerging market cycle can be done—but it takes a tremendous leap of faith. You need to identify a country at the earliest stages of the development cycle, when the country is still experiencing economic stagnation, capital flight by the country's elite, and (usually) political instability. If the country has some promise, such as natural resources that will eventually attract international capital, it pays to be early. An example is Viet Nam, which in 1991 had defaulted debt priced at 10 percent of face value. As the communist regime loosened up the paralyzed economy with free market reforms during the 1990s, this debt rose in price to 90 percent of face value by 1996. It then proceeded to fall in 1997. The crisis in the rest of Asia contaminated the entire region, and another stage of development began, consisting chiefly of dealing with inflexible state institutions that could not respond rapidly to market conditions.

Avis-Vieira says: "A common investor mistake is delaying entry until the economy expands to an intermediate plane and then holding on beyond the cycle's zenith, where price deterioration tendencies are strongest." In other words, you may profit by investing in a situation that *never* reaches a reasonable comfort level in terms of sovereign and country risk. In 2001, after Viet Nam opened a stock market, the government still hadn't quite got the principle of free markets, and was still imposing daily price caps and other rules. You will never want to "hold forever" in an emerging market that remains weighed down with unworkable socialist beliefs or some other serious drawback. But you can buy low and sell high if you can identify the cycle stages and don't get greedy and hold too long. This is an ideal example of blending fundamental analysis—where the country is located in the development cycle—and technical analysis—following the price action on a chart.

## 3. Bond Futures

Some of the top users of financial futures are financial institutions that are engaged in asset-liability management. A bank takes in short-term deposits but makes longer-term loans, and if the deposits are at a floating rate while the loans are at a fixed rate, in a rising rate environment the bank will quickly go broke unless it has hedged the exposure. You can imagine many other instances beyond the basic balance-sheet mismatch, such as dealing with a surplus of cash coming in at some time in the future (such as bunched insurance premium payments, or year-end bond fund investments) when interest rates are forecasted to fall. The ability to lock in high long-term rates today is a valuable tool. As a consequence of increasingly sophisticated asset-liability management worldwide among financial institutions of all stripes, the interest rate futures market is among the most liquid of all markets. Corporations, especially those that issue a range of debt paper, are also increasingly using financial futures for the same purposes.

Bond futures prices are determined chiefly by current interest rates, the shape of the yield curve, and expectations of changes in interest rate policy by the central bank of the country involved. Many complex arbitrage and spread trading strategies are possible—including across maturities over two countries—but they are beyond our scope here. If you have an affinity for forecasting interest rate policy, though, outright bond futures are relatively straightforward. For example, the saga of how the European Central Bank (ECB) struggled with the policy choice of growth versus inflation in 2001 has been a fascinating study in institutional behavior. On one side, the ECB is determined to gain the same anti-inflation credentials as its best predecessor central bank, the German Bundesbank. This meant no cuts in interest rates as long as inflation remains over the maximum allowable level of 2.5 percent. But because of energy price increases and food price increases (due partly to hoof-and-mouth disease), inflation in the eurozone was rising, not falling. In addition, the falling euro automatically created some price inflation because of the rise, in euro terms, in the cost of imported goods, both U.S.- and yen-denominated. At the same time, the slowdown in economic activity was beginning to be obvious. Growth estimates were being slashed left and right for the year 2001—from 2.5 to 3 percent to under 2 percent, according to some experts. There was a lot of pressure on the ECB to cut rates and to use the excuse that energy price rises were only temporary. If you (correctly) guessed that the ECB would cave in to pressure, as it did with a rate cut in May, you could have traded the insight in any number of European interest-rate futures contracts.

Figure 3.3 is a chart of the June 2001 German bond futures contract traded on the London International Financial Futures and Options Exchange (LIFFE; www.liffe.com). At the LIFFE Web site, you can get a free 30-page brochure that describes the bond futures contracts, the principle of bond futures pricing, bond issuance by country and currency, and other details. This particular contract has a nominal face value of €100,000 with a coupon of 6 percent. Each "tick" is €10. If by some miracle of perfect timing, you had sold the contract at the very highest high of 110.26 on March 22 and bought it back at the very low of 105.73, your gain would have been 453 points, or €4,530. Notice that you are trading in a euro-denominated instrument, meaning your initial margin, variation margin, and gain and loss are all calculated in euros (as explained more in Chapter 4, "Futures"). Thinking about this may give you a headache. Your U.S. broker will translate the euro margin amounts into the equivalent dollar amounts,

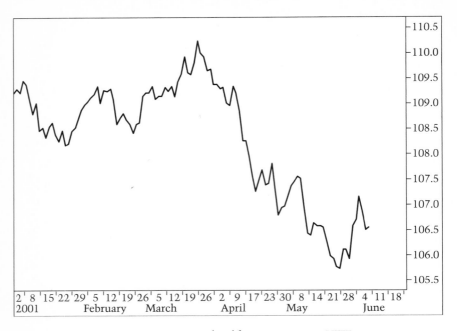

**Figure 3.3**  German bond futures contract on LIFFE.

so you do not have to keep cash margin in euros in reality, but your statement will reflect all entries denominated in euros.

Trading a foreign futures contract also gives you a foreign exchange position. Here you are short a contract denominated in euros. What if the euro were to rise against the U.S. dollar—even if the bond futures contract is going your way? You may choose to hedge the exposure or not. In this instance, the euro's downtrend was fairly well in place, and a hedge would have been a mistake. You can't know this going into the transaction without studying it, though. To trade a foreign bond or any other asset, you get a double exposure by definition, and thus, double the analytical work.

To check out what interest rate contracts are easily available through U.S. brokers to U.S. residents, go to www.ino.com and scroll through the lists of contracts, which are organized by exchange. You will find interest rate contracts of one sort or another on each of them.

## Summary and Conclusion

Bond markets around the world are large, complex, and sophisticated. Some derivative transactions are so complicated you need a flow chart to keep track of what's going on—for example, a U.S.-dollar–U.K.-pound floating-to-fixed interest rate swap. Don't be intimidated by fancy lingo and advanced math. A bond is essentially a loan from the investor to the borrower, which may be a sovereign. Repayment is taken very seriously because the ratings agencies are watching and reputations are at stake. Domestic U.S. bonds are often added to a portfolio of stocks for diversification, but nothing says that you can't add the government or government-agency bond of another country, as long as you understand the default risk. In fact, with good timing and understanding of a special situation, you can hold junk or exotic emerging-market bonds for short periods at high profitability. If you discover that you have a knack for macroeconomic analysis and interest rate forecasting, bond and other money market futures trading is another way to make high returns.

*Chapter 4*

# FUTURES

*An investor who proposes to ignore near-term market fluctuations needs greater resources for safety and must not operate on so large a scale if at all with borrowed money.*

John Maynard Keynes

"Why should I read a chapter on futures? I want to trade equities." This is probably the question you are asking yourself.

The six answers given here may surprise you. They are compelling and reasonable.

## 1. Act on Blinding Insights

Futures open up a universe of opportunity that lets you test your ideas about how the world works, and they do it in a way that equities cannot. How many times have you felt that you understand macroeconomic trends and cycles, and you know exactly what is going to happen next—but you don't know how to put your insights to use? Chances are there is a futures contract designed specifically for your situation, in currencies, interest rates, stock indices, or even a physical commodity. As described in Chapter 1, George Soros made a billion dollars on such an insight; he correctly evaluated the British economy and what policy the British government was (wrongly) going to follow. At the same time, Soros took positions in equities that he thought would benefit from the devaluation of the pound, which he expected. Equities and futures can complement or offset one another, once a trading idea has been formed.

## 2. Develop Utter Clarity of Purpose

The second great benefit of futures trading is that it imposes a need for complete clarity in your thinking. In the equity market, an old joke has it that an "investor" is a trader who forgot to get out of his position. All too often, that's true. What is really going on when this happens? Trading discipline has given way to wishful thinking: "it will come back." One of the chief virtues of the futures market, compared to the equity market, is that contracts mature. If you refuse to face a loss on an expiring futures contract, you have to roll it over to the next maturity date. This, by definition, involves closing the old maturing contract and opening a new position in the now-current contract. If you fail to close the maturing contract, your broker will ask you where to deliver the soybeans or Swiss francs, and how you plan to pay for them. So you close the old contract and you book the cash loss—a valuable reality check on whether you really want to reinstate the same position in the new contract.

Trading futures forces you to be pragmatic and realistic about trading. Nobody likes to admit he was wrong in having taken a position, especially after actively engaging in denial while losses mounted. The more you rehearse your justifications for holding a losing position, the harder it is to face the fact of loss. This is termed "Telling the market what to do." The security "should" be rising, and it's not because the rest of the market doesn't have your wisdom and analytical insight. The market is wrong and you are right. A variation on this theme is a position that went into the money (you had a big paper gain) and is now losing the gain or has lost all the gain. You had a moment of euphoria and self-validation that you were right, and the market rewarded you with a gain. Now the market is taking it away, and that's not fair. You were right when you put on the position, and you are still right.

Maybe so. But trading in futures is a constant reality check. You may be able to tell yourself that losses in equities are only temporary, because, after all, stocks have intrinsic value and markets merely overshoot in the never-ending quest for true and accurate value. This is a snare and a delusion. There is no market rule that dictates prices will be "fair," or will be more fair at some time in the future. Prices can be unfair—unreasonable and unrealistic—for long periods of time. Moreover, they can go from too high to too low without pausing at what you consider to be a fair level and thus your opportunity to enter or exit. The market is always right. The purpose of trading and investing is to make money, not to be a better factor analyst than everyone else, and not to be right about what the fair price should be. Accordingly, the professional and the sophisticated trader accept losses when the market is going against their position. Only amateurs whine that the price is wrong because of this factor or that factor. Amateurs cling to a losing position in the hope that "It will come back" due to some estimated intrinsic value that they hope and believe will be recognized someday. In futures, there is no "someday"; there is only the immediate present and whether a loss has breached a money management rule that was established in advance.

## 3. Get a Bigger Stake

Trading futures provides the opportunity to use leverage. Leverage is essentially borrowing money from the broker in order to be able to trade a higher amount of the security. In equities, the maximum leverage allowed is 2 : 1. You can borrow $2 for every $1 you have on deposit with the broker. In futures, leverage can be hundreds of times (at the maximum). In currencies today, for example, you need to deposit $1,755 to trade a Swiss franc contract worth SF 125,000 (translated at 58 cents per Swiss franc = $72,500). That's leverage of 41 times the capital stake.

Leverage magnifies both gains and losses, and thus is riskier than trading equities. Or is it? Because you *must* control losses in futures, or risk bankruptcy, your trading needs to become more disciplined and rule-based. You don't have to take every trade; you can act on only the trades that seem to have high probability. By being out of the market some of the time, you actually carry less risk. You have no risk when you are out of the market. Proponents of the "buy-and-hold" school of equity investing fail to note that inconvenient but indisputable fact.

# 4. Diversification Reduces Risk

Trading futures provides diversification. Many studies show that allocating some portion of your total capital to securities that are uncorrelated with U.S. stocks reduces risk and enhances return. At the Chicago Board of Trade Web site (www.cbot.com), you can read a brochure titled "Managed Futures: Portfolio Diversification Opportunities." It describes the managed futures industry and demonstrates some of the benefits of adding futures to a portfolio. For one thing, over the period of 1988 to 1998, the correlation of managed futures with U.S. bonds was a mere 0.32 (extremely weak), and with U.S. stocks it was 0.03 (practically nonexistent). To come up with these and other measures of risk, "managed futures" companies' performance results are used against standard stock and bond indices. Managed futures companies come in all flavors, including those that specialize in currencies, global macro, agricultural commodities, stock indices (both foreign and domestic), bonds, and so on. Therefore, each diversification exercise varies a bit—depending on which managed futures segment is being used—but in all cases in the academic journal literature and in books on managed futures, managed futures add to total return or reduce total risk, or both.

One of the managed futures studies, by Fernando Diz, an assistant professor of finance at Syracuse University, appeared in the December 2000 issue of *Futures* magazine (www.futuresmag.com). He showed that, over the 15 years between January 1985 and August 1999, a conventionally allocated portfolio (70 percent equities, 25 percent bonds, 3 percent commodities, and 2 percent cash) could have been bettered by a reallocation to only 30 percent in the S&P 500 and 70 percent in three specific managed futures indices—with substantially lower volatility of returns—even in that bull equity market. Other measures of risk show it to be superior allocation, such as the maximum loss in any month, the average loss over any losing period, the length of time needed to recover from a loss, and both the standard deviation of monthly returns and the Sharpe ratio (the annualized rate of return minus the risk-free rate, divided by the annualized standard deviation).

## 5. Hedge Your Equity Holdings

Stock index futures allow you to hedge your equity holdings today. Let's say you own a mutual fund that tracks the S&P 500. If and when the S&P takes a nosedive, you can protect your savings by going short the S&P futures contract. Gains on the short position offset losses on the mutual fund; however, it's a fine line between hedging and speculation. To the extent that the futures contract is for stock positions bigger than your own, the extra is speculation. It's only a hop, skip, and jump to trading the index futures as a security in its own right. It is sometimes said that trading equity index futures is the poor man's way of getting full participation in the stock market without having the fortune that would be needed to own each of the stocks in an index. With strict trading and money management rules, it can be the intelligent man's way to participate in the market. Without the rules, it's just the poorer man's way.

The day is coming when individual futures contracts will be available for each stock traded on the equity exchanges. This is a controversial development long in the works—and long held up in the United States because of opposition from the equities industry. In a nutshell, equity brokers fear that the existence of futures contracts on the same securities will siphon off their business. Both the New York Stock Exchange and the National Association of Securities Dealers (which runs Nasdaq) complained to Congress as the new law was being formulated. Objections were voiced in terms of protecting the individuals from themselves; the assumption is that average traders are not accustomed to working with high leverage, and the poor fools will bankrupt themselves. The other complaint is a loss of confidence, among the general public, in stock buying, once restraints against short selling are essentially gutted. "It is an important factor in market confidence to assure investors that short sellers cannot take the market down an unlimited amount," said NASD President Richard Ketchum in a letter to the SEC. This is a reference to restraints on short selling, such as the uptick rule, which allows a short sale order to be processed only after a price drop has been followed by at least one trade at a higher price.

Single-stock futures (and options on them) have the potential to replace short selling and thus to make the overall market far more volatile. The fear that a panic will develop in single issues is probably not misplaced, but, at the same time, the big institutions (mutual funds and pension funds) determine market direction, and most big institutions are prohibited from short selling altogether or are allowed only a small amount. That means true short selling will be limited to the same group that does it today—individuals, bear funds, and hedge funds.

## 6. Hedge the Currency Risk of Your Foreign Equity Holdings

You will soon be able to buy and sell foreign stocks that trade only on their own exchanges. Why would you want to do that when, in the United States alone, we have over 7,500 stocks to choose from? The main reason is *opportunity*. Stock market participation in the United States is both broad and deep. The huge success of "How to Trade . . ." books and of CNBC prove that stock market investing is more than a fad or a hobby. It has become part of the fabric of society. U.S. stocks are fully picked over. Experts advise us to find stocks "on sale," but, as a practical matter, everyone else is also looking for undervalued situations. The competition is extreme in the United States. This is not the case in most foreign countries, where stock market participation among the public is limited, and even the professionals may be asleep at the switch, especially when it comes to upstart new companies in high-tech fields that they do not understand and where they do not have much of a track record. Savvy U.S. investors who are willing to do hard research may be able to find undervalued gems in foreign countries, and get in on the ground floor.

Unfortunately, when you buy a foreign stock, you automatically take on a second risk: the currency. Unless you plan to retire to that foreign country, you always want to maximize your home currency returns (meaning U.S. dollars) when you invest. There's no point in having a wonderful foreign stock that rises 40 percent if, at the same time, the currency falls 40 percent. You need to learn how to hedge currency exposure, and the safest—as well as the most efficient—way to do that is in currency futures.

Those are the six reasons why you should learn about futures, even if your primary focus is individual U.S. equities.

## What Futures Are and What They Are Not

A futures contract is a written contractual agreement between two parties that, on some date in the future, one party will deliver goods and the other party will pay for them. It's possible that futures contracts were devised in prehistory, judging from some of the inscriptions on ancient pottery and stones. This is not really surprising because a futures contract is a direct result, and a useful tool, of trade between geographic regions. In more modern times, a rice futures contract was invented around 1710 in Japan, and eventually gave rise to a form of technical analysis named "candlestick charting," which is still used in Japan (and elsewhere). The Chicago Mercantile Exchange (CME), the parent of the International Monetary Market, evolved from a produce exchange developed in 1874 to trade butter, eggs, poultry, and other perishables. Grains are traded at the Chicago Board of Trade.

A futures contract allows a farmer to know the price he will get in September for the crop he is putting in the ground in May. It also allows a bakery to know how much flour will cost. Futures contracts are tools of purchasing and inventory management. If a storm wipes out most grain producers, prices will rise but the bakery has effectively purchased insurance. The farmer with a good crop, however, does not benefit from other farmers' misfortune (unless he gets out of his contract to sell grain at what is now too low a price). But in the event that every farmer has a fabulous crop that year, our farmer is protected against the resulting fall in prices caused by a rise in supply.

A futures contract is a financial instrument, whatever the underlying product. This is hard for people to grasp. They consider that the futures contract is a "derivative" of the "real thing," whatever the real thing happens to be—soybeans or Swiss francs. But the futures contract itself is just as real as the underlying commodity and remains inexorably linked to it. When the contract matures, the price of the futures contract is always equal to the spot price of the commodity, no matter how much it may have diverged from it over its life. Supply and demand of a financial instrument can seem to become quite divorced from the supply and demand of the underlying product, but that is an illusion. It is a function of speculators' having joined the market. Speculators have participated in futures markets from the very beginning and are welcomed as providers of additional liquidity. Speculators are seen as smoothing the volatility that invariably accompanies a market with few participants, although, on occasion, they are blamed for causing exaggerated price fluctuations.

Futures are often mistaken as being purely speculative. This is not so. The relationship between the spot price of any commodity and its price for future delivery is actually quite stable and, generally, only a function of the time value of money. The price of a commodity futures contract may seem sometimes to vary unreasonably from the price of the underlying components, but its original purpose of facilitating trade and hedging the real supply and demand of real goods remains the core of futures trading. To verify this, you only have to look at the "Commitment of Traders Reports" published by the exchanges. These reports are broken out into two categories: (1) "hedgers" and "speculators" or (2) "commercials" and "noncommercials," depending on the commodity (www.cftc.gov/cftccotreports.htm). You will often see that hedgers are predominantly long while "specs" are taking the other side (short), or vice versa.

This is useful information. We may consider that commercials/hedgers will be closing out their position under two conditions: near the maturity date of the contract, whereupon they will put on the same position in the new contract, or when the price of the underlying is moving in their direction and the hedge is no longer needed. By watching what percentage of total commercial positions is either long or short and how that changes, we can figure out what direction they believe the price is moving. Similarly, if all the speculators are in the same position, either long or short, and the absolute number of those positions is at or near record highs, we can deduce that any adverse price movement will result in covering (i.e., closing out the positions by selling if long or buying if short). Short-covering panics can often be seen in the currency market, for example, if the price moves near support or resistance, which suggests a trend correction. Reading the "Commitment of Traders Report" is very difficult, even the "short form." Fortunately, Trading Systems Analysis Group (www.tsagroup.com) offers the data in an understandable format (and an affordable price). You can download the data into any number of different software formats and see, graphically, commercial and spec positions differentiated by color. You can also see the percentage of each group that is either long or short, reflecting the intensity of market sentiment. The "Commitment of Traders Report," now published weekly, is a relatively new tool that is gaining rapid acceptance.

## Financial Futures

For a commodity to qualify for futures trading, it must be divisible into homogeneous units (each of which has more or less the same quality). It has to be standardizable, gradable, and of limited perishability. Supply and demand have to come from many parties (no monopolies or cartels) and be subject to uncertainty about future supply and demand. Nothing is more standardized, gradable, widely dispersed, and uncertain than money, credit, and stocks, and so developed futures contracts in interest rates, foreign exchange, and stock indices.

The ability to hedge risk in interest rates is useful to financial institutions such as banks, mortgage lenders, and insurance companies. The ability to hedge foreign exchange risk is useful to small importers who have to pay for goods (to be delivered in the future) in the currency of their supplier. The ability to hedge stock market risk is useful to investment managers, mutual funds, and individuals. The fact that, in each of these markets, there are speculators who have no underlying positions to be hedged does not detract from the markets' usefulness to those who do. It is true that the speculative component of futures trading has taken on a life of its own, but there is no moral judgment that is crying out to be made.

Many observers of the equity culture feel that it is a bigger gamble to plunk down your life savings on stocks willy-nilly, with no risk management plan, than it is to speculate in futures with a highly disciplined risk management plan—and these observers have logic on their side.

# Mechanics

Education and training in futures trading are offered by brokers, the National Futures Association, the exchanges on which futures contracts are traded, and the Commodity Futures Trading Commission, the U.S. Government's regulatory authority for futures. Some specialized lingo and a few conventions must be mastered, but futures trading is only a little more complicated than trading stocks outright, and the principles can easily be absorbed.

The first thing you have to keep in mind is that the instrument will mature and expire at some date in the future, unlike a stock certificate (which does not expire). Each commodity has contracts that are the most traded and thus the most liquid. In currencies and most stock indices, for example, the contracts expire in March, June, September, and December. A broker can advise you which ones are the most traded in the security you choose. The point is that futures trading is *always* a short-term undertaking.

The next thing to keep in mind is that you don't have to pay for the contract in full. You have to pay a minimum specified by the exchange. The amount may be raised by your broker, but it will still be a very small portion of the total value of the contract. This is the famous *leverage* that has gotten so many people in trouble. The exchanges change the minimum amount (the "initial margin") from time to time, depending on the volatility of the security. The initial margin to trade the Japanese yen is always much higher than the initial margin to trade the Canadian dollar, for example, because the Japanese yen is more volatile. That brings us to *variation margin*. This is the extra money you need to have in your brokerage account, beyond the initial margin, to cover the day-to-day change in the value of the contract. If you buy a Japanese yen contract and the yen falls that day, you need to make up the cash difference so as to maintain the same ratio of cash to borrowed money. And make no mistake—your broker is lending you the balance of the value of the contract not covered by your initial and maintenance margin money. This is a credit relationship, just like your relationship with the bank that gave you the mortgage on your house, or issued your credit card. If you fail to come up with the needed variation margin every day, the broker is allowed—in fact, is duty-bound to the brokerage house and the exchange—to close out all your positions and to come after you for any remaining losses. Each broker is responsible for evaluating the creditworthiness of a client. If the client fails, the broker must make whole the other party. In the background, the exchanges guarantee every trade.

There is always another party. For every purchaser of a contract, there is a seller. Technically, this is true in the stock market, too, but it is not as obvious as in the futures market. In stocks, some portion is held by long-term investors such as insiders, mutual funds, and pension funds. In the "Commitment of Traders Reports" mentioned on page 123, you can see that long positions exactly equal short positions at all times. It can be quite interesting and instructive to see how the net long or short positions of hedgers and speculators change over time. For example, in January 2001, speculators were net long the euro futures contract against the dollar by a very large amount—over 25,000 contracts. Commentators noted, at the time, that this exceptionally large number could potentially cause a crash in the euro if market sentiment soured against the euro. This is exactly what happened, although, by May, speculators were still net long the euro (by about 6,000 contracts).

The final thing to keep in mind is the "tick"—the dollar value of every point price move in the futures contract. The value of a tick is determined by multiplying the minimum tick size by the contract multiplier. In the case of the S&P 500, the minimum tick size is 0.10 index points, so the minimum tick is $250 \times 0.10$, or $25.00 per contract. The Nasdaq 100's multiplier is $100 with a minimum tick size of 0.05, so the minimum tick is $100 \times 0.05$, or $5.00 per contract. The Swiss franc tick is $12.50. If the Swiss franc falls 100 points, from $0.5850 to $0.5750, those 100 points are worth $1,250.00, or 100 times $12.50. If the average daily move in the contract is 300 points, you need to keep an extra $3,750 in your account in the event your trade goes against you, or risk having the broker close your position if he can't reach you to top up your account with more cash. If you are in the happy position of having made the 300 points that day, your daily brokerage statement will reflect that the current value of your account is $3,750 richer. You may choose to use that money to buy another Swiss franc contract, assuming you have another $3,750 in the account to cover the *next* day's maximum price excursion. This is named pyramiding.

Many futures traders concentrate on the relationship of the cash they have in their account relative to the average daily tick range, and this is indeed the practical consideration. Newcomers might be a little startled by the size of the contracts, though. Stock index contracts, for example, are valued at the "contract multiplier": the tick value × the index level. For example, if the S&P 500 futures price is 970, the value of the contract is $242,500 ($250 × 970.00). If the Nasdaq 100 futures price is 1100, the value of the contract is $110,000 ($100 × 1100.00). The Swiss franc contract is $71,815 ($12.50 × 5754).

At the Web site of each exchange, you can get information on contract maturity dates, minimum and maintenance margin, and the value of the tick at the "contract specification" section. The CME Web site is particularly well done and offers excellent materials, including a 105-page essay on stock indices that is useful in its own right, as well as live, real-time simulated trading; free trading kits; strategy papers; charts and data, and a wealth of other information.

## Sample Futures Trades

Let's say that you had invested $50,000 in Nasdaq stocks at the beginning of 1990, when the Nasdaq index was 459. It is now March of 2000, and you have a tenfold gain. The Nasdaq stands at 5049 on March 10, 2000, and your $50,000 has grown to $500,000. By some miracle of timing, you decide to hedge your investment in the Nasdaq at exactly the high. You do this by selling one Nasdaq contract on the futures market. Its value is $100 × 4605, or

$460,500. On April 24, 2000, the Nasdaq futures contract is at 3168. By another miracle of perfect timing, you cover your short sale at this point. You have made 1437 points × $100 per point, or $143,700. This offsets the loss you took by continuing to hold your Nasdaq stocks. If you paid your broker $50 per "round turn" (both the sale and the purchase), you keep nearly all of the gain. If you had given the broker initial and maintenance margin in the form of a T-bill, you would have earned interest on it, as well. As of May 2001, the initial margin required to trade the Nasdaq 100 futures contract was $33,750, and the maintenance margin was $27,000. To be on the safe side, you would have had to buy T-bills worth a little more than $60,750. For a lesser portfolio of Nasdaq stocks, you could have hedged using the e-mini Nasdaq contract, for which the initial margin today is $6,750 and the maintenance margin is $5,400.

The reason Figure 4.1 looks a little strange around the March 10 period (the time when you are selling the Nasdaq futures

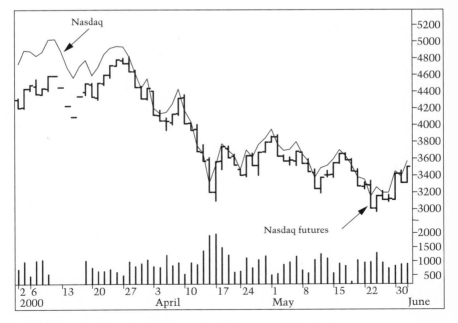

**Figure 4.1**   Nasdaq futures versus Nasdaq.

contract) is that this is a data series from Reuters that "rolls over" the March contract to the June contract to create a "continuous contract" in order to get a price series that is usable for technical analysis and other historical comparison purposes. Therefore, the principle is sound but the exact prices are not accurate because they reflect the adjustment.

Notice that this hedge, while achieving your objective of protecting your portfolio, was not without its scary moments. After making a spike low on April 17 at 3,578, for example, the futures price rose to 3,638, or 60 points, by May 2. Each point is worth $100 to you, so 60 points is $6,000 less value in your contract on a mark-to-market basis—in two weeks. You already had accumulated gains from 4,605 to 3,578, or 1,027 points, which is $102,700. Perhaps $6,000 doesn't seem like much in that context, but you can easily imagine that if you were carrying the short Nasdaq position as a speculation instead of a hedge, you would be worried.

# Day-Trading

Some people have an affinity for day-trading. They are able to see patterns in 10-minute bars that are the equivalent of patterns in daily bars, reflecting the fractal nature of markets. Usually, concentrating on a few patterns that they know well, in a security they follow every day, they are able to place high probability trades that last only a few hours. Therefore, over 99 percent of the time, they are out of the market and taking no risk at all. One trader we know trades only the Swiss franc and only when he sees the particular pattern shown in Figure 4.2. The pattern consists of a breakout from the linear regression channel formed over at least ten 10-minute bars, combined with a stochastic oscillator *going in the opposite direction.* He has found that this is a reliable reversal signal. The Swiss franc may trade in a daily range of 80 to 120 points, but he aims to make 20 to 30 points (or $250 to $375) per trade. If he can do this once a week, that's $1,000 to $1,500 per month per contract. If he trades 10 contracts each time, that's $10,000 to $15,000 per month. He always uses a stop placed 20 points below his entry when buying or 20 points above when selling, and only about one trade in 10 is a loser. He executes only four trades in an average month, so he averages one

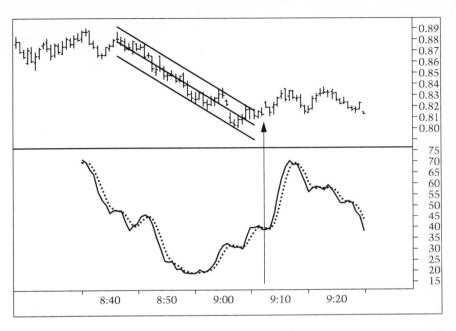

**Figure 4.2**   One day-trading technique.

loss per quarter. Not every day trader is as patient and disciplined as this man, but his trading is a far cry from the high-risk, wild-eyed gambling usually depicted.

Of course, this pattern may not appear every week. It can be boring to sit around watching the quote screen waiting for it to appear. Also, a stop placed only 20 points away risks getting hit on random moves when the holding period (a few hours) has an average range of 60 points. Still, he is trading a pattern with a high reward-to-risk ratio. Many such patterns can be found.

## Single Stock Futures

Single stock futures were authorized in the Commodity Futures Modernization Act of 2000, but it may be a while before the public can actually trade them. The Act allows for both equity and futures brokerages, and their brokers, to deal in single stock futures contracts, so, in theory, there will be no need for an additional license designation, but that does not make the equity broker competent to trade futures contracts. On the other side, Futures Commission Merchants (FCMs) are also at a disadvantage, because the new contracts are being called "securities" and therefore are traded differently from futures contracts. Futures contracts are one of a kind and are traded on one exchange, whereas securities can be traded on multiple exchanges. Therefore, the infrastructure will have to be put in place for the best price designation on each order. FCMs do not have that technology right now.

A straw poll of two very large brokerage houses reveals that no plans have been made to train equity brokers in the commodity futures business or to develop a back-office system for futures, which obviously can be a very expensive undertaking. Single stock futures pose a real problem for the equity brokerage industry because the brokers are not familiar with futures trading practices and conventions, and are seldom licensed by the National Futures Association ("Series 3") as well as the National Association of Securities Dealers ("Series 7"). Special licenses for single stock futures may be devised, but the brokerage houses would still have to incur expenses in training and oversight. Another issue is the expense of new back-office systems. The extent of what will be needed depends somewhat on whether settlement will always be in cash, or clients will be allowed to deliver the goods (i.e., actual stock).

As for delivery, in futures markets, "commercials" and hedgers can and do deliver the physical commodities they trade; speculators settle in cash before delivery. Some individual traders of single stock futures will be hedgers and some will be speculators. How will the brokerage houses calculate credit risk and margin when the client does own the stock versus when he does not? What happens when the client owns the stock, with Merrill Lynch as custodian, but trades single stock futures at Refco, a futures commission merchant (commodities trading house)? The tangle of credit and hypothecation could become mind-boggling. It's a theoretical risk-management issue as well as an accounting issue. In London, where single stock futures already trade, cash settlement has been decided as the rule, and this will probably occur in the United States, too. The three big futures exchanges—the Chicago Mercantile Exchange (CME), Chicago Board of Trade (CBOT), and Chicago

Board Options Exchange (CBOE)—have a task force in place to deal with questions like this. Meanwhile, another straw poll of commodity futures brokers shows that they are champing at the bit and expect to dominate the industry. (Their back offices are already set up.) Stay tuned.

Trading in single stock futures should begin by the end of 2001, although there is much left to be decided by the Commodity Futures Trading Commission (CFTC) and the Securities and Exchange Commission (SEC) regarding margin requirements and other regulatory matters. Single stock futures are now being traded (since January 2001) on the London International Financial Futures and Options Exchange (LIFFE) under the name "Universal Stock Futures" (USFs). The www.liffe.com Web site has educational materials under the label. It must be admitted that the growth of volume is slow (about 200 contracts per day on each of the 30 listings available so far). About 10 new contracts are offered each month; a total of about 100 per month is expected in the end. The USFs currently traded on Liffe are based on some of the biggest stocks in Britain, continental Europe, and the United States, including Nasdaq-listed stocks (such as Microsoft and Cisco Systems). LIFFE signed a deal with Nasdaq, in the spring of 2001, to bring single stock futures traded on the LIFFE to U.S. investors—during U.S. trading hours and using LIFFE's electronic trading platform. This may keep a fire lit under domestic plans.

Perry Dahm, whose company offers free training seminars on single stock futures (www.futuresonstockscentral.com), says single stock futures have the potential to bring the individual onto the same playing field as institutions and funds. A chief benefit will be the ability to hedge specific stocks held long-term in IRAs and 401(k) plans. For hedging, Dahm agrees with our basic approach of determining the average daily trading range of the underlying stock, and converting the daily average range to a percentage of the current market value of the stock. Since you are long the stock, you go short the futures contract as a hedge. If you have a daily average movement of 12 percent, you would want to place your stop loss order for the futures contract at least 15 percent away from yesterday's closing price. Be sure to adjust the daily average range according to the stock's behavior and according to the new mark-to-market value you hold in the stock.

| Date | Action | Price($) | 100 Shares ($) | ROI (%) | Futures on Stock Contract ($) | | | ROI (%) |
|---|---|---|---|---|---|---|---|---|
| | | | | | Entered | Exited | Profit | |
| Feb-97 | Purchase 100 Shares of Caterpillar | 38.13 | 3,812.50 | | | | | |
| Feb-97 | Held active order for Trailing Futures Contract | | | | | | | |
| Sep-97 | Futures Contract engaged (Sold) | | | | 55.45 | | | |
| Oct-97 | Bought Futures Contract | | | | | 55.45 | — | |
| Oct-97 | Futures Contract engaged (Sold) | | | | 55.45 | | | |
| Dec-97 | Bought Futures Contract | | | | | 48.80 | 665.00 | |
| Dec-97 | Futures Contract engaged (Sold) | | | | 47.70 | | | |
| Jan-98 | Bought Futures Contract | | | | | 47.70 | — | |
| Jan-98 | Held active order for Trailing Futures Contract | | | | | | | |
| Jun-98 | Futures Contract engaged (Sold) | | | | 54.70 | | | |
| Oct-98 | Bought Futures Contract | | | | | 43.00 | 1,170.00 | |
| Oct-98 | Held active order for Trailing Futures Contract | | | | | | | |
| Dec-98 | Futures Contract engaged (Sold) | | | | 47.00 | | | |
| Jan-99 | Bought Futures Contract | | | | | 45.00 | 200.00 | |
| Jan-99 | Held active order for Trailing Futures Contract | | | | | | | |
| Jan-99 | Futures Contract engaged (Sold) | | | | 47.70 | | | |
| Feb-99 | Bought Futures Contract | | | | | 46.30 | 140.00 | |
| Jun-99 | Futures Contract engaged (Sold) | | | | 59.80 | | | |
| Sep-00 | Bought Futures Contract | | | | | 33.00 | 2,680.00 | |
| May-01 | Marked to Market | 53.20 | 5,320.00 | | | | | |
| | | | | | | | 4,855.00 | 127.34% |
| | Gain on underlying position | | 1,507.50 | 39.54 | | | | |
| | Gain on Futures Contracts | | | | | | 4,855.00 | 127.34% |
| | **Total Gain** | | **1,507.50** | | | | | |
| | | | **4,855.00** | | | | | |
| | | | **6,362.50** | | | | | **166.89%** |

**Figure 4.3** Investment in Caterpillar hedged with single stock futures.

132

Dahm provides a case. Let's pretend single stock futures already exist, and let's say you bought Caterpillar in February 1997. You wanted to hold it long term, but you were not willing to take a large hit on it, so you used a Caterpillar Stock Futures contract as a stop loss. You determine that the average daily range is 8 percent. You place your initial order for the futures contract at 10 percent under your purchase price.

Figure 4.3 is the history of your stock ownership and futures hedging. Here is how to start reading it:

- February 1997: Buy 100 shares of Caterpillar at $38.125; cost: $3,812.50. Place an order to short a futures contract if the price falls 10 percent to $34.31.
- September 1997 Update: Stock is at $61.625, short futures order is at $55.45. Stock falls to $55.45 and you are now short one futures contract (for October 1997).
- October 1997: The stock rallies again and you exit the futures contract at the same $55.45 for no gain or loss.

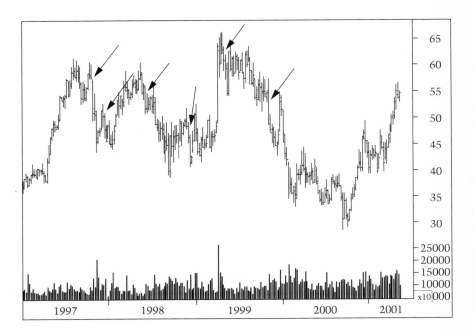

**Figure 4.4**   Caterpillar single stock futures hedge.

If you had only held the stock without hedging, your profit would be the unrealized gain of $1,507.50, or 39.54 percent over the four-year period. By adding the futures hedges, you made an additional cash gain of $4,855.00, and your total return becomes 166.89%. (See Figure 4.4.)

## Summary and Conclusions

Futures offer opportunities for you to use analysis and imagination in ways that stock ownership does not. Futures also allow you to take advantage of greater leverage than is available in stock trading, and, at the same time, give you the ability to hedge stock positions. It is not hard to trade futures; free educational materials abound on the Web sites of the major exchanges and brokerage houses. The single biggest obstacle to trading futures is getting into the correct mindset. Specifically, you are not entering into ownership of an asset with intrinsic value that can be set to one side and forgotten; rather, you are taking positions in an instrument for a specific purpose—either speculative profit or hedging a related holding—and the instrument has a limited life, so you must attend to it conscientiously.

# Chapter 5

# SOME PEOPLE JUST DON'T GET IT

*The test of a first-rate intelligence is the ability to hold two opposed ideas in the mind at the same time, and still retain the ability to function.*

F. Scott Fitzgerald

There's nothing more humbling than to watch a trader who is sitting at a screen and yelling out "Buy" and "Sell," and to learn, at the end of an hour, that he has made a tidy profit without knowing anything about the security beyond its ticker symbol. A natural-born trader can (and will) trade anything. Put a sugar trader on the Swiss franc desk, and, in an hour, he has the rhythm of the market. Some people seem to have a trader's gene.

## The Trader's Gene

When you look a little more closely at these natural-born—or well-trained—traders, they share a few characteristics that at first seem odd and irrelevant. One is: they do not read. You don't find magazines and books in the homes of traders. The newspaper on their desk is opened to the crossword puzzle or maybe the sports page. They don't watch television news. In fact, they may not know about major events like elections and wars unless they are trading a related commodity. Traders will talk with one another endlessly about the news pertinent to the security they are trading, but their knowledge is shallow and they rarely do real research.

Moreover, natural-born traders are aggressive and often rude. They don't suffer beating around the bush, and they may get to the point without much nicety. In the old days, they often used foul language; that has become politically incorrect. Like police officers who view all nonofficers as another class of human beings ("civilians"), they can recognize one another. A trader will accord another trader far more respect than he will concede to any non-trader. In the hierarchy of respect, having the job title of "trader" in an institution is not enough, especially if the "trader" is unlucky enough to have an MBA or, heaven forbid, a PhD. Credentials like these cast a black cloud of doubt over the person's ability to trade—and it is often an accurate prejudice. Street smarts are not the same as book-learned smarts. If a book-learned trader becomes successful, that is, makes money, he will be forgiven for having those degrees, and true acceptance into the traders' club will be signaled when the traders start teasing the MBA about them (or, sometimes, when they stop). Analysts who are now increasingly being attached to trading desks at financial institutions find they have no influence—unless they can correctly name entry and exit points, and never mind how they arrived at them.

Real traders usually have no understanding that the institution they work for has a corporate identity and a purpose aside from their own function. They have little interest in either. Tell a bond trader at Citibank that the credit card division makes the most money of all divisions, and his eyes glaze over instantly. (If you hint that there is going to be an earnings contest between his trading desk and the credit card division, that will perk him up.) In any business meeting of traders and nontraders in a firm, the traders contribute practically nothing except when it comes to their position limits or other conditions specific to their jobs; they simply refuse to think about other business issues and don't get the point of strategic planning, marketing, public relations, or sales.

An uncanny gift for warp-speed arithmetic calculations is another characteristic of professional traders. In currencies, for example, some traders can instantly calculate the reciprocal of the spot price (say, 110 yen to the dollar) to get the futures price (9090, and forget about the decimal point). Most traders can perform complex calculations of probabilities in their heads. (Famous trader Russell Sands was the 1980 Backgammon World Champion.) Sometimes, probability calculations seem to be little more than common sense, but when you ask a trader why he exited a position when the security was still rising, underneath the flippant response ("It was going too far") is a deep knowledge of what has happened in the past and an estimate of exactly at what level further gains became improbable. If you were to check the math using a probability-based decision-rule formula, you'd find that the trader's instinct was mathematically correct.

## Gambling

For entertainment, traders love to tell fish stories to one another—and sometimes to civilians, who respond the same way they respond to golf bores. No detail is too minor or exact. Traders remember in lurid detail, even years later, every important trade they did, down to the last penny. That doesn't mean they don't embellish the stories, like the fish that becomes 24 inches when it was actually eight. Exaggerating the story afterward is one of the rewards of being a trader. Traders will even go on, at length, about bets they have made off the trading floor: how many inches of snow fell in Central Park at New Year's, or who won the coin toss at the Super Bowl. Michael Lewis's brilliant *Liar's Poker: Rising through the Wreckage on Wall Street* (W.W. Norton & Co., 1989), is a wickedly funny and coldly accurate depiction of traders' culture, from the brass-balls bluff on the serial numbers on a banknote to the rapacious wiles of Big Swinging Dicks.

Are these silly side bets for entertainment and to relieve stress, or do traders have a disproportionately bigger problem with compulsive gambling than the general population? Nobody knows for sure, but Wall Street has funded many a junket to Las Vegas and Atlantic City, complete with bodyguards and suitcases loaded with cash. Van K. Tharp estimates that of the thousands of traders he has evaluated, about 10 percent are compulsive gamblers. This is more than ten times the incidence of compulsive gambling in the general population, which was put at 0.9 percent by the National Gambling Impact Study Commission in June 1999. The report also noted that although half the population of the United States plays the lottery in any given month, 5 percent of ticket buyers account for 51 percent of ticket sales. So the number is a little under 1 percent and up to 5 percent, which makes Tharp's 10 percent estimate of the incidence of compulsive gambling among traders especially noteworthy. Most observers who have spent any time on a trading floor would (impressionistically) put the percentage much higher: over 50 percent.

Gamblers Anonymous states that a compulsive gambler has an inability and unwillingness to accept reality, is emotionally insecure and feels comfortable only in the gambling environment, and is immature, wanting instant gratification without hard work and responsibility. This is interesting, and not a little bizarre, because the essence of successful securities trading is accepting reality (losses), believing that one's position is correct (secure in the trading decision), and knowing that trading *is* hard work. Thus, professional traders who become compulsive gamblers are seeking feelings and conditions that are exactly opposite from the ones that pertain to their main job. We can guess that the reason insurance companies now offer "rogue trader" insurance is that some traders step over the line between disciplined speculation and gambling, which should not be possible if operations safeguards are properly in place.

The stress of trading is so severe that many traders become substance abusers too, although, understandably, we don't have any statistics on that outcome. Traders deliberately set out to pump up their adrenaline level ahead of the trading day, and then have to find ways to come off the high. Nick Leeson, in *Rogue Trader: How I Brought Down Barings Bank and Shook the Financial World* (Warner Books, 1997), tells of the daily drinking to excess, with the other traders, that anesthetized him to the fraud he was committing. Other traders use a healthier way to let off steam. Sports often do the trick; famous trader Victor Niederhoffer is a five-time U.S. National Squash Champion. Balestra's Jim Melcher was on the U.S. Olympic fencing team.

Adrenaline is a metaphor for energy, but it is a real substance, too, produced in the adrenal glands. Adrenaline raises blood pressure and stimulates the liver to release sugar. Its effect on the mind is called the "flight-or-fight" syndrome, and you can trigger the release of adrenaline by drinking caffeine or ingesting other substances, most of them illegal. You can also trigger its release by *thinking.* You can think about emotional situations in the past that got your juices flowing, or you can engage in a little aggressive horseplay in the office to serve the same purpose. Psychologist Adrienne Laris Toghraie writes: "Many traders press that internal panic button all day long, until the mechanism becomes so sensitive that it becomes trigger happy." The result can be permanently high blood pressure, kidney damage, and adrenal failure (a lack of function that leads to insomnia). This is the physical manifestation of true burnout, and recovery can't be achieved in all cases.

The most noticeable characteristic of a natural-born trader is cockiness. Cockiness is more than self-confidence. Self-confident people can be quiet, humble, and self-effacing. Cocky people are loud (boastful), prideful ("full of themselves"), and seeking to be the center of attention. Cockiness is one step below arrogance, although plenty of traders go several steps beyond it. Think of Michael Douglas in the movie *Wall Street.* The character was arrogant and ruthless, and the only criticism of his portrayal, among those who know trading rooms, was that the moviemakers left out the practical jokes. In reality, the junior trader (Charlie Sheen) being groomed by Douglas would have been subjected to a coolness test in the form of cruel practical jokes, as well as the test of his ethics (the story of the movie). Trading rooms can be the scene of the most awful (and juvenile) practical jokes. They are also a hotbed of jokes in really, truly bad taste.

The natural-born trader has a short attention span, but he is decisive and can turn on a dime. He reacts very quickly, without losing his cool, in tense situations where large sums of money are at stake. After a particularly difficult trade, he may throw his chair across the room or destroy the telephone, but while the trade is in progress, he's totally in control of himself and fully focused on the trade and only the trade. His concentration is complete. The building can start burning down around him and he literally will not notice.

People who aspire to quitting their day jobs and becoming traders admire them and want to emulate them. But here is the portrait of the natural-born trader: he has limited knowledge and doesn't read or do research, even about his own specialty. He is

aggressive and rude, and treats nontraders badly. He can do sophisticated mathematical calculations in his head at lightning
speed, but is so focused on his work that he doesn't grasp the bigger picture of the institution he works for. He can be a real boor,
and a bore to boot, and the story he is telling you at excruciating
length may not even be true. He is prone to a compulsive gambling problem and perhaps drug or alcohol addiction. He is cocky
without necessarily being self-confident, and he is likely to make
a farting noise into your telephone when you are speaking with
your most valuable customer.

Because traders have a reputation for being limited and obnoxious, they often find it hard to find a job after trading. One says
that to have "trader" on your resume is tantamount to saying you
spent the last 10 years in the state penitentiary. Prospective employers think you will have bad habits or at least be a bad influence. The transition to another kind of work is perhaps harder for
traders than for others. If they burn out and literally can't do the
work any more because of physical damage, they blame themselves and feel paralyzing guilt. If they were fired, their outsized
egos take it harder than people whose jobs did not require so
much pumping up of self-regard. Worse, most jobs require a far
wider worldview and broader knowledge than trading. Old traders
often say that they literally aren't good for anything except pumping gas. Even those who succeed in reinventing themselves and
finding new careers get a wistful look in their eyes when they
reminisce, as though being on a trading desk was nirvana and
those years were the golden age of their lives, never to be surpassed. Traders like to boast that they had the most stressful job
after air-traffic control—and to be an ex-trader is almost, by definition, to have burned out. The few exceptions, like former Treasury Secretary Robert Rubin, are well and truly exceptional.

## So You Want to Be a Trader?

This description of a trader is a collection of impressions gar-
nered over the years. It describes traders at institutions. It's a bit
of a caricature, but, like all caricatures, you can recognize the person despite (or because of) the exaggerations. There are plenty of
well-read, well-balanced, well-mannered traders out there. They

have broad interests, grasp the nature of business beyond their own, and enjoy humor for people over the age of 14.

The point is that when people fail at trading, there are hundreds of reasons, while all successful traders have one thing in common: the ability to concentrate on one thing to the exclusion (sometimes unhealthy) of everything else. They believe deeply and passionately in every position, but will dump it in a nanosecond. This is like cognitive dissonance in that two contradictory ideas are held at once, but it is more than cognitive dissonance because *action* is required. This is the source of the stress associated with trading. In essence, to be a good trader you have to believe you are right but at the same time be willing to act against that belief when proof appears that you are wrong, and you have to take that action immediately. The decision to make a trade is a rational one, requiring data, logic, and memory, but the decision to exit is an instinctive one, involving the subconscious. If the left brain is the side of the body that is rational, deductive, and analytic, it is engaged in the first half of the trade. The right brain is the one that controls the exit, the side that is intuitive, inductive, holistic, and emotional.

This sets up tremendous tension and conflict. People who want to quit their day jobs, people who admire traders because of their ability to pull the trigger, forget that the stress that comes from holding two contradictory beliefs can transform you into a mass of insecurities, physical illnesses, and general bad behavior. You may escape the worst of the characteristics of the institutional trader because when working at home, you do not have the peer pressure of others egging you on (to take a weekend jaunt to Las Vegas or to head straight for the bar at the end of the day), but the very skill that will make you a good trader will also arouse old internal conflicts that eventually may damage your trading.

All commentators on trading as a profession emphasize that when you embark on a career as a trader, the journey involves more self-discovery than learning nuts and bolts. Jack Schwager says in the preface to *The New Market Wizards, Conversations with America's Top Traders* (John Wiley & Sons, 1992):

> The secret to success in the markets lies not in discovering some incredible indicator or elaborate theory; rather it lies within each individual.

Fred Gehm, author of *Quantitative Trading and Money Management: A Guide to Risk Analysis and Trading Survival* (Richard D. Irwin, 1995), says: "Every human mind conspires against itself. The trick is to recognize how, and work around it by adopting the right attitude." Markets are in a constant state of change. In the face of uncertainty, the mind responds with anxiety defense mechanisms such as denial, rationalization, and avoidance. Every trader brings to the job emotional baggage. One piece of baggage might be the need for continuous "approval" by the market (making profits), which leads to trading mistakes—in this instance, over-trading. Opposite approval might be indecision—freezing when it's time to pull the trigger—arising from a fear of commitment and thus a lack of commitment.

Psychologists, psychiatrists, and others who work with traders agree that *everyone* sabotages himself one way or another. Nearly all have a fear of success ("I don't deserve to make money because trading isn't real work, like going to work with a lunchpail to pound stakes in railway ties, or roof a house."). Robert Krausz, profiled in *The New Market Wizards: Conversations with America's Top Traders* (John Wiley & Sons, 1992), a hypnotist rather than a psychiatrist or psychologist, says that the conscious and subconscious minds must be in harmony for a trader to be successful. The conscious mind may be asserting that the trader is in it for the money, but his subconscious mind must also agree that he *deserves* the winnings. An "alarming" number of people simply shouldn't try trading—they are trying to punish themselves through the market. One case involved a man who was trading only for the excitement and thrill, and was taking big losses that he refused to acknowledge. He hid the unopened brokerage statements and blamed his wife for hiding them. He really wanted to quit his self-destructive trading, and he did close the account after finally opening the statements, an outcome brought about through treatment.

Self-sabotage comes in many forms. Each of us has unique experiences, many of which constitute deep-seated unresolved psychological conflicts and all of which contribute to our individual mindsets. A mindset is a perception of how the world works; on a subconscious level, mindset determines behavior. Psychologists call it the "paradigm." Someone who has had a devastating childhood trauma may seek to play the drama out over and over again in trading. The trader may have a puritanical outlook and be self-denying, working hard rather than working effectively. Or he may be self-indulgent, working in a lazy fashion and seeking instant gratification. The trader's mindset may make him blame everyone but himself for losses—it's the broker's fault, it's the market's fault. He may be overly dependent on others' opinion and defensive against possible criticism by some nonspecific outside agency. Adrienne Laris Toghraie is one of the coterie of psychologists and psychiatrists who specialize in helping traders overcome their personal demons in order to become good traders, or better traders, or even "master traders." In addition to coauthoring, with Jake Bernstein, *The Winning Edge—How to Use Your Psychological Power to Succeed in Trading and Investing* (Target, 1996), she writes articles for the magazine *Technical Analysis of Stocks and Commodities*. The articles have titles like "The Whole Brain Trader" and "Strategies for Overcoming Fear," and in them she recounts stories of trader-patients and how to overcome specific emotional components of the mindset.

Ari Kiev, a New York-based psychiatrist who was the first psychiatrist to the Olympic Sports Medicine Committee in the 1970s and author of *Trading to Win: the Psychology of Mastering the Markets* (John Wiley & Sons, 1998) and *Trading in the Zone: Maximizing Performance with Focus and Discipline* (John Wiley & Sons, 2001), says that even successful traders are invested in limiting mindsets arising out of their past. How much profit you make does not depend on the market, but rather on your own conceptual system. A good trader makes money whether the market is going up or down, and up or down a little or a lot. The market is not the enemy; you need the market to inform you how to adapt. A good trader is able to adapt because he can identify and overcome personal limitations.

## The Testosterone Trap

Women make better traders than men. In a study by Terrance Odean and Brad Barber, titled "Boys Will Be Boys: Gender, Overconfidence, and Common Stock Investment" in the *Quarterly*

*Journal of Economics* (www.gsm.ucdavis.edu/~odean/papers /gender/gender.html), the authors found that men overtrade far more often than women, and get lower returns as a result. Odean examined more than 35,000 accounts at a discount brokerage firm from 1991 to 1997, and found that men trade 45 percent more than women. On a risk-adjusted basis, women made 1.4 percent more money than men. Moreover, when single men are compared to single women, the men trade a whopping 67 percent more—and the women get 2.3 percent more gain on a risk-adjusted basis. Odean credits the outcome to overconfidence by men. If you are able to visit a trading floor at a financial institution, you will find a good cross-section of persons represented—women, minorities, the handicapped. Markets are truly equal-opportunity employers, color- and gender-blind, and indifferent to handicaps if the performance is there.

## Trading to Win

The first step, and a step that has to be taken over and over again, is to commit to a specific money goal. In Ari Kiev's extensive experience, nearly every trader strenuously resists this step. Traders would prefer to say that the market will determine how much money they will make in the next week, month, year. But, in practice, Kiev finds that setting a target helps the trader to focus, and focus leads to discipline. Discipline encompasses risk management as well as planning the trade, tracking and reviewing each decision, and controlling emotion so that the trader feels authentic self-confidence. Controlling emotion includes recovering from previous trades, whether gains or losses, through rational processes such as statistical risk analysis (e.g., the Sharpe ratio), but also through physical processes such as relaxation exercises and mental processes such as visual imagery of successful trading situations. The trader has to be aware of negative thoughts and make an effort to banish them.

Kiev's principles for sustaining success start with becoming aware of the sequence of events associated with success. This is the intellectual work of deciding on a specific trade, and also an awareness of where a belief system might be intruding. You need to base the trading decision on the market, not on what your mindset leads you to expect. You need to let go of anxiety by accepting that trading is an anxiety-inducing business, but not letting emotional investments get in the way, such as associating guilt with profits. You also need to let ego go, especially in recognizing losses. Don't waste time and energy covering up that losses make you feel bad. Go ahead and feel bad—but then analyze the loss both in terms of risk management and in terms of any behavioral error you might have made. In the end, the secret is to accept reality, and that entails clarifying your vision by removing psychological obstacles.

In *Mindtraps: Mastering the Inner World of Investing* (Dow Jones-Irwin, 1988), Roland Barach identifies 88 psychological traps that traders fall into. Destructive patterns of behavior include perfectionism ("I would rather be right than make money"), guilt ("woulda, coulda, shoulda"), and falling in love with your position ("I'm going down on this wonderful ship"). Like Toghraie, Kiev, and others, Barach recommends examining the beliefs and values that skew the mindset to unprofitable behaviors, and then applying the visual imagery of neurolinguistic programming to overcome them. You identify the self-destructive behavior and make a list of defects to be overcome. You imagine having corrected them and how it makes you feel. You list the specific tasks you will have to perform in order to achieve the corrections, and then you practice correcting them, one at a time. Neurolinguistic programming is a field of psychology which holds that, by some mysterious but effective feedback process, when you imagine what it feels like to be successful—seeing it in your mind's eye in detail, smelling and hearing it, and even imagining the position of your body—the imagined images become self-programmed into the mind. If you *feel* successful, you will *be* successful.

## Good Traders Think Differently

Those who have made a study of the subject universally believe that a "real" trader thinks differently from the rest of us. He may be obnoxious, cocky, and limited, but he has achieved the mindset that is required to trade successfully. *Trading in the Zone*

(New York Institute of Finance, 2000), by Mark Douglas, empha-
sizes that the successful trader simply thinks differently from the
mass of wannabe traders who fail. The original subtitle of the
book is *How to Create a State of Mind That Eliminates the Fear,
Stress, and Anxiety From Your Trading* and was changed to *Master the Market with Confidence, Discipline, and a Winning Attitude* (Prentice-Hall Press, 2001). All the keywords are in the
subtitles. Douglas says the chief cause of internal conflict is unwillingness to accept the risk inherent in trading. We accept it
with the rational mind, but do not accept it psychologically, creating fear. To banish stress and anxiety, we have to take responsibility. The market is neither your friend nor your enemy; it is
what it is. Unknown forces are always at work in the market, and
while you may know that your trading system will deliver eight
gains out of the next 12 trades, you don't know which ones they
will be. All you need to focus on is that the odds are in your favor
because you have developed a trading system that works—your
"edge." Everything else is probability. You don't need to know
what is going to happen next in order to make money, and in fact,
anything can happen:

> [I]f you don't expect the market to make you right, you
> have no reason to be afraid of being wrong. If you don't ex-
> pect the market to make you a winner, you have no reason
> to be afraid of losing. If you don't expect the market to
> keep going in your direction indefinitely, there is no rea-
> son to leave money on the table. Finally, if you don't ex-
> pect to be able to take advantage of every opportunity just
> because you perceived it and it presented itself, you have
> no reason to be afraid of missing out.

In the end, "every moment in the market is unique" and unlike anything that has ever happened before or will happen in the
future. When you let go of all expectations about the market, you
are at peace with not knowing what is going to happen next. This
is the best state of mind, the "zone," where you are at one with
the market.

Edward Toppel, in *Zen in the Markets, Confessions of a Samurai Trader* (Warner Books, 1994), expresses the same view more

poetically. Interspersing the text, which is as hardheaded as any trading book, albeit with chapter headings like "Hanging Out in the Present," are Samurai Trader's Maxims:

We do not see things as they are but as we are.

The greatest warrior is one who conquers himself.

The ideal action is one that leaves not a split second between the urge to action and the action itself.

Expect nothing, be prepared for everything.

Probably the single book that combines all the elements is Alexander Elder's *Trading for a Living—Psychology, Trading Tactics, Money Management* (John Wiley & Sons, 1993). Elder is a psychiatrist who trains and coaches traders, and who trades himself. He correctly focuses on losses, and he equates trading losers with drunks who have not yet found Alcoholics Anonymous. He says brokerage records show that 90 percent of people trading today will be out of the picture in a year. "Very few traders will begin the process of change and growth." But, for the rare individual, "the pain of hitting rock bottom will interrupt the vicious cycle of getting high from winning and then losing everything and crashing. When you admit that you have a personal problem that causes you to lose, you can begin building a new trading life. You can start developing the discipline of a winner." Elder thinks we should have a "Traders Anonymous." In a sense, we do. All over the world are traders' clubs with an ostensible purpose of sharing software formulas and trading insights. In practice, the conversation at these meetings is often directed to personal trading problems (usually, not being able to pull the trigger or pulling it too often) and alternative money management approaches.

## The Art of the Trade

Most people who decide to become traders start out looking for a guru who will provide them with a trading system or at least a set of tips. There are hundreds, if not thousands, of trading advisors in every conceivable market. Some of them are charlatans who publish dishonest performance track records, but many of them are honorable and offer good advice. Oddly, most beginning traders lose money on advisors' advice. Not really so odd: to replicate a track record, you have to take every trade. You can't cherry-pick the ones that seem most appealing and then complain that the blended track record was high only because it contained some trade you didn't take.

Disappointed in advisors, beginning traders next typically decide to design their own trading system. Trading system software, books, and training courses abound. Experienced traders call this the search for the Holy Grail, or the best-ever, foolproof trading system. The significant word is "foolproof." Even if the would-be trader can bring himself to finish the system, this approach often fails, too, because he finds that, in real time, he can't resist second-guessing and overriding it. One of the top system developers in the commodities industry, Keith Fitschen, found that he could not resist tampering with his Aberration system, but after giving it in black-box form to someone else (a broker) to execute, profits are consistently in the 100 percent-plus region. (The Aberration system is well-worth exploring, www.trade-system.com, for a clear and graphic demonstration of the trade-off between risk and return, the use of stop-losses, and the virtues of diversification. See also Fitschen's www.qualitystocktiming.com.)

So which comes first, the trading system or the personality adjustment that makes it possible to get into the "zone," or to achieve a Zen-like oneness with the market? To trade successfully, you have to have a system, and you have to believe in it fully so that you implement it without hesitation. R. E. McMasters writes, in *The Art of the Trade: Mastering the Analystic and Intuitive Elements of Successful Trading* (McGraw-Hill, 1999): "The best way to select a trading system is to figure out what fits you and your psychological profile." The most effective trading system for a hypertense person is a day-trading approach. The best system for a laid-back person would be a trend-following system. A risk-averse middle-of-the-road type might be best suited to breakout or swing trading. As McMaster says, no one strategy is inherently better than any other. Each system is only as good as the person executing it. It's important to preserve "psychological capital" in the quest for financial capital. Significantly, the publisher of McMaster's book had originally titled it "Investing with Both Sides of Your Brain." The book is concerned with integrating the rational and analytic with the intuitive and emotional. You must do the intellectual work of building a system, but, in the end, you need to step outside yourself and let intuition and insight rule.

Van K. Tharp, another psychologist who is also a trader, writes, in *Trade Your Way to Financial Freedom* (McGraw-Hill, 1999), that when you really understand the Holy Grail metaphor, you will indeed have found a magic methodology that works for you. That's the secret—it is a system that works for *you.* Success in the market comes from internal control, and to design a system that suits you, you must recognize and overcome (or compensate for) your mental biases. Whatever system you develop, the single most important component is position-sizing—not entry rules or timing, as you might expect. In fact, you could use a coin toss to determine entries and still make profitable trades if you also employed correct money management.

This goes well beyond the usual tired old clichés of "Take losses early and let your winners run," or "Don't try to pick tops and bottoms," or "Never add to a losing position, only to winning ones." Tharp, who surveyed over 4,000 traders, discovered that the one criterion that distinguished winners from losers was the presence or absence of absolute position-sizing rules that are always followed and never overridden. This is what distinguishes a trading *plan* from a trading *system.* As Krausz also says, the reasons traders cite as the reasons they lose money (lack of confidence, fear of loss, bad execution) are actually the result of not having a trading plan. They may have a computer program (a system) that dictates the timing of trades, but without a money management plan, the system is doomed.

As Tharp explains, position-sizing is what most people vaguely call "money management." Position-sizing is not defining the maximum loss you will take, nor is it risk control. Rather, it is that component of the trading system that "answers the question 'How much?' throughout the course of a trade." It will have the effect of dictating when to take profit and loss, but the purposes of the position-sizing rule are to prevent you from being kicked out of the game in ruin and to maximize the gain that can be made from any specific trading strategy, whatever the initial account size. It starts with an understanding of loss. Every trader takes losses and must accept that losses are inevitable. He must also accept that to limit losses and to return to a net winning position, he must accept and internalize Table 5.1.

"Drawdown" refers to the loss that you take in any single trade, and the "gain to recovery" number is how much you have to make in the next trade or set of trades merely to return to the starting equity stake. The most important measure of any trading system is its biggest losing trade. In the book, Tharp shows the results of a single trading system (based on a 55-day volatility breakout concept) using four different position-sizing rules (two of a Martingale variety that adds to winning positions, and two that do not). Stops and reentries are different in each of them, and the outcomes are very different. In fact, there are hundreds (if not an infinite number) of position-sizing rules. Only a handful will be appropriate to your trading system and to you.

By now you should be suspecting that endless hours spent toiling at the computer to find the optimum two moving average crossover mode, or the best breakout system, or unlocking the mysteries of Elliott Wave counts, should be the *last* activity in the process of creating a trading plan, not the first and not even the most

**Table 5.1.** Recovery after Drawdowns

| Drawdowns | Gain to Recovery |
|-----------|------------------|
| 5% | 5.3% gain |
| 10 | 11.1 |
| 15 | 17.6 |
| 20 | 25 |
| 25 | 33 |
| 30 | 42.9 |
| 40 | 66.7 |
| 50 | 100 |
| 60 | 150 |
| 75 | 300 |
| 90 | 900 |

*Source:* Van K. Tharp, *Trade Your Way to Financial Freedom* (McGraw-Hill, 1999), p. 283.

important. Ralph Vince, in *Portfolio Management Formulas: Mathematical Trading Methods for the Futures, Options, and Stock Markets* (John Wiley & Sons, 1990) and *The Mathematics of Money Management: Risk Analysis Techniques for Traders* (John Wiley & Sons, 1992), has a clever way of expressing it: "The trading system is simply a vehicle to give you a positive mathematical expectation on which to use money management." In other words, don't spend time optimizing profit. Instead, direct your "energy to maximizing the certainty level of a marginal profit."

Vince observes that reinvesting profits can turn a winning system into a losing system if returns are not consistent—an important warning. He argues that fixed fractional trading is mathematically always the best way of managing your "stake" (equity). Fixed fractional trading is a function of account size and the performance of the trading system, but, at its root, you shouldn't make a bet if you don't have an expectation of a positive outcome. Obviously, you can't be innumerate (lacking knowledge of probabilities) and hope to master position-sizing. Fortunately, you can learn the theory of gambling and statistical logic, and you should make that effort before buying into any system, including your own. Probably the most readable book in this area is Fred Gehm's *Quantitative Trading and Money Management: A Guide to Risk Analysis and Trading Survival* (Richard D. Irwin, 1995)—but note that Mr. Gehm, who, for many years, advised the largest trading organization in the world (the Abu Dhabi Investment Authority), believes that the theory of the risk of ruin always precludes pyramiding (increasing the amount invested in winning positions).

## Some People Just Don't Get It

The press often reports that the vast majority of individuals who try to become traders fail. It's not clear that this statistic is accurate. Perhaps 90 percent of people close their brokerage accounts with losses, but who is to say what percentage of new brokerage accounts are not opened by people who failed once before and are now succeeding? In fact, it seems highly likely that the second system—this time including money management rules and thus a "plan"—is the one that the trader can now believe in and therefore implement successfully.

Trading-software houses like Equis (Metastock), Worden Brothers (TC2000), and Omega continue to prosper. Omega is a public company that claims over one million systems sold. Equis has sold about 1.5 million copies of Metastock since it began in 1983. The pages of trading magazines such as *Futures, Active Trader,* and *Technical Analysis of Stocks & Commodities* remain brim-full of four-color, double-page advertisements, plus smaller ads for specialized systems that have been around since the 1970s. Individuals are certainly continuing the quest, and we have no proof of what percentage fail. For all we know, there may be hundreds of thousands—a million? more than a million?—of successful self-directed traders.

Can people learn to become traders? It would seem that some people don't get it and never will get it. "It" is the burning desire to take advantage of market moves, buying at lows and selling at highs. Show them a chart where the price is going to an obvious extreme and ask them what they should do, and they look blank. The chart does not convey useful information to them. They can't see what they are looking at. Tell them that the market is up 80 percent and their stock is up 120 percent, historical anomalies, and they will not understand that the right thing to do is get the hell out of Dodge. Their trading ideas are a hodgepodge of trite aphorisms and snippets of wise sayings that are actually dangerous out of context. They have no systematic way of viewing the market. They might even believe that every price is random and there is no point in trying to trade. The only thing you can do is buy and hold. But these people are not dummies and, in fact, may be intelligent and talented in their own fields. To some extent, they don't get it because getting it requires a lot of work— such as understanding probability theory—and the truth is, they have no taste for the work. To learn requires motivation to learn.

Those who do have a yen to trade can certainly be taught to trade. In *The New Market Wizards* (John Wiley & Sons, 1992), Schwager interviews several "Turtles," people who were selected for a training experiment by famous trader Richard Dennis, who made a bet with his partner that he could teach people to trade. The Turtles had been sworn to secrecy for five years and were unwilling to reveal anything about the system they were taught. Later, we found out that the 23 persons who were handpicked by Dennis to take part in the experiment had tremendous success—a 32.4 percent per annum collective return over the period from January 1985 to January 1996, handily beating the 16.5 percent annual return of the Commodity Trading Advisors Index published by TASS Management, and well over the 12.8 percent return on the S&P 500 over the same period. Dennis reported that the Turtles, who were initially staked by him at $100,000 each (later, the stake was raised to $1 million), made about $35 million for his firm before they broke up in 1988.

The Turtle trading system used the trend-following style, normally not the most exciting and action-packed variety. But the Turtles spiced it up with aggressive money management rules, pyramiding (adding to positions and increasing leverage), combining pyramiding with equal volatility weighting of each position (whatever its nominal size), and a strict limit of a maximum 2 percent loss of the total stake risked on any one trade. Two-thirds of trades did, in fact, result in losses of 2 percent or less. Diversification was across a broad range of commodities "because you never know which ones will be big." After a loss, each Turtle had to reduce the size of each trade but not the number of markets traded, in order to catch a trend if it developed.

Some other trading rules have emerged over the years, such as buying at any 20-day high and closing the position at the first eight-day low, and waiting three days after a trend reversal signal to execute a trade. But the trading rules are not the point—the point is that trading can be taught, if the student is motivated and if the trading system also includes a money management *plan*, exactly as the psychologists, psychiatrists, and trading coaches have discerned.

## The Plan

Don't even think of becoming a trader without a *plan*. Even with a plan, as a trader you are seeking to find the "sweet spot" represented by the intersection of all the circles in the chart, and it is very, very small. First you have to get in tune with market psychology. Some people have a tin ear and cannot hear what the market is telling them. Next, your trading system has to be relevant to the market you are trading. It may be wonderful in equities and dreadful in soybeans. This is a somewhat controversial statement, because many people believe that a winning system can be applied in any market. In many cases, this is no doubt true, but it depends to some extent on the nature of the system. For example, a breakout system works beautifully on some securities (buy when the last highest high has been surpassed), but in others you should do the exact opposite (sell when a higher high is reached).

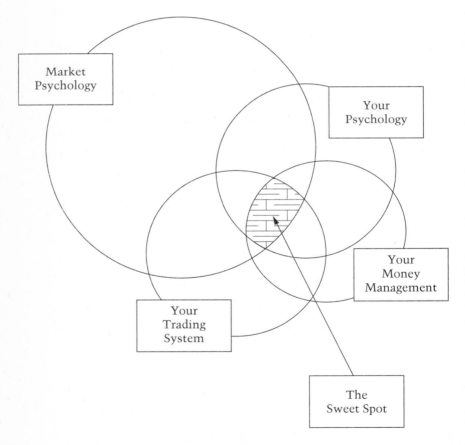

**Figure 5.1**   The sweet spot.

Finally, your money management rules need to match the trading system and your personality—and be suited to the market you are trading. If the market typically moves 100 points every day with a net gain in the direction of the trend of 75 points, you would be using the wrong system to target gains of 20 points with a stop loss of 10 points. It's conceivable that you could have a winning trading system and a winning money management system that would work in a market different from the one you are trading (see Figure 5.1)—but not in the one you *are* trading.

## Summary and Conclusions

Natural-born and trained traders are different from the rest of us. They have an innate combination of personality traits that together make up what is needed for success in trading. They may or may not be well-balanced in the conventional sense of the word, and anyone attempting to acquire their traits runs the risk of acquiring some of the side effects, too, like a gambling problem or early burnout. Still, traders can be trained, although learning to become a successful trader is not what most people think it is— buying a software package and a live-quote screen subscription. Instead, it is an intellectual and spiritual endeavor. Some of the smartest people will never become successful traders because following prices endlessly in wait for the planned setup can become boring and soul-numbing. Trading is not a part-time hobby; it is a career just like becoming a *cordon bleu* chef or an astronaut. The best advice you will get from the psychiatrists, psychologists, and coaches is to *practice* in advance of putting down any actual cash. Keep a simulated trade ledger and a diary. (You can pretend-trade at several Web sites, including the Chicago Mercantile Exchange, www.cme.com, and visit www.auditrack.com.) Most of all, go back and look at Table 5.1, "Recovery after Drawdowns." If you lose 75 percent of your stake, you have to make 300 percent to get back to your starting point. Is it realistic to expect your market, your personality and work habits, your trading system, and your money management system to deliver that?

# Chapter 6

# FOREIGN EXCHANGE

*There is no field of endeavor in which it is easier to give the appearance of wisdom than in matters of foreign exchange.*

Winston Churchill

Tokyo taxi drivers know the value of the Japanese yen against the dollar, the euro, and the pound, and in what direction the yen is trending in each instance. Six out of 10 people in Europe can tell you the value of the euro against the dollar and maybe the yen and the pound. In the United States, in contrast, hardly anyone knows the value of the dollar against any other currency, except those who live along the Canadian and Mexican borders and those about to make a trip abroad. This anomaly is due, of course, to the sheer size of the country and its economy. Americans don't need to know foreign exchange rates or how the foreign exchange market works, and so they don't. Not knowing, however, puts us at a distinct disadvantage when it comes to global trading and investing. When you buy a foreign stock such as Sony or Nestlé, for example, in most cases you are buying an ADR (American Depositary Receipt), denominated in U.S. dollars. You receive all the company's financial information presented in dollar terms; even the dividend is in dollars. You can buy and sell an ADR as easily as a domestic stock. It's easy to forget that, in fact, you are taking a foreign exchange risk—and it may be far bigger than you know.

157

The foreign exchange market is fascinating. It encompasses economics, politics, demographics, and culture, as well as business. On one day, the dollar may sharply lose value in Tokyo against the yen because an Air Force spy plane makes an emergency landing in Chinese territory—but the next day, the dollar rises because the United States is a safe haven for investment money, even though a U.S. airplane is in the headlines and the United States is engaged in a diplomatic tussle. The foreign exchange market is also exasperating; it may place an unrealistic price on a currency for a very long period of time when "everyone knows" that, on the basis of fundamentals, the currency should be at a different level. The Australian dollar is a case in point. According to many studies, the Australian dollar is at least 35 percent undervalued, and maybe more. On a purchasing power basis—that is, if a basket of common goods were priced equally in each country—the A$ should be worth about U.S. 85 cents. Instead, as of this writing, it is about U.S. 50 cents. Explanations for this mispricing include the outlook for commodity prices, with which the A$ is thought to be correlated; the Australian stock market, which lists mostly "old economy" companies instead of hot high-tech companies; and so on. But nobody really knows why the A$ is undervalued, or why the undervaluation persists.

To be involved in global trading requires an understanding of the foreign exchange (FX) market, whether you will trade foreign exchange as an asset class, hedge foreign currency-denominated assets, or perform intermarket analysis. Understanding the foreign exchange market has another benefit, too—it helps to understand what seem to be purely domestic events and policies. The Federal Reserve, for example, consults conditions in the FX market before it changes interest rates. A strong dollar allows Americans to buy foreign goods cheaply, thus restraining inflation. It also attracts foreign investors who buy dollar-denominated assets—everything from shopping centers to shares of stock and whole companies outright. Were the Fed to drive interest rates too low, the dollar would fall, instantly and automatically raising the rate of inflation in the form of the price of imported goods, and perhaps also chasing foreign investors to other places. What is "too low"? Nobody knows. It is a living experiment.

# How the Currency Market Works

The foreign exchange market is the textbook "perfect market." It is the largest and most liquid market in the world, with daily trading volume of $1.3 trillion. It is a worldwide, 24-hour market, and it possesses superb electronic news and rate information networks. Market participants include governments, professional dealers at banks and other financial institutions, multinational corporations, multicurrency fixed income and equity portfolio managers, importers and exporters, and individual traders on the futures and options exchanges. Over 95 percent of all the volume traded is executed by professional interbank dealers, and it is important to note that interbank dealing is virtually unregulated by any government authority anywhere in the world. Because the FX market is big, liquid, trended, and never closed, it is an ideal vehicle for individual traders.

You might feel a little frightened, knowing that some $1 trillion per day is being risked by bank traders in what is essentially speculation. Fear would be misplaced, though. For one thing, each transaction is covered by an offsetting transaction at lightning speed. A trader may execute 30 or 40 trades in a day, totaling several hundred million dollars, but the ongoing net position at any one time may be only $5 to $20 million, and the position is usually closed out before the end of the day. Although many banks have a proprietary trading group that holds positions overnight and for several days or weeks, these are for much smaller amounts, and they are managed with strict stop-loss rules.

Another characteristic of the bank FX market is netting of trades. As a result of many trades over the course of a day in any single time zone, Citibank may have $500 million due from Deutsche Bank and owe Deutsche Bank $495 million, leaving a net of only $5 million. Thus, the amounts that change hands at the end of the day (actually, in two days' time, the normal spot settlement) are only a fraction of the total amount traded. And this is the only cash involved. Banks trade with one another on the basis of the credit lines they extend to one another specifically for this purpose. The last time a bank went under because of foreign exchange dealing was the failure of Germany's Herstatt Bank in

1974, which in turn caused the failure of Franklin National Bank in the United States because of Herstatt's accepting payments but failing to make its own. Risk-reducing measures have been vastly improved since then. Big international banks are even working on instant settlements, for example.

# Trendedness

The foreign exchange market is highly trended. This is because at any one time, professional traders are all looking at more or less the same indicators. They all closely follow international political and economic events—elections, trade policies, relative gross national product (GNP) growth, inflation—in the attempt to predict where exchange rates are going. Trends in exchange rates roughly mirror trends in economic performance and interest rates, particularly relative purchasing power and capital flows, which themselves change rather slowly. (See Figure 6.1.) Economic news and, more importantly, *expectations* of economic news, cause traders to buy or sell currencies in anticipation of the real economic change. *Currency market sentiment is often a leading indicator of economic and political direction.*

Currencies exhibit the classic three trend types perhaps better than any other category of securities. We can easily identify primary trends, at least in retrospect. Looking more closely, we see that there are minitrends within the major trends (i.e., occasions when the primary trend suffers a retracement or consolidation before resuming). Retracements represent periods when traders are taking profits and/or the minority view prevails, at least temporarily. Such secondary trends are common, and it can be hard to know, at the time it's happening, whether a retracement represents the formation of a secondary trend or a new primary trend (trend reversal). In Figure 6.1, the euro has been on a downtrend since its inception in January 1999. No correction was larger than 10 percent (zigzag line) until October 24, 2000—and then the correction reversed back to a downtrend on January 3, 2001.

There are also periods when the currency appears to be untrended. Looking at historical data, we see that exchange rates are *not always* trended. When participants are uncertain about how to

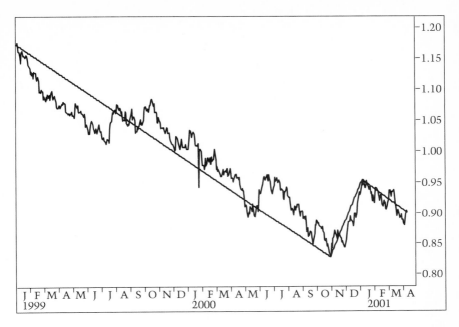

**Figure 6.1**   Trendedness (euro).

interpret economic and financial statistics, they will take the market sideways. Untrended markets are characterized by low volumes ("thin" markets) and by low volatility, which usually precedes a "breakout"—a resumption of the previous trend or a reversal of the previous trend.

Market sentiment is notoriously fickle and can change radically as new information becomes known. As market perceptions and expectations change, no trader wants to be out of step with the consensus view, and dramatic adjustments to prices occur as traders jump on the bandwagon. The "bandwagon effect" generally causes trends to exhibit strong directional momentum, although it sometimes results in minor price changes that are illogical or even perverse. An example is when the actual release of a favorable statistic causes a rate to drop (instead of going up) because the news had been so widely expected that traders had already bought the currency and are then taking profits. This is the same "Buy on the rumor, sell on the news" that we see in equity markets.

Other factors that disturb trendedness are central bank intervention, massive buying or selling by speculators (usually named as hedge funds even when they are not the guilty parties), and one-time corporate actions such as foreign acquisitions or conversion of bond proceeds. These seldom actually change the direction of an existing trend, but they can create large random movements that sow uncertainty in the minds of traders. When traders are uncertain how to interpret economic news or recent large counter-trend price changes, many conflicting opinions will be heard and markets enter periods of untrendedness, called sideways markets or range-trading markets, characterized by high volatility and small but frequent price changes. Then traders wait for the next significant piece of news to resume the original trend—or reverse it. Often, when a currency is going sideways against the dollar, it is going somewhere against a different currency. If the market feels a high level of uncertainty about where to take the Japanese yen against the dollar—say, because the Bank of Japan has been making noises that it might intervene—the market may shift attention to

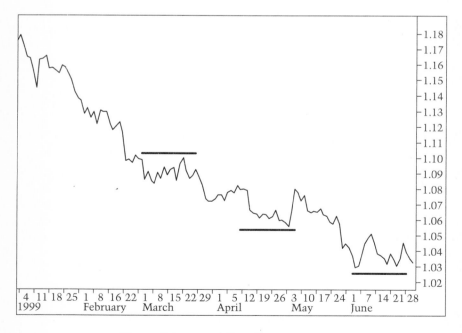

**Figure 6.2**   Euro/dollar sideways movements.

the yen cross-rates, such as the euro/yen or pound/yen. If the market feels uncertain about where to take the euro against the dollar, it may do nothing, which results in a flat or horizontal linear regression line. These shifts in focus happen all the time.

A shift in focus, from one set of exchange rates to another set, occurred in March 1999. Figure 6.2 shows that uncertainty gripped the market about the future direction of the euro, which was only two months old at the time, having been invented out of the currencies of the European Monetary Union in January 1999. The consensus of opinion in the market was that the euro, launched at a value of $1.17, would rise to $1.35. Instead, in the first two months of its existence, it fell to $1.08. This was confusing, to say the least. Economists and analysts were saying one thing ($1.35), but traders were doing another ($1.08). The market decided to take a pause. Over a three-week period from March 4 to March 26, it changed a mere net 0.0023 cents, closing at $1.0841 from $1.0864. Against the yen, however, the euro fell from €133.27 to €129.47, or 2.9 percent. (See Figure 6.3.)

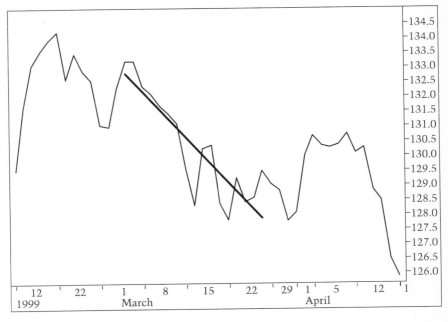

**Figure 6.3**  Euro/yen trendedness.

Another way to look at this is to say that the yen strengthened by 2.9 percent against the euro. But at the same time, the yen was strengthening by 2.9 percent against the dollar, too. Figure 6.4 shows that over the same period, it moved from ¥133.27 (to $1.00) to ¥129.47 (to $1.00). In sum, the yen was trending against the euro and the dollar, but the euro was not trending against the dollar. That makes it a euro story, not a yen story.

This example of untrendedness points out a valuable feature of trading the foreign exchange market: the amount of new research you have to do to shift focus is minimal. When a stock trend is exhausted and the stock goes into a sideways period, you have to find another stock, perhaps in a different sector. This occasions fresh fundamental and technical work. Not so in currencies; you can simply shift focus from one set of rates to another, with no additional work. Something is always trending in currencies.

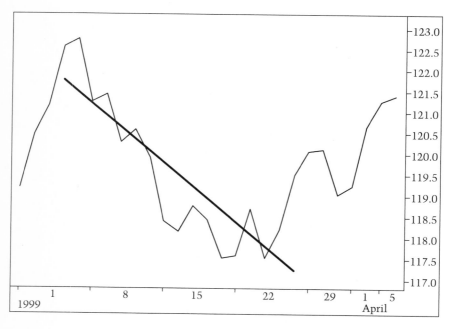

**Figure 6.4**  Dollar/yen trend.

# A Note about the Dollar Index

Is the so-called dollar index important to foreign exchange traders? In March 2001, the front page of the *Financial Times* blazed with the headline: "Equity gloom sends dollar to 15-year high." Apart from the dubious assertion that big stock market declines around the world were causing capital flight into the dollar, what "dollar" was the *FT* talking about? The dollar was certainly not at any long-term high against any major traded currency at the time. Near the end of the article, readers found out that "the dollar" in question is the Federal Reserve's traded-weighted "broad" dollar index. This is prepared by the statistics division of the Board of Governors of the Fed in Washington, reported daily in newspapers and at www .federalreserve.gov/releses/H10/update. The dollar index is constructed from the exchange rates of trading-partner countries, weighted by each country's share of trade with the United States (both imports and exports). (See Table 6.1.)

The Federal Reserve Board also prepares a dollar index against "major currencies" and another against "other important trading partners" (OITP). The underlying exchange rates used by the Board come from the New York Fed, which publishes the exchange rates of every country, daily. The New York Fed is the designated regional Fed office responsible for foreign exchange, which encompasses the tracking of rates, managing U.S. Government foreign reserves, and foreign exchange intervention when directed by the Treasury Department. The Federal Reserve in Atlanta calculates a dollar index, too. This index is a little different (and more realistic) from the one published by the Fed Board of Governors, and its Web site has the virtue of carrying several well-written research papers on the subject of calculating the index, and related matters (www.frbatlanta.org). To get the Board's research papers and commentary on the dollar index, you need to surf the Fed *Bulletins;* the major article on the dollar index was published in the *Bulletin* dated October 1998 (www.federalreserve.gov/pubs/bulletin).

Looking at the weights in the broad dollar index, right away you can see that Canada has almost as much weight as the 12 countries of the eurozone and more weight than Japan, and Brazil has a higher weight than Switzerland. That means that the Canadian dollar is as important as the euro and the Japanese yen in the

**Table 6.1.**   Federal Reserve Board of Governors

| U.S. Dollar Index Weights: Broad Measure* | |
| --- | --- |
| Country/Region | Trade Weight |
| Euro area | 17.086% |
| Canada | 17.183 |
| Japan | 13.214 |
| Mexico | 9.345 |
| China | 7.395 |
| United Kingdom | 4.572 |
| Taiwan | 3.731 |
| Korea | 4.076 |
| Singapore | 2.731 |
| Hong Kong | 2.643 |
| Malaysia | 2.345 |
| Brazil | 1.762 |
| Switzerland | 1.737 |
| Thailand | 1.592 |
| Philippines | 1.310 |
| Australia | 1.247 |
| Indonesia | 1.147 |
| India | 1.114 |
| Israel | 1.156 |
| Saudi Arabia | 0.821 |
| Russia | 0.814 |
| Sweden | 0.909 |
| Argentina | 0.598 |
| Venezuela | 0.517 |
| Chile | 0.541 |
| Colombia | 0.413 |
| Total | 100.000% |

*Source:* www.federalreserve.gov/releases
/H10/weights.

*As of February 1, 2001.

index, and the Brazilian real is as important as the Swiss franc. This is out of line with the relative size of the individual economies; Japan is the world's second largest economy in terms of GDP, while Canada and Brazil rank well down the list. Moreover, the Canadian dollar, euro, yen, and Swiss franc are freely floating currencies and their price is determined moment-by-moment by the foreign exchange market, whereas the Brazilian currency and many others on the list are either at fixed exchange rates against the dollar or in a "managed float," meaning their governments have capital controls that allow them to fix the price of the local currency against the dollar. In practice, U.S. exports are dollar-denominated and U.S. imports are denominated in the currency of the country of origin if that currency floats and is traded, or in dollars if the local currency is fixed. Saudi Arabia, nearly 1 percent of the total weight, conducts all its business with the United States in U.S. dollars; the Argentine peso is linked one-to-one with the dollar (although perhaps moving to a euro and dollar "basket" at some point in the future). Therefore, the dollar index does not really represent a "summary measure" of the dollar, as it is intended to do. You would be hard-pressed to impute "demand for dollars" for trade purposes from the dollar index, or to calculate true changes in the importance of various regions (Asia, Latin America) to the United States in the formulation of U.S. policy, although this is exactly what was done in the debate over the North American Free Trade Agreement.

The dollar index also suffers from the "index number problem," inherent in all indices, and that is the date that is chosen to be the base year. All indices are constructed by nailing down the first number in a series as equivalent to 100 and adding the percentage change from the first number to the second number as 100 plus the change. The percentage change from the first number to the third number is then expressed as 100 plus that change. The base is 100 and every other index number after it represents the percentage change from the base. If we take the rate of inflation in 1990, for example, and set it to 100, then the rate of inflation 10 years later, in 2000, is 33.93 percent higher if the 2000 inflation index is 133.93. Notice that the index number for 2000 does not include the inflation rate in 1990, only the change from 1990. Indices have the virtue of displaying acceleration or deceleration of the rate of change in a series, but, at the same time, you always have to question the choice of the first data point.

In practice, the Fed does not re-base the dollar index series very often. The broad dollar index was re-based in January 1997, as was the OITP series, but the major currencies index is still based at March 1973 = 100. In 1973, when the dollar was floated, the Japanese yen was at 203.4 yen to the dollar; it has been as low as 79 to the dollar (1995).

Using a very long time line does not eliminate the base-year problem; in fact, it compounds it because of inflation. A nifty Web site, www.westegg.com/inflation, will calculate the cost of an item in current dollars and compare it to the cost in any year in the past, using U.S. Government inflation statistics. What cost $100 in 1800 would cost $976.38 in 2000. Looking at it the other way around, something that cost $100 in 2000 would have cost $10.24 in 1800, or $5.01 in 1900 (implying that prices fell by 50 percent during the 1800 to 1900 century). The Ford automobile that cost $500 in 1910 would cost $9,243.44 in 2000—when we know that a Ford today costs a great deal more. On the other hand, the loaf of bread that cost 25 cents in 1956 would today cost $1.55—not a bad comparison to the actual price in 2000 for the same kind of bread. The pack of cigarettes that cost 25 cents in 1965 should cost $1.34 today, but it costs more than twice as much because of taxes. In addition to taxes and other price distortions, inflation is tricky because changes occur in the type and quality of goods, the actual number of pounds and ounces in a package, and many other factors. To get a realistic estimate of inflation, you need to compare the same basket of goods in both periods—but the basket changes beyond recognition, and sometimes in a very short period. Some items that were astronomically expensive in 1900, such as oranges and bananas, are commonplace and cheap today. Lamp oil, candles, and coal, cheap in 1900, are expensive today. Comparing the cost of lighting the home in 1900 and lighting the home in 2000 entails a far more complicated series of comparisons than you can perform using inflation statistics. Shorter time frames are susceptible, too. A typical basket of consumer goods in 2000 is not the same basket as in 1975, only 25 years earlier, when the CD had not yet been invented, let alone designer water and organic cat food.

Inflation is the chief reason that calculation of a dollar index is problematic. Both the Board of Governors' and the Atlanta Fed's dollar indices are in nominal terms, that is, not inflation-adjusted. In fact, the value of a dollar index depends, to a large extent, on inflation being more or less the same in each country, so that the relative price of the currency accurately reflects purchasing power and thus the trade situation. We are assuming not only that domestic purchasing power has not changed from the base year, but also that purchasing power in the other countries has not changed. Even when a dollar index is inflation-adjusted, what inflation index is being used? The Atlanta Fed published an article in its *Economic Review* (www.frbatlanta.org/publica/eco-rev/rev_abs /3rd99.html) showing that the nominal and inflation-adjusted dollar indices are little different from one another. This, however, is not convincing. We know, for example, that Brazil often suffers from hyperinflation that is only sporadically reflected in the dollar value of the real. Japan has suffered from price deflation [a falling Consumer Price Index (CPI) since 1998]. For political reasons, inflation statistics in every country are suspect, even in the United States after the re-basing of the official CPI by the Commerce Department in 1999.

In sum, the dollar index is a fiction. It reflects the blended external value of the dollar in a highly distorted way that becomes ever more distorted as the time from the last re-basing increases and in the absence of accurate adjustments for inflation. You should not look at the dollar index as a summary guide to the value of the dollar. The Fed's dollar index is of use mostly to academic economists and newspaper reporters. It is misleading to speak of "the dollar" as though it had one value or price, when it may be strong against the yen but weak against the euro or Swiss franc.

And yet, when the dollar index makes a new 15-year high, it is an important indicator of *something*. We know from technical analysis that any time a price makes an extreme high or low, we need to perk up and take notice. It is a warning that an unsustainable situation has developed. Current foreign exchange positions may be too high (the problem) or too low (the opportunity). In most contexts, an American resident has no foreign exchange rate exposure or risk to the U.S. dollar. It is his home currency. As a wage earner, consumer, or investor, very little changes in his life when the external value of the dollar rises or falls. The chief effect is on the cost of foreign-source consumer goods, which could constitute a rather high proportion of total spending when housing and energy are excluded. Just try to buy a U.S.-manufactured TV set; there are none. But it is also true that, from a global perspective, the average American is overinvested in the dollar, literally and figuratively. Thus, the risk that a U.S. resident has to the dollar is an opportunity risk.

## The Tradable Dollar Index

The New York Board of Trade (NYBT) offers a futures contract named (and trademarked) "the dollar index," and this contract is optionable. The New York Board of Trade is the parent company of the Coffee, Sugar and Cocoa Exchange (CSCE) and the New York Cotton Exchange (NYCE), but it also trades various cross-rate contracts like the euro/yen, euro/British pound, Australian dollar/Canadian dollar, and others. The NYBT dollar index contract is constructed from the trade-weighted geometric averages of the currencies shown in Table 6.2.

Here we have to question the relative weights of the euro and yen, not to mention the inclusion of the Swedish krona at 4.2 percent of the total when U.S. trade with Sweden is less than 1 percent of total trade with all countries, according to the Fed. The NYBT dollar index has fallen in popularity among retail currency speculators in recent years for the obvious reason that big moves in the euro dominate the index and the Japanese yen is still big enough to constitute a wild card when the euro is falling but the yen is rising. The volatile U.K. pound also contributes to confusing countertrend effects. The dollar index does not appear on the list of the 45 most liquid futures contracts published monthly by *Technical Analysis of Stocks & Commodities* magazine. Some

**Table 6.2.**   The New York Board of Trade U.S. Dollar Index®

| Currency | Currency Weight (%) |
|---|---|
| Euro | 57.6 |
| Japan/yen | 13.6 |
| United Kingdom/pound | 11.9 |
| Canada/dollar | 9.1 |
| Sweden/krona | 4.2 |
| Switzerland/franc | 3.6 |

*Source:* "Contract Specifications," www.nybot.com.

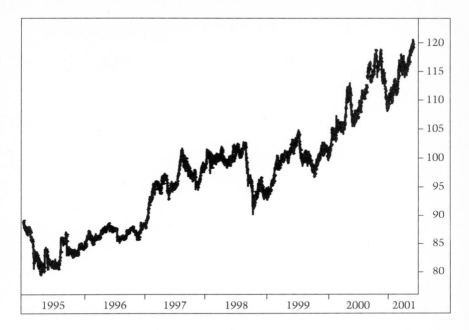

**Figure 6.5**   U.S. Dollar Index.

advisory services, such as Dollar Trader (www.dollartrader.com), have stopped offering analysis of the dollar index for this reason. (See Figure 6.5.)

## A Note about Quotation Conventions

The dollar is the main world currency for transactions in commodities (oil, metals, grain, and so on) and is also the main currency held as reserves by sovereign nations. About 50 percent of world trade and about 65 percent of world reserves are dollar-denominated. For this reason, most currencies are quoted in terms of the European quotation convention, or how many units of a currency one dollar will buy. Today, one dollar will buy 2.1900 Deutschemarks, for example. This is phrased as "dollar/mark." The yen is also quoted in the European quotation convention, and phrased "dollar/yen." One dollar will buy 125 yen today. We would never say that the yen is worth 0.0080 cents, even though it is perfectly accurate, because the phrasing would be awkward.

In contrast, the pound is always quoted in terms of how many dollars it will buy, such as $1.6500. This is a custom held over from the days (before World War II), when it was the main world currency. Possibly because the Chicago futures market trades foreign currencies denominated in dollars and cents, this is called the American quotation convention.

You can convert a currency quote from the European quotation convention into the equivalent American quotation convention by dividing into one, a process named "reciprocation." Before the euro came into existence, each continental European currency was quoted in the European quotation convention. As noted, when the dollar/Deutschemark was quoted at 2.1900, it meant that it took 2.1900 DM to buy one dollar. A tourist or a futures trader may say that the DM was worth 46 cents, or 2.1900 divided into 1.00, but professionals always quote the DM in the European quotation convention and always to the fourth decimal point (except for the yen). When the euro came into existence, however, the Europeans decided to put its name first in each currency pairing, so we have the euro/dollar, meaning that now we are asking how many dollars (or cents) you can get for one euro. When we say the euro is 8500, we mean one euro will buy 85 cents. In naming the new currency, the Europeans chose to use the non-European quotation convention, which is named—the American convention. Getting its name first in the pair was evidently more important than the name of the quotation convention.

The choice of name had an unintended consequence, too. We already had something called a "eurodollar." A eurodollar is a dollar that lives permanently outside the United States, manifested as dollar-denominated deposits and loans held at banks in London or other money centers. The interest rate is called the "eurodollar rate" or just "the eurodollar," and it is typically lower than the rate paid or charged in the United States because these funds escape Federal Reserve Bank reserve requirements and deposit insurance costs. Eurodollar interest rates are calculated as a discount from U.S. Treasuries of the same maturity. You can become horribly confused when you look up "the eurodollar" and see "95," the price of a three-month eurodollar deposit with the rate calculated as 100 minus the 5 percent yield. At the same time, the euro/dollar, the currency price, may also be at 95, meaning 95 cents. It is necessary to specify what you are trading: an interest rate or a currency pair. Many a mistaken trade is still being done today. Many market participants have taken to calling it "the eurocurrency," but this is not satisfactory because the second currency of the pair is not explicit.

When you see a price quote of 7.7990 and you don't know which convention is being used, it's usually safe to assume that you are looking at the European quotation convention, that is, how many units of a currency one dollar will buy. In this case, one dollar will buy 7.7990 Hong Kong dollars. We could as easily say the HK$ is worth 12.82 cents, but we do not, any more than we say the dollar is worth 60.5 British pence. The Canadian and Australian dollars are quoted both ways. The A$ may be quoted as 2.0600, meaning it takes 2.0600 Australian dollars to buy one U.S. dollar, or you may see it at 48.50, meaning 48.5 cents. The same thing is true for the Canadian dollar.

The European quotation convention can take some getting used to. It's hard to see a number going up and to understand that the dollar value is going down. When the yen rises from 110 to 125, the yen is getting weaker in dollar terms—one dollar will buy 15 more yen. When the yen is at 110, it is stronger than when it is at 125; again, how many do you get for one dollar? When you get fewer yen for the same dollar, the yen has become stronger. The pound, euro, and all futures prices are far easier to understand. Up is actually up, and down is actually down, in the dollar value. A higher number really does mean a more valuable foreign currency unit, and a lower one means a lower dollar value.

The quotation convention is relatively easy when you are dealing with a cross-rate, which, from an American perspective, is any currency pair that does not include the U.S. dollar, such as euro/Swiss franc, euro/yen, pound/yen, and so on. As you might imagine, professional arbitrageurs buy and sell each currency pair, so any opportunity among rates is fleeting. When you see that the euro/yen is 112.10, you know that one euro buys 112.10 yen. It is the price of the euro denominated in yen. If you also know the price of the euro in dollars, you can derive the dollar value of the yen; and if you know the dollar/yen, you can derive the euro. If the euro/yen is 112.10 and the euro/dollar is 0.8993, you divide the yen price of the euro by the dollar price of the euro and get 124.65 as the price of the dollar/yen. If the euro/yen is 112.10 and the dollar/yen is 124.65, you divide the yen price of the euro by the yen price of the dollar and get 0.8993 as the dollar price of the euro.

## Trading Currencies as an Asset Class

Nearly all individuals trade currencies as an asset class on one of the futures exchanges. Foreign exchange is traded in futures markets at the International Monetary Market division of the Chicago Mercantile Exchange (CME) (www.cme.com), the Mid-Am affiliate of the Chicago Board of Trade (www.cme.com), and the New York Board of Trade (www.nybot.com). The instructional materials offered by the exchanges are excellent—and free. The CME offers simulated trading and risk management, as well as Saturday seminars (worth attending if you are in Chicago). The National Futures Association (www.nfa.futures.org) also offers free educational material, including how to avoid being swindled, options on futures, mediation and arbitration, and other topics.

In foreign exchange, the most heavily traded contracts are March, June, September, and December, although contracts maturing in other months are available. The best liquidity is to be found in the major currencies (euro, British pound, Japanese yen, Swiss franc, Canadian dollar), although if you really wanted to trade Czech koruna, you could do it on the Budapest Commodity Exchange after you open an account there. The dollar, as one half of a currency pair, can be traded on futures exchanges in Budapest, Manila, Seoul, Transilvania, St. Petersburg, Siberia, Brussels, Paris, Madrid, Milan, London, Amsterdam, Caracas, Santiago, Singapore, Hong Kong, New Zealand, and Tokyo.

The essence of futures trading is that, for the price of a good-faith "performance bond" deposited up front (initial margin), the individual may take a position in a contract that will mature at some time in the future. If the price of the commodity rises, he can sell the contract for a profit. If the price of the commodity falls, he will be asked to deposit more money to cover the loss.

Positions are marked to market every day (revalued as of the final "settlement" price at the close of business), and you receive a telephone call, e-mail, or fax telling you the status of your positions after the close every day. If your trade was profitable, the new cash value of the contract is added to the account total, as though it were cash. If the gain is big enough, you can use it as initial margin to execute another trade, in the same or in a different contract (pyramiding). If your account gets low on cash—that is, you do not have the maintenance margin, the amount stipulated by the exchange to cover daily variations in the closing value of your positions—your broker will ask you for a fresh cash infusion. This is the famous "margin call." If he can't reach you or the request goes unanswered, he is allowed to close your positions.

The initial margin to buy or sell a contract is quite low in comparison to the value of the contract, usually $750 to $3,000 to "control" a contract worth $50,000 to $150,000. The exchanges raise and lower the minimum initial and maintenance margin amounts periodically, as volatilities change. Brokers may require more margin than the exchange minimum. The CME makes it hard to discover the initial and maintenance margin of specific contracts. You have to wade through each "advisory notice" issued on the Web site, scrolling through lean hogs, feeder cattle, forest products, the E-Mini Nasdaq, the Goldman Sachs Commodity Index, and so on, until you find the contract you are looking for.

## Leverage

Table 6.3 holds the key to why critics say commodity trading is inherently high-risk and virtually every first-time commodity trader fails in the first year: leverage. If we calculate leverage using only initial margin, leverage in the British pound contract is 57.86 : 1. In other words, one dollar controls $57.86. Regulators dislike the word "control" and, in official publications, warn futures managers against using it, presumably because it could be applied in an advertising context to impress and entice the unwary.

Leverage is wonderful when your trade is winning, and awful when your trade is losing. Let's say you believe the Swiss franc will rise. You buy a Swiss franc contract and have to put down

**Table 6.3.** Chicago Mercantile Exchange IMM

| | | Currency Futures Contracts* | | | |
|---|---|---|---|---|---|
| Futures Contract | Local Currency Amount | Dollar Equivalent | Initial Margin | Maintenance Margin | Maximum Leverage |
| British pound | 62,500 | $ 89,862.50 | $1,553 | $1,150 | 57.86 |
| Euro | 125,000 | 111,475.00 | 2,673 | 1,980 | 41.70 |
| Japanese yen | 12,500,000 | 101,887.50 | 2,025 | 1,500 | 50.32 |
| Swiss franc | 125,000 | 73,437.50 | 1,620 | 1,200 | 45.33 |
| Canadian dollar | 100,000 | 64,180.00 | 743 | 550 | 86.38 |

*Source:* www.cme.com.
*As of April 13, 2001.

only $1,620.00. The Swiss franc rises by 20 points and each point is worth $12.50, so you have made $250, or a 15 percent return on your initial investment. Considering that the entire trade can take 15 minutes, this is intoxicating stuff. Even if you include in the calculation the maintenance margin on deposit with the broker (which may be in the form of an interest-bearing T-bill), your return is still 9 percent. Of course, you actually have to execute the trade that closes the position, and pay the broker his commission. Let's say you pay $25 for the "round trip," plus some $7.00 in exchange fees. Now you have a return of $218 on $2,820, or 7.7 percent (plus the T-bill interest). In comparison, no risk-free investment (a U.S. Government security) pays as much as 7.7 percent per annum, the rate of return, net of expenses, that you just made in 15 minutes.

People go a little crazy when they realize the power of leveraging. If you traded six hours a day and made one trade every 15 minutes, you could make 24 trades a day, times $218 per trade is $5,232 per day, times 220 trading days is $1.15 million per year. And that's trading only one contract. Of course, you could use your gains to buy more contracts, a process called pyramiding, and become obscenely rich in no time. Such greed-inspired fantasies are the real reason first-time futures traders tend to lose their shirts. They simply forget that the trade can go against them in 15 minutes, too.

Instead of using the full leverage allowed by the exchange, let's say you prefer leverage of 3:1, meaning you have cash on hand in the account equal to one-third the value of the contract. In the Swiss franc example, that would be $26,145.83. Now the $218 gain, expressed as a rate of return, is only 0.83 percent. It's also 44 percent per annum over the course of the year, if you take no losses and do not pyramid your gains. In the same way, when you lose the 20 points instead of gaining them, the loss is only 0.83 percent of your stake, instead of 7.7 percent.

You need to determine how much leverage to use, in advance of making the trade, if you have any hope of putting gains and losses in perspective. Some managers will risk 10 percent or 20 percent of capital in any single trade. If you had a 10 percent stop loss against the highly leveraged trade, that would be 28 points, or $280. Today, the Swiss franc futures contract average daily high-low range is well over 100 points. You would be sure to be stopped out at a loss on any long trade that was not initiated at the day's low. In contrast, if you had a 10 percent stop-loss rule in the 3:1 leverage situation, you would be willing to lose as much as $2,615, or 209 points. Your loss of 209 points is wider than the normal daily high-low, so you can place your stop-loss order with a fair chance of not being stopped out by a mere random move. A high-leverage trader can't afford to be stopped out, and so he is; the low-leverage trader can afford to be stopped out, and so he can hold a position longer and for greater gain—a virtue in a trending market. The high-leverage trader has a high volatility of returns; the low-leverage trader has a low volatility of returns. It has nothing to do with currencies or with futures, and everything to do with the choice of leverage. You have heard the maxim that you need enough capital to trade. This is why.

*Volatility of returns is not necessarily a function of the security being traded, but rather a function of leverage.* Stocks are, statistically, more volatile than currencies. If everyone traded stocks on the maximum leverage allowed (50 percent), as many first-time traders would go broke as are reputed to go broke in commodities. John Meriwether took Long-Term Capital Management (LTCM) into bankruptcy by trading the least volatile of all securities: U.S. Government bonds. In each trade, he was often looking for less than 20 points—but on thousands of contracts and with no stop-loss orders. In some trades, the leverage was infinite, because LTCM had sweet-talked the banks and brokers into booking the trades with no cash deposit at all. Everyone was so beguiled by theoretical elegance that they all forgot the most basic rules of trading and money management.

Leverage requires discipline. You can have a so-so trading system that dictates entries and exits, but if you have great money market discipline, you can succeed. If you decide to trade currencies as an asset class, or any other commodity in the futures market, you must repeat to yourself every night, preferably 25 times, before going to bed: *volatility of returns is more often a function of leverage than of the security being traded.* Your results are more traceable to your trading plan (including money management) than to "the market."

## The Newfound Popularity of FX

You have probably seen an advertisement touting foreign exchange as an investment, or you have received an e-mail, like this one from "joe454@hongkong.com":

Do You Have the Yen to Be a Millionaire?

100% return in less than 90 days! Unique Strategy Trading in the International Currency Markets! Largest MarketPlace in the World! Get our Reports, Charts and Strategies on the U.S. Dollar vs Japanese yen and euro dollar.

Example: A $5,000 Investment in the yen vs the dollar, "properly positioned," on 08/18 could have returned $15,184.45 on 09/19/99. For a "FREE NO OBLIGATION" Just Click Below to visit our website . . .

When you follow up on these ads, you find that the "broker" will open an account for you for as little as $5,000 and direct you to buy or sell options on currencies, for which you will be charged $250 for entering the trade and another $250 on exiting the trade, also on the "broker's" advice.

What's wrong with this picture?

Aside from shamelessly overcharging in trade commissions, *nothing*. It is perfectly true that buying a call option on the Japanese yen on August 18, 1999, and selling it a month later could have resulted in a very large gain. From 113.10 yen to the dollar on 08/18, the yen appreciated by 5.26 yen to 107.84 on 09/20/99. We can deconstruct the transaction like this: a $5,000 premium on a $300,000 option (1.667 percent of the face amount) would have returned $14,632.80, very close to what the "broker" is claiming you "could" have made. (He doesn't actually say anyone did.) We don't know the strike price of the option, so that is just the raw gain on a spot-to-spot basis. September 19 was a Sunday in 1999, so we can question the exact arithmetic, but the principle is sound. So how do we know that succumbing to a bucket shop come-on like this is foolish?

First, the purveyors of this particular account will not send you a track record of their recommendations. A track record is absolutely essential before you accept any advice. It must contain every recommendation, not just the ones that yielded a profit, and it must display the ratio of winning trades to losing trades. In options, when you have a losing trade, the most you lose is the option premium (and the commission), but obviously it only takes one bad trade to lose the entire $5,000 stake. This specific e-mail was sent in early 2001. Why is it naming one trade from 18 months earlier? Doesn't the broker have a more recent success?

Second, who is this "broker?" It is one of the anomalies of the modern trading world *that spot foreign exchange is unregulated by any government authority anywhere in the world.* In the United States, the Commodities Futures Trading Commission and the National Futures Association may grind their teeth, but their authority to regulate the currency futures market does not extend to the spot market. In the spot market, every trade is a private transaction between parties—in this case, you and the broker. There is no "board" or exchange where the price of a trade is posted. If the "broker" tells you that the premium to buy a call option is 1.667 percent of the face amount, you have no way of checking it (except to consult several such "brokers").

The word "broker" is put in quotation marks because many of these companies are not registered and regulated banks or brokers within the generally accepted meaning of those terms. Real banks and brokers are licensed by governments and subject to various rules and audits. Among those rules are the requirements to segregate funds by client account (except in the case of a "pool"), to report every transaction to the owner of the account, and so on. In the case of spot foreign exchange transactions, the "broker" has to execute the trade by booking it with a bank. Just as stock brokers and their clearing firms are the ultimate repositories of equity share certificates—proof of ownership—banks are where money is deposited. If you buy a yen contract and fail to offset it, at the maturity date you would literally be expected to pay the $300,000 (in dollars) into a bank and in turn receive the yen amount in a bank account in Japan. There may be several intervening counterparties, but, in the end, the "broker's" counterparty is always a bank. You want to know whether the bank is in fact a true bank that is likely to be around to make the payoff on the maturity date—and there is no deposit insurance on foreign exchange transactions. They are a contingent liability and not actually deposits unless and until delivery is made. You are therefore taking the credit risk not only of the "broker," but also of his bank. If you made this transaction and the yen did rise but you never received your cash gain, to what agency would you direct your complaint?

In this particular case, the broker is peddling options, the right but not the obligation to deliver. On the surface, this seems somewhat safer than an outright purchase or sale of currencies, but since the broker is not taking the trade for his own account, he, in turn, is laying it off to a bank. It is this bank that must make the payment of profit to the broker and thence to you, so you have the same credit risk of the bank as in a direct trade.

When you conduct your trades with a properly registered futures broker, each of your trades is guaranteed by the exchange of which the broker (or his clearing broker) is a member. In addition to their own capital, members must contribute to a pool of contingency funds held by the exchange to take care of the customers in the event of a brokerage failure. As a political preference, many people think the less government regulation, the better. In trading markets, however, government regulation does serve to protect the consumer. The Exchange Modernization Act of 2000 calls for spot brokers to become registered FCM's; as of the summer of 2001, only a few have done so.

## Ponzi All Over Again

This is not to say you should reject foreign exchange trading as a way of reducing total portfolio risk via diversification into a mostly uncorrelated asset class. It is to say that because spot foreign exchange trading is unregulated, you need to be careful. Legitimate spot FX brokers, most of them online, are emerging. One of the first was Midas DK, a firm in Denmark that is regulated by the Danish government's Financial Services Agency. The Midas site (www.tradingforex.com) is named among the top ten finance sites by the *Financial Times*. Midas offers spot foreign exchange trading, with excellent analytical support materials, for accounts as small as $10,000. Midas takes care to disclose the risks of trading foreign exchange and to control its customer accounting at the highest level of clarity and transparency.

Another broker is Money Garden (www.forex-mg.com). Its site states, up front, that accounts can be opened for as little as $1,000 and leverage can be up to 200:1. This is the real secret of the current appeal of foreign exchange trading. In stocks, the most leverage you can get (outside of options) is 50 percent. In spot foreign exchange, 200 to 1 is commonly advertised. Other sites include FX-Trade, MatchbookFX, actforex.com, hotspotfx, and equotefx.com. All these sites (and others) offer free, live quotes and vast amounts of analytical material, including advanced charting capabilities and commentary. Some are only matching services, like equity ECNs, which of course limits liquidity.

As discussed in the futures trading section above, 200-to-1 leverage sounds great but is a surefire way to the poorhouse. $1,000 is far too small a capital stake to allow good money management. These kinds of enticements make even respectable companies seem like con artists because the appeal is, at heart, a self-directed Ponzi scheme. The idea is that you will make a fast, high return and by reinvesting at high leverage (pyramiding), get rich quick. We mustn't forget that Ponzi's original fraud was also a form of foreign exchange trade—the purchase of international postal certificates, in a now-devalued currency, that were redeemable at an outdated fixed exchange rate in another currency. Ponzi had a valid arbitrage concept—he just didn't execute it, and instead was able to give high returns to old investors out of the initial capital from the new. Nobody is suggesting that the new spot brokers are fraudulent or are running a Ponzi scheme—instead, they lure you into running a Ponzi scheme on yourself with dreams of unrealistic returns based solely on leverage.

Assuming you had sufficient capital and eschewed high leverage, why would you want to trade in the unregulated spot market instead of in the regulated futures market? There are three issues here: (1) regulatory protection, (2) the price advantage of round-lot trading, and (3) liquidity. Regulatory protection has developed over many years in the futures market and is not to be dismissed lightly. More on this subject below. As for round-lot trading and liquidity, proponents of spot trading claim that the far greater degree of liquidity in the spot market permits greater volumes to be traded at any particular level without moving the market. This is only partly true. The CME recently introduced big-lot trading for blocks of 100 contracts or more, but up to now a 100-lot might skew the intraday price trend in futures as the broker chased the bid or the offer to satisfy the client. Even today, a 50-lot might have this effect. In the spot market, though, the same dollar amount would be a mere flea bite and could be executed without a second's thought. The very size and speed of the spot market, however, warns us of a hidden danger in trading spot: no matter what the spot broker tells you, the quote you see for retail trading is not the same as the actual interbank spot rate, and this is true whether the notional amount is a round number or an odd number. In spot, a round number would be $1 million and an odd number would be $43,000.

Spot brokers who offer trading services to individuals are not getting the real interbank spot price for you. By definition, interbank spot is a price exclusive to interbank market participants. Every participant is a market maker, meaning he must make a two-way quote (both a bid and an offer) and be prepared to stand by the quote. This is what gives a financial institution its membership card in the interbank fraternity. The only way an interbank market participant can disown his electronic or voice price quote is if the counterparty names an off-market size for the quote, either vastly smaller or vastly larger. Each currency is traded in a normal size (which changes over time). The pound, for example, is traded in $5 million increments. If a bank hits another bank's offer for pounds at $1.6505 and afterward stipulates that the size of the trade was only $100,000 or $50 million, the offering bank has a right to be annoyed—the offering trader either already had a position that he was squaring, or may have already *in the same moment* offset what he thought was a $5 million trade. The interbank spot market is unimaginably fast. An unexpectedly too-small or too-large trade throws a monkey wrench into the smooth operation of this very fast market. It's not done, or at least it's not done very often if the interbank participant wants to stay in the club. In sum, the interbank spot price is reserved for professionals who stand prepared to make a two-way market at agreed-on sizes with one another, based on credit arrangements already established. Brokers almost certainly do not qualify for credit lines at the big trading banks. Most trading today is done over specialized electronic platforms (which eliminates, to some extent, any misunderstanding over size), and the major world banks join one or more new electronic dealing networks as market makers. Atriax, for example, is a network of about 50 banks that, together, control about half of the total daily volume. Atriax will allow major multinationals, and some brokers, access to their screens. Atriax is owned by Chase Manhattan, Citibank, a unit of Citigroup Inc., Deutsche Bank, and Reuters, and no doubt they and their customers do want the smaller retail business, but it's unlikely to be at the same prices as for prime names.

One reason is that if they are true brokers, they do not make a two-way price but only hit the bid or offer of the specific banks with which they have a credit relationship. When you read the fine print of the spot brokers enticing the retail market, you see that they typically have a relationship with only one or two banks, or a handful at the most. Even if the brokers could aggregate several retail trades at once (the brokers say they do not), the average size of each trade falls well below the real size of the normal interbank trade. It's only logical that the bank offering the supposed spot service has already marked up the trade by widening the bid-offer spread, just as they do for multinational corporations and any other counterparty that does not reciprocate with a two-way market-making price of its own. Therefore, when a broker says you are getting the interbank spot price, it's almost certainly not true. There is only one way you can check the price quote you see or hear from a spot broker: you would have to have access to the same screens as the professionals. On Bloomberg and Reuters, for example, which cost a minimum of $1,500/month, you could see the bids and offers of every bank in the real interbank spot market fraternity.

Another reason why you are not really getting the interbank spot quote is that the retail market is nearly all speculative. It is not motivated by actual capital flows or payment flows (for goods and services). The banks that service the spot brokers know that the retail crowd will buy in the morning and sell in the afternoon, according to some obvious technical indicators, or sell in the morning and buy in the afternoon. A popular approach, for example, is to buy the foreign currency if it opens above the previous day's close and makes a new 24-hour high within the first 90 minutes. The banks know they will be selling foreign currencies into this environment. They also know that the retail crowd will take profit and offset the trades anywhere from 20 to 40 points higher (if they are correct) or 10 to 15 points lower (if they are not). Three guesses how they skew the bids and offers. The retail spot market is a profit center for the banks, just like the corporate market. And take a second look at cost. Brokers say they are adding 5 pips (0.0005) and there are no other commissions. But 5 pips on a trade worth €100,000 is $50, and you would pay the $50 twice, once when buying and once when selling—whereas you can do a "round-trip" with a futures broker for $25 or less.

Finally, a reason to worry about trading the retail spot market is: what happens when a crisis comes along? A spot trade, by definition, settles two days later. If you have a winning position and you want to roll it over into the next day, there is an interest rate charge associated with the rollover. In most cases, the yield curve is "normal"—overnight and short-term money is cheaper than medium-term and longer-term money. The retail spot trader either pays or receives the overnight interest rate, depending on whether he is long or short the higher interest rate currency. But published overnight rates are for large sums lent and borrowed by large institutions with big credit lines with one another. The smaller and less capitalized the institution, the smaller the lines and the higher the rollover interest rate. The overnight rate for a spot broker is many basis points higher than when Citibank is doing the rollover. It can easily happen that a position rolled over on each of 30 days will incur cumulative interest charges that are higher than the single 30-day interest charge embedded in a futures contract.

In a crisis, moreover, the overnight rate can leap to 50 percent or 500 percent or any other high number, depending on how determined the affected central bank is feeling. Before the euro came into existence, the French central bank did this whenever the French franc was under speculative pressure, as did the Bank of England in the 1992 sterling crisis. During the Asia crisis in October 1998, the Hong Kong Monetary Authority raised the overnight rate to 300 percent. Technically, a seller of Hong Kong dollars is borrowing them from a bank in Hong Kong, and is suddenly, unexpectedly, and irreversibly charged that rate. He is quickly motivated to close out the speculative trade. But it's too late for the retail spot trader, who will definitely get nailed with the charge in the form of a huge variance in the bid for his HK$ from the day before. Most recently, the crisis in the Turkish lira resulted in overnight lending rates at 50 percent and above. Yes, the market is perfectly liquid in the sense that there are lots of market participants—but you will not like the cost.

In futures, these one-time charges make their way into the price, too, which already incorporates the interest rate differential between the two countries. But the impact is more limited, unless the futures contract is exactly two days from maturity. When a contract has just become "top step," meaning it has about three months to go to maturity and is now the most-traded and liquid, the effect is muted.

Finally, while the emergence of a third tier in foreign exchange trading is interesting—these enterprises are exploiting the unexplored market for retail FX trading—you have to ask yourself why the big-name banks and brokers are not offering the service. The answer most likely lies in their unhappy experiences with allowing individuals to trade FX. Several cases are known in which the individual simply refused to pay up on losing trades. Some of these individuals are related to royal families in the Middle East and Europe, and some are self-made millionaires.

This is why FX trading is conspicuous by its absence in the high net-worth individual business of U.S. banks, growing by leaps and bounds out of the ashes of the stodgy old trust departments (which used to invest chiefly in U.S. Treasuries and maybe a blue chip or two, but are far more aggressive nowadays). Hardly any of these cases ever made it into the mainstream press, for the obvious reason that the deals are private contracts that don't need to be disclosed, and banks would be embarrassed if the news got out. The first rule of banking is "Know your customer," so to be stiffed by a high net-worth individual is galling. Legally, a spot foreign exchange contract is the simplest and most binding of contracts, made orally and evidenced by the confirmation notice sent by the bank. It says, in essence, "I owe you." In most cases, all the banks had to do was debit the account of the individual who had the losing trade. When important individuals complain, however, banks tend to eat the loss themselves, since most such customers bring substantial other business to the bank and there is the reputation risk that the individual would go to court or to the press, or both.

The most famous case was actually a futures case, but it illustrates the difficulty of working with prima donna high net-worth clients. It involved millionaire Henryk de Kwiatkowski, who lost more than $300 million trading foreign exchange at Bear, Stearns and took the firm to federal court—and, to the amazement of the entire industry, won ($122 million, later raised to $164 million for loss-of-interest earnings). De Kwiatkowski had a reputation as a gambler (backgammon, horses) and had, in 1992, made a $82 million gain in currency futures in the space of three months. Advised by Bear, Stearns economist Larry Kudlow and ex-Federal Reserve Board member Wayne Angell, de Kwiatkowski eventually amassed a $6.5-billion position and at one point had to increase his good-faith deposit by $250 million. On a single day (January 9, 1995), he lost $99 million. As the positions continued to move against him, he continued to hold, on the prospect of getting it back later. The court's decision hinged on his not receiving (or claiming that he had not received, although admitting he didn't open all his mail) a research advisory from a lesser analyst at Bear, Stearns, warning against his currency outlook.

De Kwiatkowski was an owner of race horse-breeding Calumet Farms and an experienced gambler; he was also an experienced trader who had made huge profits trading currencies in the past. He had signed all the risk disclosure documents pertaining to the trading account. He made a mistake in judgment for which he was unwilling to take responsibility. The case is ongoing in the appeals courts, but the banking and brokerage industries have learned a very public lesson: high-net-worth individuals think the rules don't apply to them. Retail spot FX trading is not offered to individuals at major banks and brokerages because if rich people behave this way, imagine how much worse it can be when the average Joe takes a loss in a fast-moving market.

## Electronic versus Telephone Trading

In both spot and futures trading, you have the choice of trading electronically or using a human broker with whom you speak on the telephone. Electronic trading generally is cheaper in commission cost and vastly more expensive in terms of your time spent correcting errors. Some electronic brokers lean over backward when an order goes awry; others lack the ability to track the order flow—or lack a good error-resolution process. Some individual traders report no problems with electronic trading; others run through electronic brokers like picky teenagers through blue jeans. It's hard to know whether the fusspots have authentic gripes or are just bad traders. Nearly all futures professionals favor using the telephone, whereas nearly all spot-market professionals use electronic entries, having had the capability from the early 1980s.

It is serious business to lodge a complaint against an individual or broker in the futures market, because an innocent error can swiftly degenerate into an imputation of improper behavior. Various scandals over the years, including a controversial sting operation by the FBI, have left an impression, among the public, that futures brokers are not to be trusted [David Greisling and Laurie Morse, *Brokers, Bagmen & Moles: Fraud and Corruption in the Chicago Futures Markets* (John Wiley & Sons, 1991)]. The National Futures Association (NFA), which is not a government agency but rather a private-sector industry association under the regulatory authority of the Commodity Futures Trading Association (which *is* a government agency), responds ferociously to accusations of wrongdoing—both the accuser and the accused are put under the microscope. These days, the National Futures Association claims to have a "sophisticated surveillance system" to monitor unusual trading patterns, patterns of conduct, and abnormalities in both regular brokerage activity and electronic trading. According to the NFA website (www.nfa.futures.org), NFA "specialists will investigate allegations of pre-arranged trading, accommodation trading, trading ahead of customers, crossed orders, out-trade problems or lost orders. We also will investigate complaints from public customers about such problems as improper fill prices or the mishandling of accounts. Quality is important."

The majority of individual traders in the futures market will never smell the slightest hint of any wrongdoing. The chief grievance among individuals with small accounts is that they seem invariably to lose a point or two on their fills. This usually means that they asked for a transaction "at the market" and they are looking at a live screen that shows the current bid-offer. Their fill, however, is one or two points off what the screen shows. This is called "slippage" and, over the course of a year, it can add up to a lot of money—even the difference between a winning year and a losing year. Sometimes, slippage may be a function of having a broker who is not a member of the exchange and has to pass the trade through to a clearing member for execution. Slippage can arise when you use an "introducing broker," too. Another grievance is the sometimes big discrepancy between prices on the full contract and on an e-mini contract. This occurs regularly between CME currency futures prices and the CBOT Mid-Am mini-futures prices. It's annoying but not actionable.

## The Human Computer Is the Best Computer

Placing orders with a human broker has many advantages. In using telephone orders, you have the choice of every kind of order that has ever been devised, including contingency orders ("if this, then that"). Most electronic order systems cannot accept every order type. More important, the probability of a misunderstanding or a mistake is far lower when you use the telephone. Nearly every broker tape-records client calls. If you said "sell" when you meant "buy," or if the broker misquoted a price, it can always be untangled decisively by listening to the tape. Also, a good broker knows your account. He parses it before the market opens every morning, to make sure that somebody else's soybeans were not put into your account, which deals mostly with Swiss francs. He verifies that his trade tickets from yesterday match your statement today. This is an invaluable time-saving service whether you are a fastidious or a sloppy bookkeeper. In addition, he may take it upon himself to guide you in trade selection or money management. If you really want to buy Japanese yen but he happens to know that his order flow is all on the sell side, without disclosing other clients' confidential information, he can herd you to a lesser position, the opposite position, or no position at all. If you are getting overextended by way of leverage, he may gently suggest that you have too many positions or your stops are too far away.

A good broker is an asset, but even the best broker has an inherent conflict if you, the customer, have a disagreement with his back office. You have to consider whose side it is most logical for him to take. Let's say you made a telephone call to the brokerage's overnight desk and the content of the call is in dispute. The call should have been recorded, but may not have been recorded, or mysteriously the tape can't be found or has been erased. There is a simple solution—get your own tape recorder (and obey all the relevant laws about disclosing your taping of calls to the other party). Another self-protective action you must take is to keep a log of all trades. The log, called a "blotter" in institutional trading rooms, should contain the date and time of each transaction, as well as the person with whom you made the transaction and the ticket number given the transaction by the broker, as well as the number of contracts, price, and whether it was a purchase or sale. Without this information, and your back-up tape, disputes can be impossible to resolve *in your favor.* When you receive confirmation of your trades, you need to check every entry. You have only 24 to 48 hours to dispute a confirmation or a statement, depending on the broker and the exchange. For example, say you did a euro/yen trade. The base currency is the yen, not the dollar.

Your gain or loss will be maintained on your statement in yen terms. This can be easy to overlook, especially since the standard FCM statement is extremely user-unfriendly and hard to read in the first place. If you had a gain and now the yen is falling, you could have booked a profit in your personal book-keeping system that is now rapidly disappearing on the broker's statement—but you don't notice, because the yen amount remains the same, and that is what is displayed. If you can't prove that you ordered the yen sold for dollars, or that the content of a phone call is as you say, you are out of luck. The brokerage will always take the interpretation of a disputed event that is the most favorable to its bottom line, and so will your broker, however friendly you may think the relationship. Your broker is not your friend. He is a businessman who is making a living by taking some percentage of the brokerage commission you generate on each contract traded. Stop and think about how much money you put in his pocket every year. Let's say he gets $5 per contract round-trip and you do trades involving 500 contracts per year. That's only $2,500 for the broker. It may be undignified and unseemly, but the broker is literally watching every $5. If you are a big customer, generating $25,000 per year for the broker, you may get cut a little slack and you may be invited to the Christmas party—but don't forget that any give-back by the broker is coming out of his pocket.

Do brokers offer good research and opinions? Some do and some do not. The only way you can evaluate research and opinions is to keep a log of recommendations and how they worked out—a tedious process. Keep in mind that if you are getting the advice, so is everyone else. This brings up, again, the age-old paradox of following the crowd. If the crowd is mostly wrong in the end, and few people wind up with profits, let alone extraordinary profits, why would you want to do what everyone else is doing? Besides, the order flow that your particular broker sees may be small potatoes in the grand scheme of things. Unless you have a very large account that is handled by a broker with other very large accounts, the broker's opinion may be worth little. Some critics charge that if a broker knew how to trade, he'd be a trader and not a broker. This may be true of some brokers, many of whom are out-to-pasture jocks, but it is unfair to others who are genuinely enjoying the hurly-burly of an active market: speaking with traders, making knife-edge decisions, and being in the know and part of an exciting process.

Most of all, futures brokers are highly regulated, and they take oversight by the National Futures Association and Commodity Futures Trading Commission very seriously indeed. While they make a living taking a small piece of the commission you pay, and thus have an incentive for you to trade as much as possible, at the same time they have to conduct their relationship with you in a responsible and ethical way, and there are almost no excuses for foul-ups. They are not all saints, though. In choosing a broker, you can check out the reputation of the firm or the individual broker at the National Futures Association. Its Web site has a segment named Background Affiliation Status Information Center ("Basic"), where you can type in the name of the individual or the broker and find out how many cases he has been involved in and whether there were "reparations" (money payments to aggrieved customers). The absence of disciplinary actions doesn't mean the house or the individual has never made a mistake or mistreated a client; it may mean the mistake just wasn't caught. Still, a record with lots of black spots should be avoided.

## Summary

The foreign exchange market is big, liquid, open 24 hours, and trended, all of which makes it an ideal market for individuals to trade. Any close observer of developments in international economics and finance can become qualified to trade currencies without having to learn esoteric facts, as in other commodities markets ("How is the cocoa crop responding to all the rain in Ghana?") Whether you are trading foreign exchange as an asset class or hedging a position in another security such as a foreign stock, you should go directly to the currency in question and bypass the dollar index. The dollar index is of interest to academics and newspaper headline writers; it is not a real exchange rate. Trading currencies is best done in the futures market, where regulations have been crafted over the years to protect your interests; the emerging third tier of spot brokers is intriguing, but it has yet to be demonstrated that they deliver any substantial benefits that would outweigh the absence of customer protection. Whether trading futures or spot, however, you must remember that the variability of your return is largely a function of the leverage you choose to implement your trading plan, and is not necessarily due to the volatility inherent in the currency market itself. Do not be seduced by fantasies of huge gains that are based only on pyramiding at high leverage, akin to a Ponzi scheme that you run on yourself.

# Chapter 7

# ADVENTURES IN SYSTEM BUILDING

*Success is the ability to go from one failure to another with no loss of enthusiasm.*

Winston Churchill

Technical analysis has been around in the equities market, in one form or another, since the turn of the twentieth century. Today's foreign exchange system of floating rates came into existence in 1973. Right away, analysts observed that exchange rates are highly trended, and they were among the first nontraditional class of securities to be submitted to technical analysis when PC-based software emerged in the early 1980s (first CompuTrac, then Metastock). Actually, before then, European American Bank, in 1978, and Citibank, in 1980, launched mainframe-based technical analysis of currencies. It was wildly successful from the very beginning, partly because the performance track record of currency forecasters was so dismal. Fundamentals-based forecasting remains relatively dismal today. Going into the euro launch on January 1, 1999, for example, the consensus of opinion was that the euro would immediately rise from $1.17 on the first day to $1.35 to $1.40 by the end of the year. This view was based on the euro's becoming (1) a competitor of the dollar for transactions and for reserve currency status and (2) an expected capital inflow into a newly efficient European economy, once the friction of national currencies was removed. It didn't happen. Instead, the euro fell as low as 82.50 cents.

193

# The Failure of Forecasting

The failure of currency forecasting has many perfectly reasonable explanations, plus a few that are not so reasonable. The market may choose to ignore what is normally a key fundamental factor (such as the huge U.S. trade deficit) in favor of a different factor (offsetting capital inflows into the United States). Forecasts turn out to be wrong because economists and analysts do not recognize, in a timely fashion, that minor factors are major factors—for example, the relative inefficiency and low productivity growth of European industry, due in part to rigid labor markets, that have inhibited the expected capital flow into Europe. Then there is the process of forecasting itself. Data may be old and lagging, or later revised by government agencies to give an effect that is exactly opposite from the preliminary release. Often, data are just plain bad—they don't describe what they purport to describe.

Economists and analysts are swayed by one another; they may wish to be contrarian, or to avoid the appearance of being contrarian. In one instance, a major foreign exchange advisory service persisted in forecasting the dollar higher, despite clear evidence to the contrary, because "the U.S. is the best country in the world." This patriotic point of view did not hold up in the face of the yen's rising from 240 to 176 over the period of the forecasts. (It also did not work to save Mr. de Kwiatkowski from losing $300 million nearly 20 years later, speculating that the dollar would rise "because it should," as described in Chapter 6.)

Most of all, forecasters are influenced by the factor that is fashionable at the moment, whether it "should" be dominant or not. There are just too many factors to follow all at once. The art of economics has not delivered a unified and coherent theory of how modern economies work, let alone a single model of what determines exchange rates. Michael Rosenberg, in *Currency Forecasting—A Guide to Fundamental and Technical Models of Exchange Rate Determination* (Richard D. Irwin, 1996), summarizes the various theories: purchasing power parity and the balance of payments model, the monetary approach, the portfolio balance approach, and so on. The list can make you dizzy.

Worse for the currency forecaster, it is hard to extrapolate foreign exchange action from the globalization of capital markets. Up to about 1998, relative inflation and relative bond yields reliably predicted capital flows. In his book, Rosenberg presents a chart showing the dollar/Deutschemark exchange rate overlaid on the real (inflation-adjusted) 10-year bond interest rate differential between the United States and Germany. The correlation is well-nigh perfect. If you perform the same exercise today, however, you see big unexplained divergences. (See Figures 7.1 through 7.3.)

Now we have equity flows to contend with, and, unlike inflation and interest rates, equity fund reallocations and merger-and-acquisition deals are private and not disclosed until the very last minute, if then. This is a real wild card for currency forecasters. Finally, currency forecasters have gotten an undeserved bad rap because of the ridiculous procedure of averaging a group of forecasts—a wrong-headed process used by newspapers, magazines, and consulting groups. Invariably, this results in a blended forecast that is practically the same as the current price. This outcome arises naturally enough because roughly half of

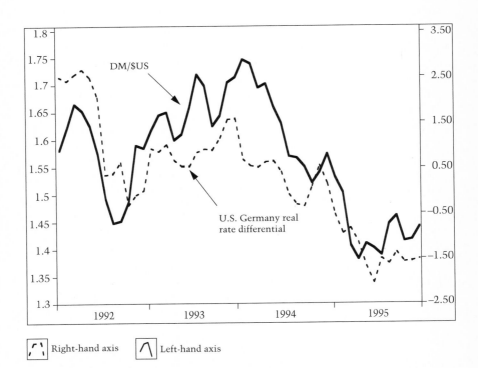

**Figure 7.1**   United States and Germany.

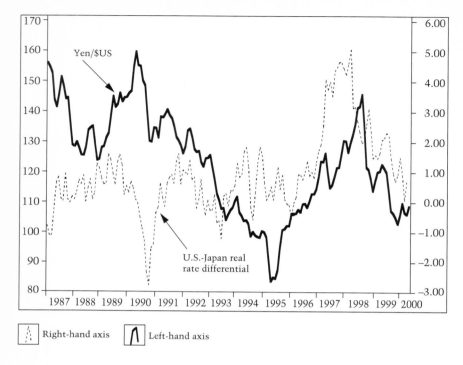

**Figure 7.2**   United States and Japan.

forecasters will see a higher rate in the future and the other half will see a lower one. Multinational corporations that need forecasts for budgeting often throw up their hands in despair and conclude: "nobody can forecast exchange rates." The averaging process is simply not valid in the first place, and, in practice, many individual forecasters have a far better than 50–50 performance record, at least over short time frames (30 days). Still, on the whole, fundamental forecasting of exchange rates tends to be pretty poor, especially for periods longer than 30 days.

## Everybody's Doing It

Already by 1985, academic economic and financial researchers had discovered that the majority of interbank currency market

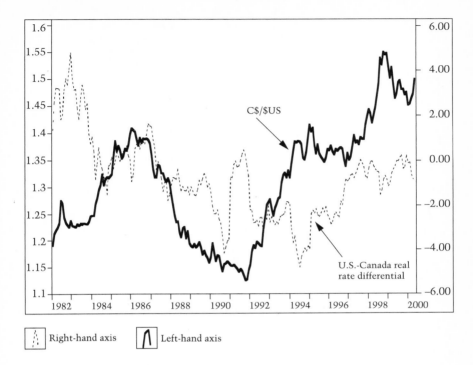

**Figure 7.3**   United States and Canada.

professionals were using technical analysis to time their trades. A study of the Group of Thirty in that year showed that a whopping 97 percent of traders at banks and 87 percent of traders at securities brokerage houses agreed that the use of technical models was having a significant effect on currency trends. That meant the price of nearly $1 trillion of daily trading volume in currencies was being set by lines on charts, and not by serious study of the economic and financial policies over which governments labor so diligently and self-importantly. The Group of Thirty study, and later studies, including several from the Federal Reserve, dished up a real puzzle to the academic community: if markets are efficient, as theory has it, how is it that financial institutions persist in trying to exploit inefficiencies in this market, with huge amounts at stake—and succeed?

## Inefficiencies Galore

The answer, obviously, is that the market is not efficient. *Any* move in exchange rates may be random, but not *every* move. Trading is not the same as a series of coin tosses, in which the outcome of each toss is independent of all the others. If a currency has been moving in a particular direction, the mind searches for a reason. The purported "cause" of major trends can usually be summarized in a sentence or two. Minor trends in currencies have been known to occur because a large enough group of traders believed a rumor or a theory that later turned out to be perfectly wrong. (See Figure 7.4.) The foreign exchange market is often rumor-ridden for hours or days at a stretch. Sometimes the rumor is started by someone whose position is going against him (akin to malicious postings in stock market chat rooms). At other times, the rumor is true ("Treasury Secretary Rubin is resigning"), if not particularly relevant to the underlying trend.

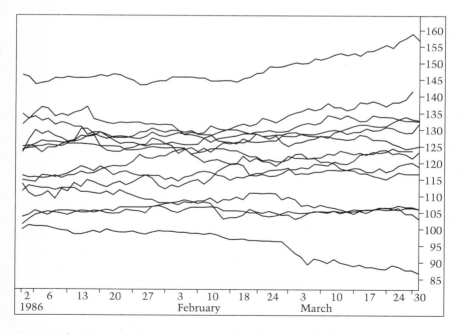

**Figure 7.4**     The myth of yen repatriation—value of the yen in the first quarter over 14 years.

Forecasters and traders alike can't help but have a mental construct of where each bit of rumor or news fits into the grand scheme of things, and the grand scheme of things is not one of randomness. Because we have so many theories of how exchange rates are determined, and most are mutually exclusive, only one idea can hold sway at any one time. This is the one to bet on—but the *size* and *duration* of the bet will vary according to how well it fits into the individual trader's mental model. At some level of consciousness, no foreign exchange trader is immune from having a model of what *should* happen next in the foreign exchange market, based on what has just been happening. John Maynard Keynes, who was both an economist and a successful commodities speculator, said: "Practical men, who believe themselves to be quite exempt from any intellectual influences, are usually the slaves of some defunct economist."

Professional foreign exchange traders pretend to be hardheaded and purely market driven, but at the same time, they must respond—and fast—to developments in the news. These include economic statistics like the Consumer Price Index (CPI) and industrial production, sentiment indicators like the Conference Board and University of Michigan consumer confidence indices, changes in interest rates by central banks, intervention by central banks, statements by important figures, and many other factors. The important point is that *any* news could be a catalyst in the foreign exchange market, whereas in other markets the relevant and market-moving news is generally confined to a narrow set. This makes "event risk" in foreign exchange higher than in any other market.

In addition, all the major financial institutions see order flow. This is supply and demand in the purest sense, and it is also "inside information" in the true meaning of the phrase. An international mutual fund may be raising its allocation to the eurozone and reducing its allocation to Japan, for example. When Fidelity and Vanguard call their banks to buy euros and sell yen, the amounts can be enormous—hundreds of millions of dollars. The same thing happens when a multinational corporation decides to repatriate funds for a dividend, or repatriate the proceeds from a foreign bond offering, or just to "sweep" cash out of its foreign subsidiaries to avoid having to borrow at home. Cross-border mergers and acquisitions have become commonplace, and many of them are numbered in the billions of dollars, pounds, euros, and yen. In some instances, the amounts are so large that the trades have to be spaced out over the course of several days or weeks, to avoid moving the market. Who is to say that the banks do not put on the same positions for themselves? In most securities markets, including the equity market and futures market, such "front running" is illegal, but it is not specifically prohibited to banks conducting their own and their clients' business. Knowledge (or expectations) of order flows will influence the forecast, even when this information may be incorrect. Traders may be making the fallacy of composition—because they are buying yen for fund managers to get into Japanese stocks, everybody must be doing the same thing.

Another kind of transaction where big financial institutions can anticipate or see order flow is the "carry trade." This is a deal in which a party borrows a sum of money in a low-cost currency such as the Swiss franc or the Japanese yen, and converts the proceeds to a currency in which high returns can be made. If the loan is made at a fixed interest rate and the investment is also made at a fixed interest rate (notes or bonds), the investor has a surefire return in the form of the spread between the two—as long as the currency in which he has borrowed does not become more expensive to repay. As soon as the borrowed currency appreciates to a level near the borrower's break-even point, he can be expected to "cover" the loan. Because of the incorrect euro forecast mentioned above, many European companies got themselves in a bind with euro/yen carry trades.

Over the past few years, the covering of dollar and euro/yen carry trades has been a primary influence in accelerating the rise of the yen once an uptrend begins, and exacerbating the problem by triggering successive covering action at higher and higher levels. Often, it seems that virtually all yen carry trades are periodically squeezed out of the market, whereupon momentum in the yen uptrend abates. In other words, managers using the yen carry trade sometimes exit at precisely the worst moment (and, presumably, at a loss). The financial institutions conducting the foreign exchange leg of carry-trade transactions know how much yen volume is likely to be out there at various levels (which is easy enough to calculate). More importantly, they know which side of the yen bid-offer is going to be hit. Who is to say that they do not skew the yen deliberately to flush out the owners of yen carry trades?

Newcomers to the foreign exchange market often ask whether there is seasonality in currencies. Commodities are being traded for U.S. dollars, but producers of commodities are located everywhere, and they can be expected to convert U.S. dollar proceeds into their home currencies on a seasonal basis when the commodity itself (e.g., Canadian grain) is seasonal. On the whole, seasonal influences are minor, except for the myth of the Japanese fiscal year-end repatriation. Japanese companies close their books on March 31 each year. To dress up their balance sheets, it is believed, they wait until the final quarter of the fiscal year (the first calendar quarter) to repatriate overseas funds into yen. Whenever the yen rises in a first calendar quarter, people nod their heads sagely and pronounce that it's due to repatriation. This is simply not so. From 1986 to 2001, the yen fell in more years than it rose during the first calendar quarter. The story seems to have started in 1995, when the yen appreciated, for the second year in a row during the first calendar quarter. It didn't rise in 1996, 1997, 1999, 2000, or 2001—but it did do it once more, in 1998.

A study performed for this book by Stuart Johnston, founder of Software & System, shows that if you had bought the yen on February 4 of every year from 1978 to 2000, and sold it on March 29 or March 30 of the same year, you would have had gains in only 10 of 23 years. The average gain was 2.558 points in futures—but the average loss would have been higher: 2.621 points. Figure 7.4 shows a different study: the spot price of the yen, over the relevant period, for 14 years. There is no seasonal trend. In short, it would be dead wrong to count on any yen-boosting "repatriation effect." It's a myth. Oddly, there *is* a slight seasonal effect from mid-August to end-September over the past 14 years. Japanese companies close their books for the half fiscal year at end-September. But this effect is deemed weak, when statistically it is the only significant instance of seasonality.

# The Big Kahuna of Inefficiency—Intervention

Another reason we know the foreign exchange market is not efficient is the prevalence of central bank intervention. Aside from the
occasional foray into stock market support, generally done only by
Japan and by a few emerging-market governments such as South
Korea, foreign exchange is the only "security" in which governments feel they have the right to fiddle with the working of a free
market. On a few notable occasions, the U.S. Treasury (working
through the New York Federal Reserve Bank) has intervened to
change the value of the dollar against other currencies. The first occasion was an emergency dollar defense taken in November 1978,
when confidence in the dollar was at a low. The second occasion—
the Plaza Accord, in September 1985—was designed to do exactly
the opposite: bring down the too-strong dollar. In each case, foreign
central banks were enlisted to help in what is named "coordinated
intervention." Former Fed chairman Paul Volcker, with former
Deputy Finance Minister of Japan Toyoo Gyohten, wrote a wonderful book titled *Changing Fortunes: The World's Money and the
Threat to American Leadership* (Times Books, 1992), about these
and other events. The book is 10 years old but is tremendously useful for anyone trying to discern how governments think about such
matters (if governments' thinking is not an oxymoron).

When they intervene, the central banks literally call up commercial and investment banks like any other customer, and buy
or sell foreign currencies in the spot market. Amounts may range
from a few million dollars to $5 billion per day, and, in rare in-
stances, more. The Federal Reserve, the Bank of Japan, and other
central banks usually confirm that they are intervening, since
they are going after "the announcement effect" rather than trying directly to move the $1-trillion-plus daily market. All the re-
serves of all the major countries do not add up to $1 trillion, so
wishes must be horses when it comes to government currency
intervention. Usually, a single day of intervention is all it takes
to get the message across. Traders who have the wrong position
take a loss and are reluctant to put on a new position that is contrary to what the central bank wants. That doesn't mean they
put on the position that the central bank *does* want. Instead,
trading slows down to a scared crawl, and that is the desired

effect—to stop "speculative excess," which is deemed to be the rate of change and the absence of a two-way market rather than solely the direction of the change.

Where do the central banks get the money? From the tax-payer, the origin of all government money. Foreign reserves can be thought of as a country's savings. Reserves are denominated in gold or other countries' currency (actually, their notes and bonds) for the simple reason that governments can print their own, so using their own currency would hardly reflect the true situation. Intervention is always a political decision and is thus determined by the Ministry of Finance or the Treasury Department of the countries involved, and then implemented through the national central banks. (See Table 7.1.)

After the Plaza Accord, the Bank for International Settlements (BIS) issued a research paper on whether intervention actually serves the purpose for which it is intended. The paper concludes that intervention does not change trends. The BIS's latest Working Paper, "Perceived Central Bank Intervention and Market Expectations: An Empirical Study of the Yen/Dollar Exchange Rate, 1993 to 1996," says perceived intervention (which may be different from confirmed intervention) had no statistically significant effect on exchange rate levels or on the trend bias expressed by traders in news stories. It just increased uncertainty (www.bis.org/publ/work77.pdf).

**Table 7.1.** Government Reserves: Selected Countries

| Country | Official Reserves (in U.S. Dollars, Billions) |
| --- | --- |
| Japan | 361.5 |
| People's Republic of China | 171.3 |
| Hong Kong | 114.3 |
| Taiwan | 110.1 |
| Germany | 84.4 |
| United States | 65.0 |
| France | 62.6 |
| Switzerland | 52.7 |

*Source:* www.imf.org; *The Economist,* April 14, 2001, p. 100.

This hasn't stopped governments from trying, and, in recent years, we have seen many cases. The Japanese yen rose from 159.21 in April 1990 to 80.50 in April 1995, punctuated by many interventions both jointly with the United States and other countries, and by the Bank of Japan alone. At the time, the press delighted in reporting that the land under the royal palace in Tokyo was worth more than the state of California. More to the point, Japanese investors bought Paramount Pictures, Rockefeller Center, numerous golf courses, and many other properties; mispricing of currencies can have important social and political effects. Ironically, by the spring of 1998, the United States and Japan were intervening together to prevent the yen from getting too weak (less than ¥150 to the dollar). This was a direct response to China, which had been making threatening noises about devaluing its currency in the face of trade competition from Japan. At the same time, China was hinting in public that it might agree with top officials from France and Germany that it would be a good idea to diversify its reserves into the euro, which was then about to be launched. Note that when the reserves of China, Hong Kong, and Taiwan are added up, the sum is $395.7 billion, more than those of the current leader, Japan.

According to stories collected daily from the BridgeNews service, Japan intervened no fewer than 16 times during 1998, to prevent the yen from becoming too weak. Notice that sometimes the Bank of Japan was intervening "with the wind"; translated, it was buying even when the yen was already strengthening. Sometimes it worked a little and sometimes it worked a lot. It wasn't until October 6 of that year, however, that the yen finally obeyed the government's wishes. This occasioned the announcement of a ¥16-trillion plan to rescue the 20 largest banks with an injection of government capital, reinforcing the point that central bank intervention does not change sentiment toward a weak currency— or a too-strong one, either. It's the health of an economy and its financial sector that counts. (See Figure 7.5.)

Of all the world's governments, Japan is the most interventionist, or at least the most openly interventionist. Between May and December 1999, Japan spent $50 billion of its reserves in an effort to halt the strengthening yen trend. It didn't work—the yen rose from 124.62 in May to 101.41 in December. You can see the

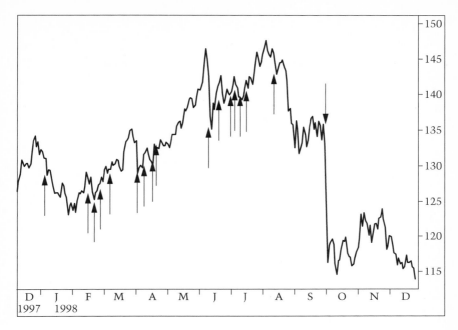

**Figure 7.5**   Intervention in the dollar/yen, 1998.

official history of Japanese intervention at www.mof.go.jp /english/feio/eO34_133.htm. Elsewhere, other central banks intervene, too, but often the intervention is not publicized. The central bank of Sweden, which intervened on behalf of the krona in 1998, announced, in April 2001, that it may do it again to restore equilibrium—or it may just raise interest rates. The Canadian and Australian central banks have intervened, as have the central banks of Russia, Turkey, Brazil, and the Hong Kong Monetary Authority—all within recent memory.

The new European Central Bank (ECB) took over responsibility for intervention from the national central banks comprising the European Monetary Union, although some of them (notably, the German Bundesbank) have been seen in the market making "adjustments" to the amount of reserves they retained, after handing over the highest proportion to the ECB. Miraculously, the adjustments always seem to be needed just when the euro is weak. The ECB itself was dilatory in making a decision to intervene to prop

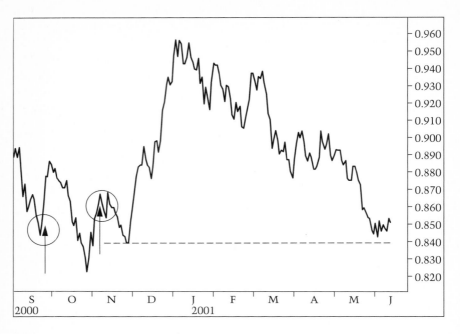

**Figure 7.6**   Intervention in the euro/dollar.

up the ailing euro, but finally did so on September 22, 2000, and again, on three days starting November 6. On the first occasion, the United States and all the other major central banks (Japan, the United Kingdom, and Canada) coordinated with the European Central Bank, but the second batch was solo. (See Figure 7.6.)

Notice that intervention seemed to do the trick for a while. Or did it? After a few months, the euro resumed its downtrend and, in June 2001, it was below the level at which the ECB had intervened during the previous November.

## Inefficiencies and Technical Analysis

Practical people think that the debate over whether markets are efficient is a waste of time. Theoretically, no advantage can be gained from technical analysis (or any other kind of analysis) if a market is truly efficient, because all participants know all the news, and they all know it simultaneously. Obviously, this is not true in the foreign exchange market, which is the extreme case of a market in which *any* news can be a catalyst for a change in prices. Because every participant cannot, literally, know everything (such as another bank's order flow), the market cannot be efficient. When relevant news does become widely known, market participants behave rationally on most occasions; however, rational trading decisions still require interpretation of events, and interpretations can be wrong as new theories evolve. Therefore, we see an ebb and flow of prices that is trended about 70 percent of the time. Cornelius Luca, the head of the foreign exchange unit at BridgeNews and author of two books on foreign exchange, agrees with this estimate of trendedness. The degree of trendedness is calculated by academics to be as low as 20 to 30 percent, but practitioners know better. A market that is big, that has many types of participants with different interests, and that is open virtually 24 hours a day—and is trended—is the technical analyst's dream come true.

## Support and Resistance

Periodically, we get forecasts and break-even export exchange rates from the Confederation of British Industry, Japanese Association of Businesses (*Keidanren*), or other industry associations and research institutes around the world. These may be taken as important support or resistance levels. In some cases they are vague, and in other cases they are quite specific; Japanese exporters like Sony, Honda, and Toyota, for example, will tell you the level they are hedging export sales, and sometimes their break-even rates. In the United States, the National Association of Manufacturers (NAM) does not publish exchange rate forecasts, although the Conference Board forecasts the euro and the yen in the monthly newsletter "Straight Talk," by chief economist Gail Fosler. The publication costs $395/year but occasionally its information and insight make it into the mainstream press (www.conference-board.org).

Usually, however, the forecasts heeded by market participants come in the form of a support and resistance range estimated by banks and brokers for their own use and the use of their clients. Some daily foreign exchange advisories run to 10 or more pages, but the most consulted nugget is the support and resistance range for the day. Today's trading range is not the only forecast—or, arguably, even the most important one—but it is the most ubiquitous and the easiest to understand.

A Federal Reserve study, on the assumption that the support and resistance band is the most important technical indicator, reviewed the daily support and resistance estimates of six financial institutions for January 1996 through March 1998. After some serious statistical analysis, the author found that "Consistent with the market's conventional wisdom, exchange rates bounced quite a bit more frequently after hitting published support and resistance levels than they would have by chance . . . 60.8% of the time on average." (Carol Osler, "Support and Resistance: Technical Analysis and Intraday Exchange Rates," *Federal Reserve Bank of New York Economic Policy Review*, July 2000, p. 61.) The author also finds that numbers ending in "0" or "5" occur more often (95 percent of the time) in the support and resistance forecasts than if they had been chosen randomly. The estimates have predictive power five days out, meaning that you could still make good trading decisions on Friday, based on support and resistance ranges estimated on Monday, although not as good as on Monday itself.

## Getting Oriented

We may argue that estimating support and resistance bands is an indirect way to arrive at entry and exit decisions. After all, support and resistance are outer limits, or extremes, and we do not expect prices to reach extremes every day. The lines are important, however, because they help us become oriented. Is it going up or is it going down? Is it moving evenly or is the move choppy? Is the slope of the trend shifting? Professional foreign exchange commentators say that demand emerges at support, and supply emerges at resistance, although we have to question whether supply and demand, in the true economic sense, have much to do with it when over 90 percent of FX trading is purely speculative. Nevertheless, it is a form of supply and demand, even if no real capital flow is being priced. On a practical level, it is often true that old resistance, once decisively penetrated, becomes new support. All the major purveyors of trading advice in the foreign exchange market name support and resistance levels, although, curiously, they do vary— and by rather a lot.

This is because there is no single correct way to estimate support and resistance. The easiest way is to draw a straight line connecting highs and another one connecting lows, and to extend them out into the future (at least one day). Now you have the problem of deciding whether to follow a strict "no penetration" rule, as famously recommended by Victor Sperandeo in *Trader Vic— Secrets of a Wall Street Master* (John Wiley & Sons, 1991), or to connect the majority of highs and lows without regard to a penetration or two. In foreign exchange, "sloppy" support and resistance are preferred to the perfectionist versions, probably because the market does frequently have an odd spike arising from one of those inefficiencies mentioned earlier—a single big deal that takes a while to digest, a mini-rally based on a false rumor that is just as quickly reversed, and so on. At the time, nobody had an explanation for the spike in the Swiss franc shown in Figure 7.7.

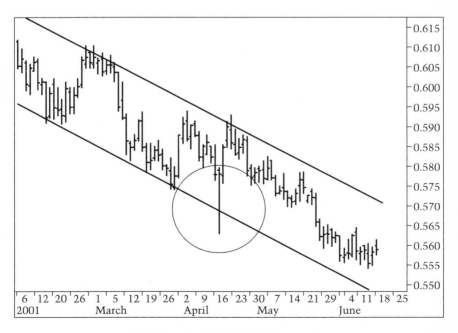

**Figure 7.7**  Mysterious Swiss franc spike.

Figure 7.8 shows the support and resistance lines in the euro leading up to the September 22, 2000, intervention by the European Central Bank and others. In this instance, just-beforehand support was being heavily taxed and was neared or met every day over several consecutive days, which presumably is what alerted the European Central Bank to an excess of negative sentiment. At the time of the intervention, the ECB stated that its goal was to restore a "two-way mentality." Intervention, however, failed in the sense that the euro resumed a steeper downtrend afterward (one of the times when old resistance failed to become new support for more than 10 days).

Newcomers to technical analysis often question why support and resistance lines are drawn parallel to one another when that doesn't always accurately describe the situation. There is no answer except the universal longing for order. Straight parallel lines are a convenient organizing principle. Notice that, in this instance, the support and resistance lines lost all their usefulness as

**Figure 7.8**  Euro support and resistance.

soon as the significant event occurred. The more important question is: do the support and resistance lines really define the trend and its range? Highs and lows are not the only measure of a security. We also have the close, the average, the median, the moving average, and so on.

Support and resistance are critical to making the correct trading decision at the correct level, but even more important is knowing the main direction of the trend. We assume—and many studies have confirmed—that trading with the main trend is the best approach. It is more profitable than any other approach, and causes less stress to the trader. Keep it in mind when you consider very short-term "set-ups" (patterns) recommended by self-styled trading advisors.

## The Magic of Linear Regressions

The only way to display support and resistance that is nonjudgmental and therefore scientific (i.e., replicable by anyone) is to draw lines parallel to a linear regression line. The linear regression is the purest form of a trend line. It is the line that minimizes the distance between itself and every point on the chart, using the least-squares method of calculation. Nearly every charting software program contains it. You have to use common sense in deciding where to start and end the trend line—usually, at an obvious major high or an obvious major low.

You have two options when you draw the channel on either side of the linear regression: (1) judgmentally determined parallel lines that are completely outside the highs and lows, called a Raff channel, or (2) the standard error channel. Standard error is like standard deviation, a measure of variation away from the linear regression (instead of variation away from a moving average, as with standard deviation). The Raff channel is useful because, when the trend changes, penetration of the outer channel is almost certainly significant. The standard error version is useful because penetration of one of the channel lines alerts you to a statistically abnormal situation, whereupon you need to pay close attention to fundamental developments and other indicators.

The only book written on the subject is now out of print: Gilbert Raff, *Trading the Regression Channel: Defining and Predicting Stock Price Trends* (Equis International, 1996). You can, however, easily teach yourself how to use the channels. You will find that prices persist in testing one or the other side of the channel, usually in a wavelike pattern. In many instances, linear regression channels are nearly the same as hand-drawn support and resistance. One technique for determining whether a big event, like intervention or an election, is causing a change in the trend is to extend the trend lines from the Event date into the future. When a channel has been in place for a while and we have a reason to think the trend might be changing, we have a terrible dilemma—which of the two channels is valid? Figure 7.9 illustrates the point.

First, we have reason to believe the trend might be changing because of a new reformist prime minister in Japan, gains in the stock market that might prefigure foreign capital inflows—and, technically, the gap that appeared just before the price bottom, which occurred about one week before the Japanese election. In

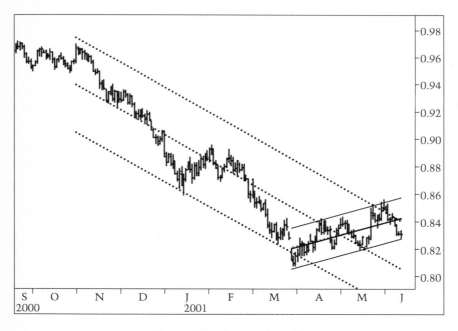

**Figure 7.9**    Two yen channels.

support of the idea that the smaller, more recent channel is the correct one, we can note that trends often end with a last convulsive move like the one shown. Second, the up move took prices above the center linear regression line for all of May and June to the date when the data end. The price has not, however, sustained a move above the top of the bigger, older channel, and in fact had only two days on which the price was entirely above it. Standard error channels allow for a few outlying errors bigger than the standard, so we really need a sustained breakout above the old downward channel before we can declare the new upward channel the winner. Notice that the last price is just at the bottom of the new up channel. If it breaks below there and sustains the break, we have to delete the new channel as just one of the waves within the grand scheme of the big channel. (See Figure 7.10.)

The Raff channel, which draws equidistant support and resistance lines just outside the highest highs and lowest lows, may be a little more useful than the standard error channel because a breakout is visually more compelling. In a standard error channel,

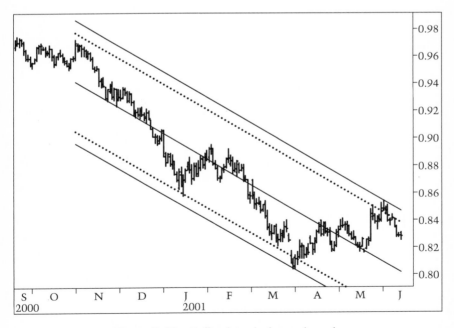

**Figure 7.10**   Raff and standard error channels.

you have to fiddle with the number of errors to make the lines "fit" the highest highs and lowest lows. Once you know the usual number of errors to use, you can predict how wide a *new* emerging channel will be when it finishes forming. This is called a "measured move" and has been a part of technical analysis lore for a very long time. (See Figure 7.11.)

By making the up channel wider, to match the width of the previous bigger channel, we do not gain anything. The lines no longer touch the highs and lows like hand-drawn support and resistance lines. On other occasions, drawing a measured move is more valuable.

The point to take away from this discussion of channels is that although the linear regression channel achieves the impossible—an objective definition of a trend and its range—it is only another tool that can be misused, and is not without risk if the user attributes too much to it or starts and ends it incorrectly. Not every top and bottom is obvious, for example, until after the fact. In currencies, linear-regression-based channels tend to be rather

**Figure 7.11**   Measured move.

long term; they last many months. It takes practice and experimentation to get the hang of drawing them correctly. When you know the fundamental and institutional picture at the same time, you may have a tendency to see changes in channels that are not there, simply because you *expect* them to be there. You can draw a series of channels from what seem to be equally valid starting points—but from which you would draw very different conclusions. (See Figure 7.12.)

By going back further in time, we see that the downtrend started long before the starting point shown in Figure 7.11. If we draw the channel starting from the highest high, the latest up move looks pretty puny—it barely makes it over the center linear regression of the longest-term channel.

Support and resistance channels, however constructed, are not a trading system. Even the most sophisticated charting software will not allow you to backtest a channel trading system when the channel starting point and ending point are determined by judgment. Channels are powerful tools that can make

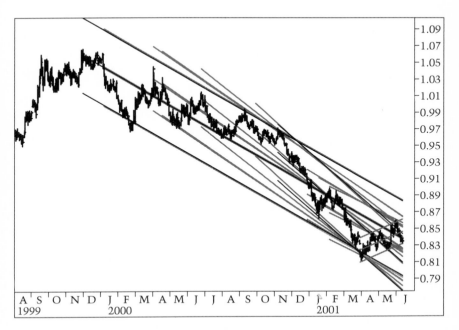

**Figure 7.12** Multiple regression channels.

all the difference in trading outcomes, but first you have to build an actual trading system.

## Average True Range Channel

Many technical indicators use the average true range (ATR) in their formulation. ATR was first described by J. Welles Wilder in, *New Concepts in Technical Trading Systems* (Trend Research, 1978). It's easy enough to understand: we know the daily trading range if we know the high and the low. Subtract the low from the high and you have the range. From this, we can easily construct a moving average of the range. When the range widens (reaches a higher number), we have two new pieces of information: (1) a struggle is going on between bulls and bears who are putting some real money behind their positions and (2) the market is getting riskier. When the range narrows, it means traders lack passion about the direction. A narrow range often precedes a breakout, so it can be as risky as a widening range.

A problem arises when we have a gap. Simply to keep subtracting the low from the high does not accurately represent what a gap means. A gap usually implies a sudden shift in perception and preferences. You can have a tiny range today after a large opening gap from yesterday. To incorporate today's range in the average would be to make the average smaller, when in fact something big happened. Thus was born average *true* range, where "true" refers to bridging the gap by changing the data that are used in calculating the range. If there is no gap, the range is the true range. If there is a gap, the average true range is calculated as the distance between today's low and yesterday's close (if it's a downward gap), or today's high and yesterday's close (if it's an upward gap). This is illustrated in Figure 7.13.

If we calculate a moving average of the average true range, we can project tomorrow's range. This is tremendously useful because it gives the maximum probable move, either up or down, from the last average price. First, we construct a moving average of the average or median price. The average is the high plus the low, divided by two; the median price is the high plus the low plus the close, divided by three, giving weight to the close

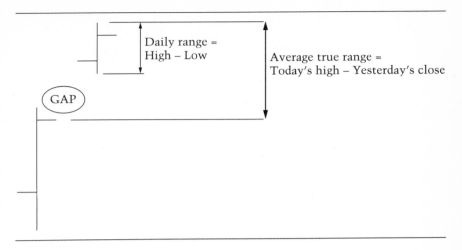

Daily range =
High – Low

Average true range =
Today's high – Yesterday's close

GAP

**Figure 7.13** Average true range.

(because, near the end of the day, many players have a stake in the close and try to move the market in the direction that favors their position). To the average or median price we add the average true range—or some multiple of the average true range, to get a channel. (See Figure 7.14.)

Now we have something we can backtest as a trading system that does not rely on any human judgment. We actually have three variables to test: (1) the number of days in the moving average of the midpoint, (2) the number of days in the average true range, and (3) the percentage of the average true range to add or subtract from the midpoint. Figure 7.14 uses six days for both the midpoint and the ATR, and 1 times the ATR. This is how we pose the question to the software: what combination of these variables would have yielded the most profit if used over the past $x$ number of days when we buy on an upside breakout of the top of the channel and sell on a downside breakout of the bottom of the channel?

Right away, there is a problem with this question. In the beginning of the period, we have a clear downtrend—and yet we have several breakouts of the top of the channel. If we buy on those topside breakouts, we will take a lot of losses. We can fiddle with elaborate rules ("Buy only on the second day of a breakout," "Buy only if the breakout is $x$ number of points over the top," and

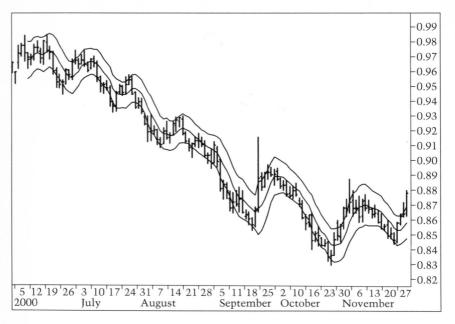

**Figure 7.14**   Average true-range channel.

so on), but these do not improve results by enough to justify the added complication. In system building, the simpler the better. We need to know the trend first and to ignore any breakouts that are not *with the trend*. Eventually, there will be an upside breakout over the channel top that *is* the real thing—an authentic reversal—but, meanwhile, we went broke because of all the times it cried "Wolf!"

One potential solution is to acknowledge that when a security is trending down, the percentage of the ATR to add to the midpoint to derive the top of the channel should be bigger than the percentage added to derive the bottom. This makes it a higher hurdle; we expect downside breakouts in a downtrend and we worry about the upside breakouts. This sounds like a good solution until you test it on real data and in real situations; remember, currencies are trended 70 percent of the time, but the transition from one trend to another is seldom a neat V-shape. If you are still using a downtrend bias for the ATR channel at the time prices are going sideways and evolving messily into an uptrend, losses become large. We can still use the ATR channel to trade currencies—it's just not a viable trading system on its own. Steve Notis, the developer of the top ATR breakout system software, acknowledges this issue (www.byte-research.com) and accordingly offers trending tools as well as directional bias, in his ATR system.

In its defense, average true range is a superior technique to Bollinger Bands as a measure of volatility. In an article in *Technical Analysis of Stocks & Commodities* (June 2001), Gordon Gustafson compared ATR with standard deviation (the basis of Bollinger Bands) on several different criteria (number of highs and lows outside the bands, and so on). ATR and standard deviation measure volatility in very different ways and are not interchangeable. He found that when he used a countertrend entry and a fixed time exit, ATR returned a higher percentage of trades that were profitable, a higher net gain—and a higher drawdown, too (meaning the system is riskier). The countertrend entry consists of *buying* after a downside breakout as opposed to the trend-following technique of *selling* after a downside breakout.

## Everything Works

Because the FX market is so highly trended, the technical indicator has not been invented that doesn't work to some degree or another, on exchange rates. This poses quite a challenge. Which ones should be used? As with your choice of leverage, the answer lies not in the market, but in yourself. We know two important facts about the market: (1) trends last for months, suggesting that a very long-term approach will be successful, and (2) the professional traders that dominate the market are in and out within the same day. That gives us two time frames to consider, and thus two different sets of technical tools.

The very long time frame—months—lends itself to the crossover of moving averages, a workhorse of a model that has been bypassed, in the public's attention, by fancier concepts or at least fancier names. Moving averages are excellent at identifying, with a high degree of reliability, trend reversals after they have occurred. Their chief defect is a lag in determining that a reversal has taken place. That lag can get quite big, the higher the number of days in the moving averages. Also, when a price series moves from one level of day-to-day volatility to a higher level of volatility, the model generates so-called "whipsaw losses." You get in only to get right back out again a few days later. The only way to prevent whipsaw losses is to use a high number of days, which circles us back to the first problem, the lag.

In Figure 7.15, two long-term moving averages are used to give buy/sell signals in the Japanese yen. In the initial sideways period, the buy/sell signals are not conspicuously successful, but then we become well-positioned to ride the long trend over the next seven months. Notice that, on several occasions, the price corrects downward before resuming the trend. This can be nerve wracking.

An elegant solution to the lag problem is the adaptive moving average, devised by Perry Kaufman, author of *Smarter Trading, Improving Performance in Changing Markets* (McGraw-Hill,

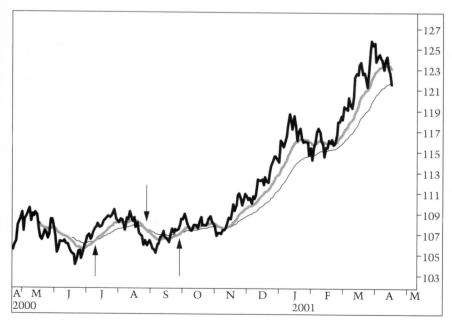

**Figure 7.15**   Crossover of two moving averages.

1995). This adjusts the number of days in the moving average according to changes in day-to-day volatility. In Figure 7.16, circles mark each crossover by the price of the adaptive moving average. You would exit and reenter on each crossover. This gives a greater number of trades than the crossover of two moving averages, but also some peace of mind.

Adaptive moving average is the backbone of the most successful currency futures trading software available, Dollar Trader (www.dollartrader.com), which has posted gains of 107.1 percent *per annum* since its inception in 1986, using leverage of 3:1. It is named as one of the top 10 trading systems of all time in *The Ultimate Trading Guide* by John Hill, George Pruitt, and Lundy Hill (John Wiley & Sons, 2000). Dollar Trader also uses other techniques, including an adjusted parabolic stop-and-reverse (SAR) and for confirmation, moving average convergence-divergence (MACD), as well as a few simple rules on entries and exits that mitigate the whipsaw effect of sideways prices.

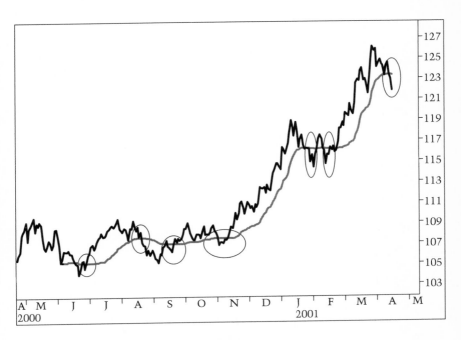

**Figure 7.16** The adaptive moving average.

## Adding Momentum

The moving average convergence-divergence indicator is a measure of longer term sentiment compared to shorter term sentiment. Another, more direct way to display the same thing is with raw momentum. This is today's price divided by the price x number of days ago, and while that sounds ridiculously simple, it is visually very effective. Combining a momentum measure with the adaptive moving average (AMA), and adopting a rule that we buy or sell only when they both agree, improves the profitability and reduces the whipsaw losses of using either model alone. In Figure 7.17, an arrow marks where the AMA alone would have given us a whipsaw from which using momentum too saves us. Circles mark two other places.

Why do we want a trading system that has as few trades as possible? Commissions and slippage (not getting the price you ask for but, instead, one that is 1 to 3 points worse) can chew up as much as 40 to 50 percent of your profits. This seems like a high

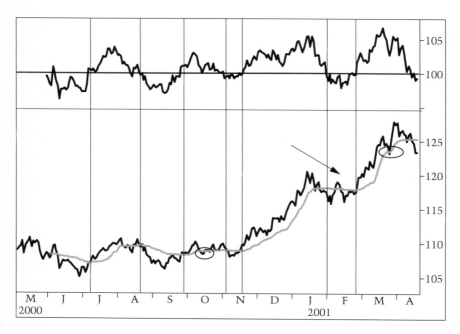

**Figure 7.17**    Adaptive moving average with momentum.

proportion, but you should test it with a few examples. It is, alas, true, even with relatively low commissions (such as $10 to $15 per round trip).

## Stochastic Oscillator

The stochastic oscillator is the central model in many trading systems in use today. Its chief virtue is in untrended or sideways markets, where it has an uncanny ability to display that a security is overbought or oversold and thus to suggest the next direction when the price line itself looks flat. The stochastic oscillator determines where the current close stands, relative to the recent trading range defined in a particular way. When the indicator is calculated at 50, the current close is at the midpoint (50 percent) of the recent trading range. The indicator is usually modified to slow it down, with a moving average crossover using the slowing parameter. The standard default parameters of the indicator are

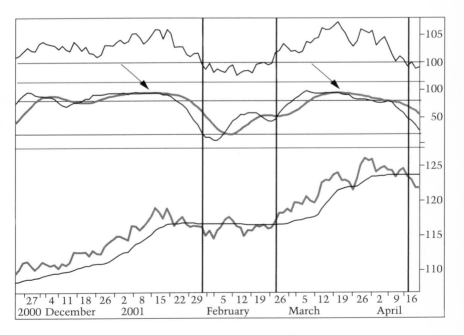

**Figure 7.18**  Stochastic oscillator.

five days slowed by three days, but you don't have to accept standard default parameters. If you are trading a security with a long-term trending habit, you can lengthen the number of days in the parameter set. In Figure 7.18, for example, the parameters are 11 and 9 days.

Zooming in on the most recent period of the same chart, we see that, on two occasions, the stochastic oscillator signaled an overbought condition (the indicator above the top line) well before the AMA or momentum generated a signal. You can use this information in a number of ways: reduce the number of contracts you hold, or narrow your stop-loss in anticipation of a reversal in the trend; or exit altogether.

## Putting It Together

Figure 7.19 shows the three-model system with the addition of the linear regression channel. Now we can see that the two over-

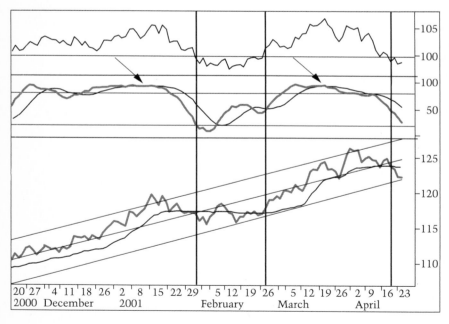

**Figure 7.19**   Multiple models.

bought warnings from the stochastic oscillator are coming at a time when the price has cycled to the top of the channel and is now likely to slide down to the bottom of the channel. Suddenly, the addition of the channel to the chart makes the warning signals understandable. The channel provides context. In the first instance, we don't know that the uptrend is continuing. We might choose to wait until the AMA and momentum confirm the expected drop—but by then we have left 262 points on the table. This is the difference between the clear crossover in the stochastic oscillator at 118.88 and the crossover of both the AMA and momentum about two weeks later at 116.26—our confirmed sell signal. In the yen, 262 points at $12.50 per point is $3,275 on one contract. You won't know whether this is a lot or a little until you evaluate how much gain you had to begin with (which this loss is reducing), how many contracts you own, and your personal risk profile—what total net gain you originally expected to make, and how much dollar loss you can tolerate.

In the second instance of the stochastic oscillator's giving an early warning, the price had slumped from the top of the channel to the midline (the linear regression in the channel) but then made another upward burst. If we had obeyed the stochastic oscillator and exited at its signal, we would have foregone 100 points or $1,250 per contract. This is the additional amount we would have made by waiting for the AMA and momentum combined sell signal, which comes three weeks later. This disappointment serves to point out that not every model works every time, or, at least, not every model works precisely the way we imagine it will. In this case, the delay in the second sell signal can try your patience to the utmost.

## Time Frames: Valuing Corrections

Our biggest problem is figuring out whether a correction is just a temporary move or a real reversal. Figure 7.20 shows a schematic chart of a prototypical price move.

Let's say that you have identified the price in Period 1 as a low ($2.00). If you buy and hold 100 units to the highest high in Period 6 ($26.81), you would make $2,681.81. Subtracting your initial

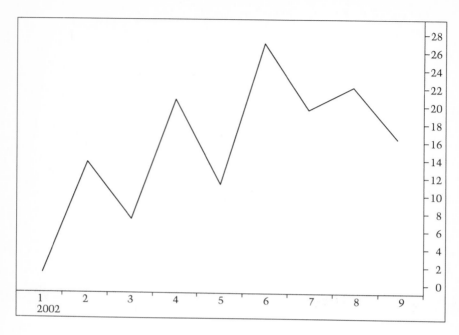

**Figure 7.20**   Corrections—A model.

stake of $200, the gain is $2,481.81, or more than 12 times your initial investment. If you could identify the two intermediate corrections, how much more would you make? We assume you can pick the correction start and correction end perfectly. (See Table 7.2.)

From an initial stake of $200, by reinvesting profits you now have a gain of $8,325.58, or 42 times your initial stake. This is better than buy-and-hold by three and one-half times. We have some unrealistic assumptions to swallow—such as the availability of exactly the number of units we want, and perfect execution—but this example demonstrates why active trading is theoretically always superior to buy-and-hold, as long as we can identify the

**Table 7.2.**   The Magic of Reentry

| Period | Entry | Exit |
|---|---|---|
| 1–2 | 100 units at $2 = $200 | 100 units at $13.95 = $1,395.0 |
| 3–4 | 178 units at $7.80 = $1,388.40 | 178 units at $20.75 = $3,693.50 |
| 5–6 | 318 units at $11.60 = $3,688.80 | 318 units at $26.81 = $8,525.58 |

corrections. *It's not enough to identify the trend.* In the buy-and-hold example, we identified the beginning and end of the trend and indeed secured a wonderful gain. It is in exiting and reentering at corrections, however, that extraordinary gains are to be made.

And you will need them. Every trader takes losses. In fact, most technical-analysis-based trading systems generate more losing trades than winning trades. You need extraordinary profits on the winning trades in order to compensate for the losing ones.

In Table 7.3, we see a correction in the euro. Following only the AMA with momentum, as indicated by the vertical columns, we would have made 985 points on the first trade, or $12,312.50. This is enough to pyramid up to two contracts, and on the next trade we make 704 points, or $17,600. Now we can have three contracts, and we make 759 points on them, or $28,462.50.

This looks very appealing until you realize that it would have taken an iron will to hold the short position through the two interventions in the fall of 2000, not to mention a number of one- and two-day moves totaling 300 to 600 points. Each point is worth $12.50, so the potential adverse moves would have totaled $3,750 to $7,500. Notice also that we have no linear regression guidance in the middle period (although we didn't know it at the time), and that, on two occasions in the last period, the momentum indicator did rise above its buy line at the same time that the close was over the AMA. Noting that the stochastic oscillator indicated an overbought condition at the same time, we would have been warned away from those small whipsaws. (See Figures 7.21 and 7.22.) One or two brave souls might actually trade this way, but, as a practical matter, few would try to conduct this kind of "position trading."

**Table 7.3.** Practical Applications—Euro

| Date | Purchase Price | Sale Price | Points | Dollars |
|---|---|---|---|---|
| 7/12/00 | 1 at 9560 | | | |
| 11/24/01 | | 1 at 8575 | 985 | 12,312.50 |
| 11/27/00 | | 2 at 8575 | | |
| 2/09/01 | 2 at 9279 | | 704 | 17,600.00 |
| 2/9/01 | | 3 at 9279 | | |
| 6/13/01 | 3 at 8520 | | 759 | 28,462.50 |

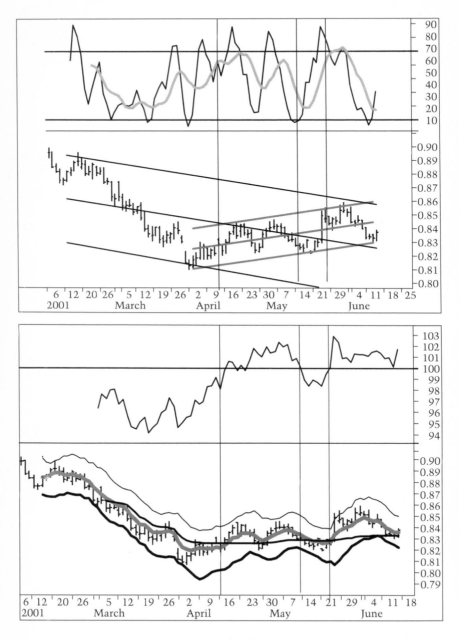

**Figure 7.21** Practical applications—The euro.

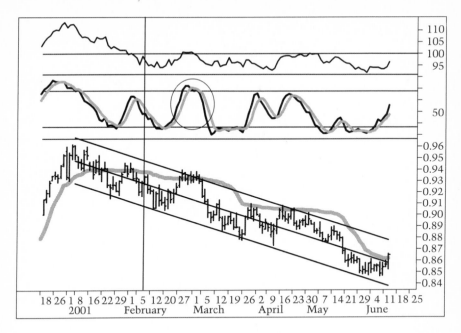

**Figure 7.22**  Practical applications—The euro 2.

Position trading is seen as extraordinarily risky because losses, under leverage, can be devastating. That is why all good traders who use leverage also use stop-loss orders. Using the average true-range channel to stop losses would have reduced gains but increased peace of mind. The problem is that it's very hard *not* to trade until a signal is perfectly clear. In this case, we have a Buy Stop on 4/20/01 and do not get a confirmed sell signal until 5/10/01. (See Table 7.4 and Figure 7.23.)

Finally, we got good results using the euro, partly because it is so highly trended and we had the benefit of perfect hindsight in preparing these examples.

While we can "prove" that trading corrections as well as the main trend is superior to trading the main trend alone, identifying corrections is very difficult. Some advisors recommend using three time frames (such as daily, weekly, monthly) and accepting a trade only when they all say the same thing. This concept can be applied to short holding periods, such as 5-minute bars, 15-minute bars, and 30-minute bars. You enter when they agree and

**Table 7.4.**    Stop-Loss Applications—Euro

| Date | Purchase Price | Sale Price | Points | Dollars |
|------|---------------|-----------|--------|---------|
| 2/9/01 | | 2 at 9279 | | |
| 3/2/01 Stop | 2 at 9362 | | (83) | (2,075) |
| 3/13/01 | | 3 at 9298 | | |
| 4/20/01 Stop | 3 at 9027 | | 271 | 10,162.50 |
| 4/20/01 Stop | | 3 at 9279 | | |
| 5/10/01 | | 3 at 8865 | | |
| 56/13/01 Stop | 3 at 8610 | | 246 | 9,225 |

exit when any one disagrees as to the trend. This is intense work and also requires a top data feed and top equipment. Some traders claim to get higher profits from this technique than from identifying "set-ups" and then having to apply a stop that might be suboptimal given the probable worst-case adverse excursion against the position.

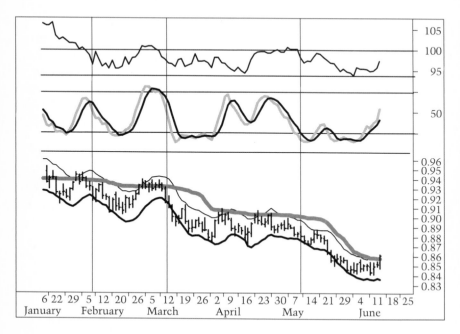

**Figure 7.23**   Stop-loss applications.

# *Chapter 8*

# THE HEDGE FUND MODEL FOR THE EVOLVED TRADER

*When you find yourself in a hole, the first thing to do is stop digging.*

Will Rogers

Since their invention in 1949, investors have been fascinated by hedge funds. They are often blamed for adverse market movements—most of which they have not precipitated. Former hedge fund managers like George Soros and Julian Robertson were either praised or despised by the press, depending on what sort of story was needed to "explain" a market's behavior. Like foreign brokers, offshore hedge funds are not allowed to solicit U.S.-domiciled investors. Because of this peculiarity in U.S. securities laws, the activities of hedge funds are often shrouded in mystery and misunderstood by the press and public alike. Actually, there is nothing mysterious about hedge funds. When properly understood, they have useful lessons to teach modern investors. The definition of a hedge fund varies widely, but the most common and accurate definition is: a fund that is long and short different stocks so that it can show profits whether the market goes up or down.

Today, a hedge fund is an onshore or offshore limited partnership that invests in publicly traded securities as over-the-counter or private transactions. Onshore funds are available to U.S. citizens, but, to avoid registration, the SEC limits onshore hedge funds to 99 investors (or 499 investors, under some circumstances). At least 65 must be accredited, which, to the SEC, means having a net worth of at least $1 million or an annual income of at least $200,000 in each of the two years prior to investing. Offshore hedge funds have no legal limit on the number of investors, but they may not accept U.S. investors.

Because offshore funds are technically not available to U.S. citizens, they are not regulated in any way by the SEC. This is so, even though many of them are located in the United States and are run by U.S. citizens. The rules are being examined constantly and do change from time to time. Oddly, the current state of affairs had George Soros testifying to Congressional committees, in 2000, that regulation of hedge funds should be stepped up. The Treasury Department and the Federal Reserve do not favor an increase in regulation.

Investing in hedge funds is a very seductive concept. They sound inherently safe; investors believe they are "hedged." In fact, this is not true, but the importance of hedge funds for intelligent investors is they can produce high risk-adjusted absolute returns that are not correlated with other holdings. Alas, you have to be a "qualified" high-net-worth individual to be accepted by a hedge fund, but you can learn quite a lot from understanding how they operate, and can emulate some of the principles—in effect, creating your own hedge fund.

The first principle to grasp is "risk-adjusted" return. This means that the fund—or your portfolio—can produce returns that are relatively high compared to the risks you are taking. This is achieved through seeking noncorrelation of returns from various investments.

The second principle is "absolute" return. This means returns that are earned regardless of what passive-tracking mutual funds in the same category are doing. Most investors are accustomed to thinking in terms of relative returns. The S&P 500 produced 21 percent in 1999. If your fund produced 22 percent, you are happy. If the S&P 500 were to lose 9 percent next year, but your fund lost only 5 percent, you would feel you were doing well. However, long-term investment success means continually compounding positive returns, even if returns are small in some years. Ideally, investors should have funds that earn an absolute return on capital every year. Hedge funds were originally designed to earn absolute positive returns.

# The Core Principle

The first hedge fund was created by Alfred Winslow Jones, a sociologist and business reporter who worked for *Fortune* magazine in the late 1940s. At the time, the U.S. economy was booming because of the release of consumer demand that was pent-up during World War II. Pension funds and endowments were just beginning to think about investing in common stocks, an investment practice that had been shunned by professional asset managers, who had favored bonds since 1930.

Like many students of the markets in New York at the time, Jones studied with Benjamin Graham, who, with David Dodd, had written *Security Analysis* (McGraw-Hill, 1997). The book was first published in 1934 and it is still in print. Graham's book is the backbone of what is now called value investing. While researching an article for an issue of *Fortune* that was published in 1948, Jones reasoned that the same rigorous analysis that Graham and Dodd applied to buying the cheapest and most undervalued stocks could also be used to identify the most expensive and overvalued stocks.

A seasoned operator could thus buy good stocks and use them as collateral to borrow the funds to cover short sales of bad stocks. If the market went up, the good stocks would rise faster than the general market. If the market went down, the bad stock would fall faster than the general market, generating a profit. Thus, 100 percent of capital could be used to get something in the neighborhood of 140 percent exposure. Jones's original turn of mind was to try for the best of the up markets and the down markets. This was the first systematic application of leverage. Until then, leverage was used only to buy, causing untold misery when markets crashed.

Jones began the first hedge fund in January 1949. The business model he used was a limited partnership of which Jones was a general partner who invested a significant amount of his net worth along with limited partners. For his efforts, Jones demanded an incentive fee of 20 percent of everything he might make over the original investment. Jones's original fund did not charge a management fee because he believed that managers should be paid only for the returns they produced. Charging a management fee of 1 percent on $100 million would mean that a manager only had to break even to make a million dollars for himself before expenses. Jones believed that management fees discouraged asset managers from working at their best. Later, hedge funds added a management fee of 1 to 2 percent to cover expenses.

Until the great bull market of the late 1960s terminated in a crash and the recession in 1970, Jones did very well for his investors, outperforming the market consistently. However, it should be noted that Jones did not do the managing himself. Instead, he hired a stream of managers whom he watched very carefully. But the general model that he created is still in place.

## The Templeton Version and the Birth of the Global Mutual Fund

A prominent practitioner of value investing was John Templeton, who said that, in the financial field, Graham and Dodd's *Security Analysis* is "the greatest book ever written." He first read the book in 1935, as an undergraduate at Yale. When he came to New York in 1938, he studied with Graham and, in 1954, founded the Templeton Fund, the first global mutual fund in the United States. Adhering faithfully to his interpretation of its principles until his retirement in 1992, Templeton guided the fund to achieve a lifetime return of 17 percent annualized. The Templeton value-investing method was simple in concept. Looking at all assets in the world, he sought to identify those that were the most undervalued and the least expensive, which he bought and held. They were replaced only when he found other securities that were 20 percent cheaper. For the first two years, 1954 and 1955, Templeton reported he lost 20 percent each year. In 1956, he changed to replacing assets that were 50 percent cheaper. From then on, he was notably successful.

Templeton never worried about when to exit the stock market to go to the safety of cash. That decision was made for him by constant analysis. When cash (money market instruments) was 50 percent undervalued to the stocks he was holding, he switched. Thus,

Templeton avoided the uncertainly of market timing. By adhering to market valuations of all investable liquid assets, including cash, he let the market make the decision. This is the same exercise as evaluating the risk-adjusted expected return on Stock A at only 2.5 percent per annum over the expected holding period, when you can get 5 percent per annum in a money market account for the same holding period. *This is a practical application of the positive expectancy idea.*

We may think that the difference between a hedge fund and a mutual fund is that hedge funds take short positions and mutual funds take only long positions. This is not strictly accurate. Some hedge funds do not go short, and some mutual funds do. What's important to keep in mind is that both hedge funds and mutual funds operate according to a diversification principle that, in theory, will result in high and consistent positive risk-adjusted and absolute returns.

## Does It Work?

Many hedge funds do not live up to the promise of noncorrelated, positive returns in good markets and bad. During the bear market that followed the crash of 1969, hedge funds did poorly and fell out of favor. They were all but forgotten by the general public until the mid-1980s, when the stock market uptrend returned. It was then that Julian Robertson got his start as a hedge fund operator and George Soros came into a constant public spotlight.

In the 15 years to 2000, the total assets invested in hedge funds grew from an estimated $80 billion to as much as $400 billion. Veteran fund operator George Van, of Van Hedge Fund Advisors (www.vanhedge.com), a consultant to potential hedge fund investors, notes that the risks hedge funds normally take are *lower*, on average, than those assumed by an investment manager tracking the S&P 500 or another benchmark. Over time, hedge funds have generally outperformed both mutual funds and benchmarks, and a chief benefit is protection when major markets are down. (See Table 8.1.)

You can get information on U.S. and offshore hedge funds, by strategy type, for 1988 to 2000 at the vanhedge.com Web site. Van

**Table 8.1.**    Total Returns, 1997–2000

|  | Annual Average Return |
| --- | --- |
| U.S. Hedge Funds | 19.4% |
| MSCI World Equity Index | 9.1 |
| S&P 500 | 16.7 |
| Average U.S. Equity Mutual Fund | 13.2 |
| Average Mutual Bond Fund | 5.4 |

*Source:* www.vanhedge.com.

also shows the Sharpe ratio (a measure of riskiness) and the beta to the S&P 500 of each strategy type.

## Mystery and Proliferation

The proliferation of hedge funds in recent years is a bit mysterious, considering that, according to SEC rules, they may not advertise. It is very hard, even for seasoned financial journalists, to discover exactly how well or badly a specific hedge is doing. This leads to difficulties for investors who are not qualified to invest in hedge funds. How can you discover a fund manager's style and performance? *MAR/Hedge* is a monthly magazine that began reporting on hedge funds in January 1994 ($695/year). It posts eight different categories of hedge funds:

1. *Aggressive growth.* Uses momentum investment techniques.
2. *Arbitrage.* Uses purchase and sale of identical securities or commodities in different markets at different prices, including asset- or mortgage-backed securities, bonds, commodities, foreign exchange, oil, precious and base metals, and stocks. Pure arbitrage is simultaneous purchase and sale; many so-called arbitrage funds do not practice pure arbitrage.
3. *Distressed securities.* Invests in securities of bankrupt or near-bankrupt companies, sometimes described as "event-driven" or "vulture" funds.
4. *Emerging markets.* Assumes there is, in emerging market securities, inherent value that is not recognized by the general run of market participants.

5. *Global macro.* A top-down investment style that seeks absolute or relative value in securities anywhere in the world.
6. *Short selling.* An investment style that concentrates a significant portion of its assets in short positions, regardless of market direction.
7. *Small capitalization.* Assumes that some percentage of new, small companies will become the corporate titans of tomorrow.
8. *Value.* Uses the Graham-and-Dodd method of security analysis.

Not every rating service uses these same categories, but rating services do exist, even though you have to claim to be an accredited investor to find out exactly how well hedge funds perform. Almost a dozen services offer comprehensive hedge fund performance data, including Managed Account Reports (MAR) in New York and TASS Management Ltd. in London. Performance information is not cheap, nor is it available to everyone. Because of SEC regulations, only professional managers and qualified investors may have access to these data, although you can register at some sites to get data and it's not clear whether the sites will actually check to verify that you are a "qualified" investor. One such site is www.hedgefund-index.com, which publishes an index newsletter and profiles on over 2,500 managers. Recently, the *Financial Times* added a regular series of feature articles on alternative investment funds and hedge funds, and you can often get data there. Note that, in the United States, managed futures are considered an "alternative investment" on a par with hedge funds. For information on managed futures performance, go to www.barclaygrp.com.

Be careful with whatever data you do get. It's easy to be misled. A *Forbes* article in the summer of 2001 contained incorrect or biassed data. Another example is the failure, in 2000, of famed hedge fund operator Julian Robertson's Jaguar fund. It was widely reported in the financial press that Robertson's lifetime investment average was about 27 percent. In fact, TASS Management, which tracks some 2,600 hedge funds, revealed that the Jaguar Fund's lifetime performance from 1986 to 2000 was 18.53 percent (arithmetic), or 17.62 percent (geometric), which is a far cry from the 27 percent the news reports claimed for all his funds. The reason for this discrepancy is that a financial reporter confused

Robertson's performance with that of George Soros's Quantum Fund. Because most reporters do not have access to hedge fund performance databases, there was no way to check the 27 percent performance figure. At the same time, it was assumed that Robertson's Tiger Fund, which closed at about the same time as the Jaguar Fund, had a similar performance which, in fact, it did— about 18 percent.

As a result of their shroud of mystery, hedge funds are often used as convenient scapegoats for market behavior that appears aberrant, irregular, and unexplainable. When the price of a stock, a currency, or gold suddenly moves up or down outside of what has been a normal trading range, the explanation offered most frequently is that hedge funds were behind it. The funds may not report their activities publicly, because it could be seen as a form of advertising, so no one can say this isn't true. However, according to MAR and TASS, some $330 billion is now invested in hedge funds throughout the world. Assuming that they are leveraged at an average of 3.5 to 1, they have $1.155 trillion in world assets under their control. Given that U.S. pension funds have some $8 trillion in assets and that total global equity capitalization is some $50 trillion, the hedge fund world is a small one. Nevertheless, when things go wrong, the damage is magnified because of leverage.

## When Things Go Wrong

The perfect case is Long-Term Capital Management (LTCM), a U.S. hedge fund run by John Meriwether, which had two Nobel prize-winning economists on its staff. LTCM was said to have made about 40 percent a year, after fees, for its investors. LTCM's strategy was convergence trading, a simple and highly profitable method of trading that works very well as long as financial conditions are "normal."

As an example, convergence trading makes an assumption that the high-yield debt securities of one country will, in the course of its life, pay all interest and full principal at maturity. Because it is emerging-market debt, it sells at a discount. The price will, however, converge to face value as maturity approaches. In order to finance it, sell the low-yield debt of an established country. This is what LTCM did. It sold U.S. debt of certain maturities and used the money it received to buy Russian debt of similar maturities. LTCM used its long positions in Russian debt as collateral to borrow U.S. securities to cover the short sales. However, periodically, certain events occur that can skew normal relationships between securities. In 1997, the collapse of several Southeast Asian economies precipitated a significant change in the perception of emerging-market debt. When this spilled over to Russia, hopeful owners of Russian debt, who had forgotten that from the first issuance of Russian Government debt in 1822, virtually no Russian government bond has ever matured, were soon disappointed by Russia's default on current bonds. This default had an enormous adverse impact on LTCM's bottom line.

Fourteen of the world's largest banks and investment houses had lent money to LTCM without bothering to check how much the firm had actually borrowed from other lenders. As a result, by August 1998, LTCM had leveraged its positions by 30 to 1. When the Russian Government defaulted on its debt, investors bailed out of emerging-market debt everywhere and moved back into U.S. Government debt in "a flight to quality." LTCM found itself suddenly squeezed on two fronts. It had shorted U.S. Government debt to raise capital to buy Russian debt. Now the Russian debt had fallen in price and the U.S. debt had risen in price. Because of overleveraging, it appeared that LTCM would never be able to pay back the $3.625 billion or so it owed to lenders, which, in turn, could cause some of them to fall in domino fashion. The Fed stepped in and organized a bailout. Today, Meriwether is back in business.

## Lessons

In the past year or two, several hedge funds have failed. Each made basic mistakes that we can learn from. In a nutshell, you have to be able to admit it when you are wrong, and you have to have iron-clad rules for getting out of your mistakes with the maximum of skin.

1. *You can't control the market; you can only control yourself.*

The main lesson from LTCM is not that convergence trades are high risk, but rather that losses are the market's way of telling you that you made a mistake. There's no excuse for sticking to a strategy that is losing money, if the strategy is failing to work because of an unforeseen Event. You can't control events; the only thing you can control is your own gains and losses. Actually, identifying the Event may be desirable for educational reasons, but not necessary. The purpose of investing and trading is to make money, not to be worldwise and not to understand every political/economic chain of links. The market doesn't care about your theory of how the world works. It's entertaining and gratifying if your theories work out, but to be wedded to a theory in the face of losses is to engage in wishful thinking, which seldom makes money. For every trade, you need to establish the amount of loss you can tolerate, and stick to it even when you are convinced you are right and the market will "come back." The only way to engage in active securities trading is with a stop-loss limit. You need to acknowledge that you will always take losses; the point of successful trading is to keep the losses small and the gains bigger.

2. *Liquidity is everything.*

During the Asian crisis, loss of confidence quickly spread to Russia, Latin America, and other emerging markets. Meriwether had a hard time exiting because liquidity dried up just when he needed it the most. As a smaller participant in the market, you should not face a liquidity problem of this magnitude, but that doesn't mean you won't face a liquidity problem with equally catastrophic effects on your position. The way to prepare for a crisis is not only to check your prices every day, but also to check the bid-offer spread and the volume actually traded. When the bid-offer spread widens from the norm and volume falls to a historically low level, somebody knows something unfavorable about the outlook for that security. This is valuable information. If you can find out the information, you may decide that it is false, or irrelevant, or "should not" be having the effect it is having. Watch out: this is to try to outsmart the market, and there is nothing smart about owning a security that you cannot sell because there is no market for it. Truly outsmarting the market consists of exiting right now and buying the security back after it has hit bottom and started back up, which it will do if it is really a "value" investment. If not, there is always something else good to buy, and, as Bernard Baruch said, "I made my money by selling too soon." The corollary, of course, is that averaging down is not smart.

3. *The Fed will not rescue you.*

The higher the leverage, the higher the losses and the bigger the mistake you are making. Meriwether's LTCM was rescued through the intervention of the Federal Reserve Bank, which strong-armed creditors into becoming equity shareholders and coughing up more money. The Fed will not rescue you, though. If you are using leverage, especially in fast-moving markets and in markets that are in a different time zone, you need to follow strict rules and discipline concerning leverage. Opinions on leverage vary widely. The sanest rule is to leverage only a security that has already made a sufficient gain to finance 75 percent of the new leveraged add-on. In most instances, you can finance 50 percent, so the 75 percent rule is more conservative. (Your car will go 100 mph, too, but that doesn't make it a wise speed under most circumstances.) Then you need to adjust your stop-loss limit—daily—to ensure that you can exit the total position with no net loss.

This rule means you should not borrow to trade a new security, but only to add to an existing position that is profitable and that you presumably know well (pyramiding). If you know the security well, you know its average daily price move. Let's say that the average daily price move is $5 and the security is trading at $80. You had originally bought 100 shares at $20, so you have a $6,000 cash profit. You can buy an additional 100 shares for $8,000, of which you have $6,000, or 75 percent of the purchase price. Your borrowing consists of the other $2,000. The question now becomes: how far can the price fall before you should exercise a stop-loss limit order? Your average price is $50. If you wait for the stock to fall to your average price, you will get back your original $2,000 on the first tranche of 100 shares, the $6,000 gain that was used to buy the second tranche, and the $2,000 you owe the broker. This should be your worst-case stop-loss.

In practice, you would never wait to sell until your stock fell 37.5 percent. Instead, you would watch the daily price move. If it exceeds the average $5, you would exit, because something is happening. It doesn't matter what it is or whether the market is interpreting new events correctly, to your way of thinking. It is just commonsense money management. The next day, it may open with a gap and fall more than your breakeven 37.5 percent, and if the market suddenly panics and becomes illiquid, you will not be able to exit at the breakeven. This is why the stop-loss limit should be entered every day. Remember, you cannot place stop-loss limit orders in most electronic trading situations.

This leverage exercise may surprise you. It uses a fraction of existing profits rather than a multiple of total capital. There's a good reason for it: the Fed will not rescue you. If your stock falls back to $20, where you originally bought it, you will have preserved your original capital, but only to pay it over to the broker (plus interest and commissions). You have failed, in the end, to preserve capital, the cardinal sin of investing. Even the most conservative of leveraging rules, like this one, carries the risk that high volatility in prices will result in catastrophic loss. That's why leverage should be applied sparingly, if at all.

## When Things Go Right

Sometimes, when things go wrong in the major established stock and bond markets, they are going right in the hedge fund and alternative investments world. As noted, getting up-to-date data can be hard. It can be even harder to figure out exactly what kind of trading is included in a particular category, or how representative the numbers may be of the entire universe of managers in a sector. At www.hedgeworld.com, you can get an overview from CSFB/Tremont, which calculates an overall index as well as subindices. (See Table 8.2.)

Table 8.2 means that the CSFB/Tremont Index outperformed all the other benchmarks named in the first five months of 2001. The components of that outperformance are in Table 8.3.

**Table 8.2.**   CSFB/Tremont Hedge Fund Index versus
Other Benchmarks

|  | **May 2001** | **Year-to-Date, 2001** |
|---|---|---|
| CSFB/Tremont | 0.83% | 1.53% |
| Dow Jones | 1.65 | 1.16 |
| MSCI World | −1.49 | −8.20 |
| S&P 500 | 0.51 | −4.88 |

*Source:* www.hedgeworld.com.

Global macro is highlighted because that is mostly what we have been talking about in this book—finding a market that is going up, an economy that is prospering, and then zooming in on specific securities (such as Chinese telecoms). By the time this book is published, Chinese telecoms may be old hat. The Chinese market may have tanked. How do hedge funds keep track of what's going on?

## Comparisons Yield Insight

One fund, which shall remain nameless, reveals its technique. This consists of ranking each class of securities (stocks, bonds, and currencies) according to "relative attractiveness." Relative

**Table 8.3.**   CSFB/Tremont Subindices

| Category | **May 2001** | **Year-to-Date, 2001** |
|---|---|---|
| Convertible arbitrage | +0.69% | +8.38% |
| Dedicated short bias | −2.73 | −0.18 |
| Emerging markets | +2.39 | +1.89 |
| Equity market neutral | +0.64 | +6.16 |
| Event-driven | +1.10 | +6.34 |
| Fixed-income arbitrage | +0.52 | +4.09 |
| **Global macro** | **+2.14** | **+10.25** |
| Long/short equity | +0.40 | −3.75 |
| Managed futures | +0.83 | +0.06 |

*Source:* www.hedgeworld.com.

attractiveness sounds vague but in fact is highly specific. Attractiveness consists of financial and economic data that are compiled into an index, with points given for such factors as liquidity, volatility, and recent return (last week, last month, year to date). Then each country is ranked according to the percentile it falls into. The greatest portion of money is put into the markets and countries that are in the highest percentiles; tiny amounts are allocated to poorly performing economies, markets, and currencies. This is done daily, and any change in the trend of attractiveness is noted for weekly and monthly reallocation decisions. For example, in May 2001, Singapore's stock market was outperforming— raising its attractiveness—but its currency was falling—offsetting the attractiveness, which was then raised a hair by falling interest rates that made the cash/bond market more attractive. Each of these attractiveness indices was then added up in the context of U.S. dollar-based returns, and [despite Singapore's small share in world gross domestic product (GDP)], a small percentage of total capital was reallocated to Singapore stocks. This would be an immensely time-consuming process were it not for computer modeling and compiling. The point of the exercise is: do not judge any single security or sector in a vacuum; regard it as relative to every other opportunity.

## Start Your Own Hedge Fund

You have probably seen an advertisement by a securities house for a free seminar on starting your own hedge fund. This is hardly surprising; a hedge fund can charge a 20 percent profit-sharing fee, and would-be asset managers like to think that they can quickly make a great deal of money on a relatively small pool of assets. Brokerage houses want the transaction business and are willing to give all kinds of accounting, tax, and operating advice to get it. You may not want to go that far, but you can learn from Jones and Templeton (as well as Robertson and Soros). Jones introduced the idea of using leverage to go short poorly performing securities as well as being long securities with high-positive expectancy. This is making money do double duty, and it requires strict discipline in managing losses.

From Templeton, we learn to invest in any single security only if it has a high probability of returning more than cash. Once it has done that, we ruthlessly abandon it for the next opportunity that has the highest probable return. The implication is that our fall-back position is not only cash, but must include a bigger universe of possibilities. Robertson famously left the U.S. equity market in 2000, complaining that value was not driving the market but rather "momentum and mouse-clicks"—and he got revenge of a sort by later shorting the market at the top. Soros, having made a fortune identifying the U.K. pound situation, later participated in the high-tech bubble just as it was about to burst, evidently losing his touch that time.

## Summary and Conclusion

Hedge fund strategies and performance have been a mystery to most people since their inception because the SEC feels that even to report performance would be an advertisement (despite limits on participation to only the wealthy). In some periods, hedge funds have underperformed the broad market benchmarks, and, in some cases, such as that of Long-Term Capital Management, major mistakes were made. In periods of distress and turmoil, though, some hedge funds outperform, due to their focus on a specific inefficiency that can be exploited, usually going both ways (long and short) and with the use of leverage. The latest wrinkle is funds that invest in a basket of hedge funds. Like mutual funds, these may become available to the average investor with less than a million dollars to place. In do-it-yourself emulation of hedge funds, it's important to become expert in whatever specialized area affords you identification of an inefficiency, and to couple that identification with a cold-hearted taking of gains and cutting of losses, as though it were a game—even though you know it is not. You goal is to obtain an absolute positive return, consistently, whatever the standard benchmarks are showing.

# Index